Monkey Business

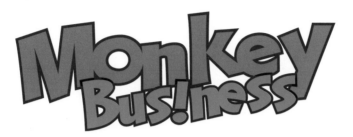

Another Cartoon Collection

by

The Flying McCoys

Glenn and Gary McCoy

Andrews McMeel Publishing, LLC

Kansas City

The Flying McCoys is syndicated internationally by Universal Press Syndicate.

Monkey Business copyright © 2007 by Glenn and Gary McCoy. All rights reserved. Printed in China. No part of this book may be used or reproduced in any manner whatsoever without written permission except in the case of reprints in the context of reviews. For information, write Andrews McMeel Publishing, LLC, an Andrews McMeel Universal company, 4520 Main Street, Kansas City, Missouri 64111.

07 08 09 10 11 WKT 10 9 8 7 6 5 4 3 2 1

ISBN-13: 978-0-7407-6843-9
ISBN-10: 0-7407-6843-3

Library of Congress Control Number: 2007925785

www.andrewsmcmeel.com

Thanks to Dr. John Adkins Richardson.

—— **ATTENTION: SCHOOLS AND BUSINESSES** ——

Andrews McMeel books are available at quantity discounts with bulk purchase for educational, business, or sales promotional use. For information, please write to: Special Sales Department, Andrews McMeel Publishing, LLC, 4520 Main Street, Kansas City, Missouri 64111.

For Mark and Kent.
We couldn't have asked for two better brothers.
We tried, but Mom and Dad said 'no'.

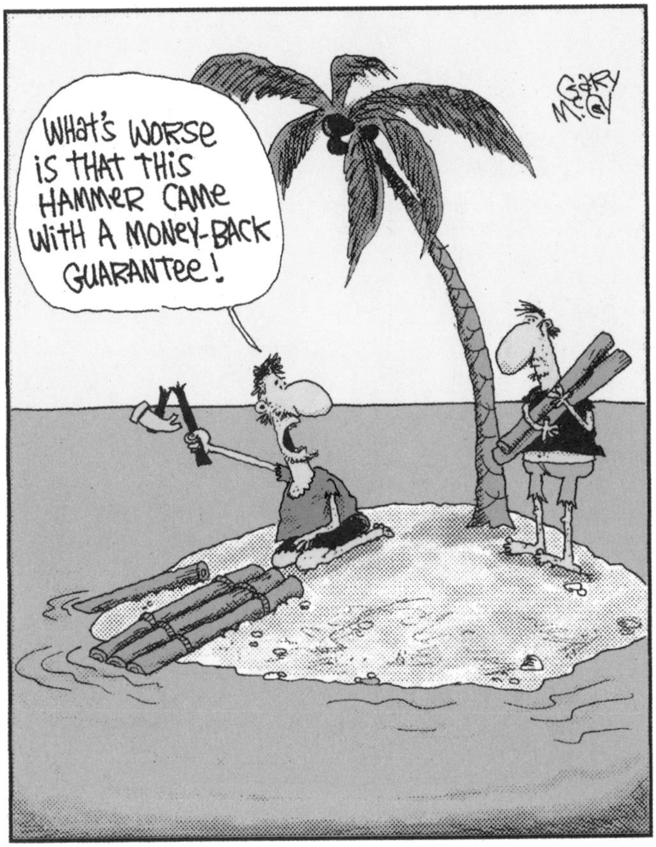
WHAT'S WORSE IS THAT THIS HAMMER CAME WITH A MONEY-BACK GUARANTEE!
GARY McCOY

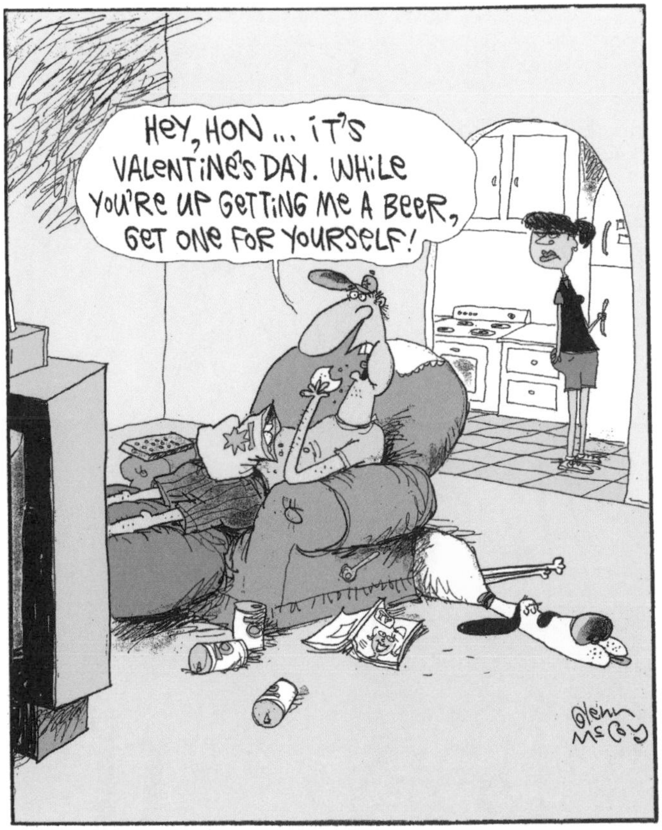
HEY, HON ... IT'S VALENTINE'S DAY. WHILE YOU'RE UP GETTING ME A BEER, GET ONE FOR YOURSELF!
GLENN McCOY

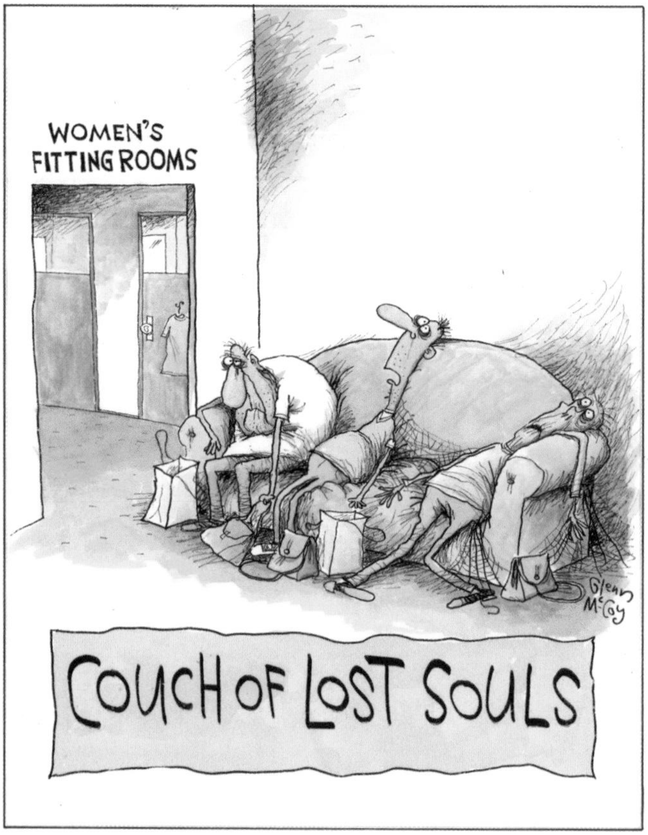
WOMEN'S
FITTING ROOMS
COUCH OF LOST SOULS

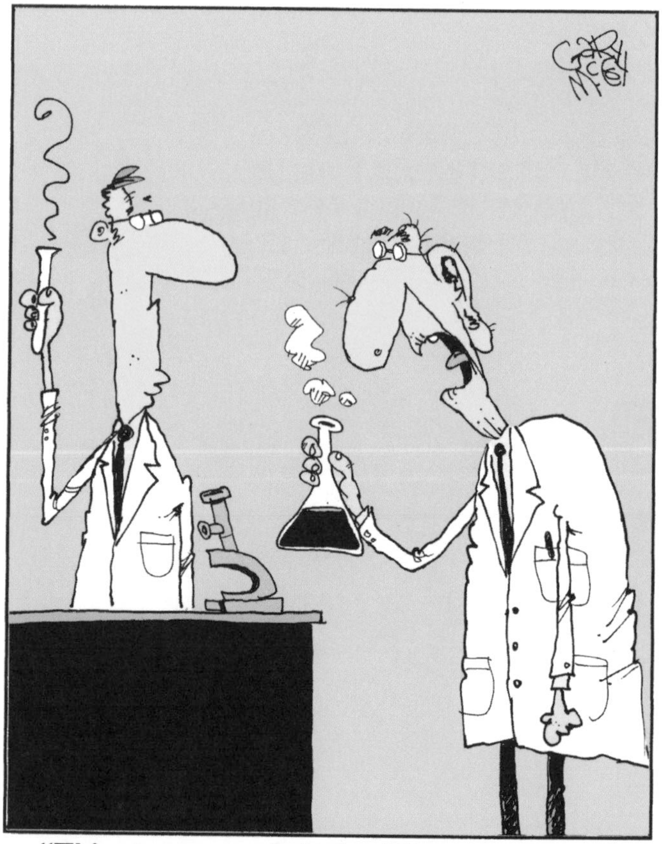

"This steams my britches! Seventy years of research, and now I discover an antiaging drug!"

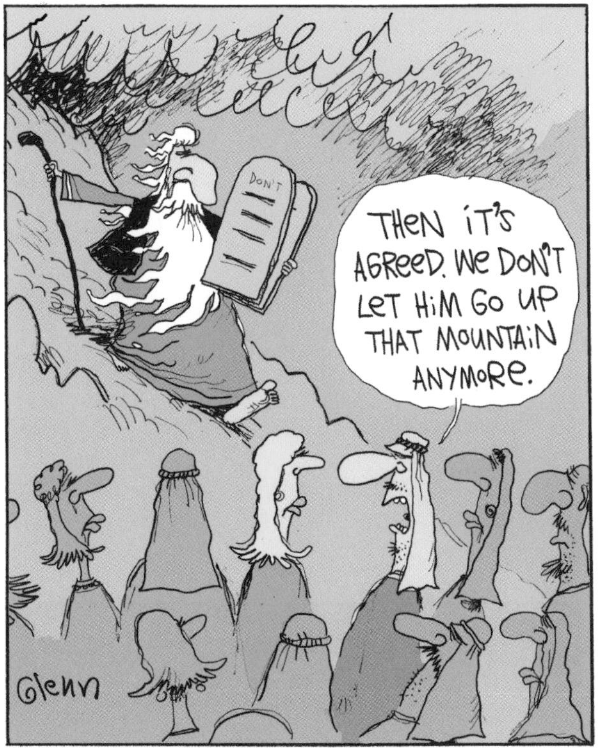
THEN IT'S AGREED. WE DON'T LET HIM GO UP THAT MOUNTAIN ANYMORE.
DON'T
Glenn

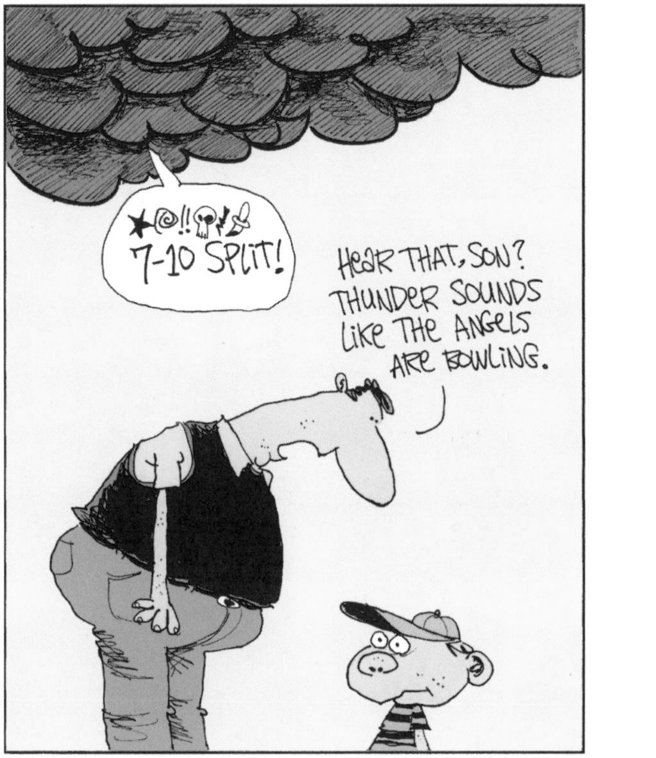
7-10 SPLIT!
HEAR THAT, SON? THUNDER SOUNDS LIKE THE ANGELS ARE BOWLING.

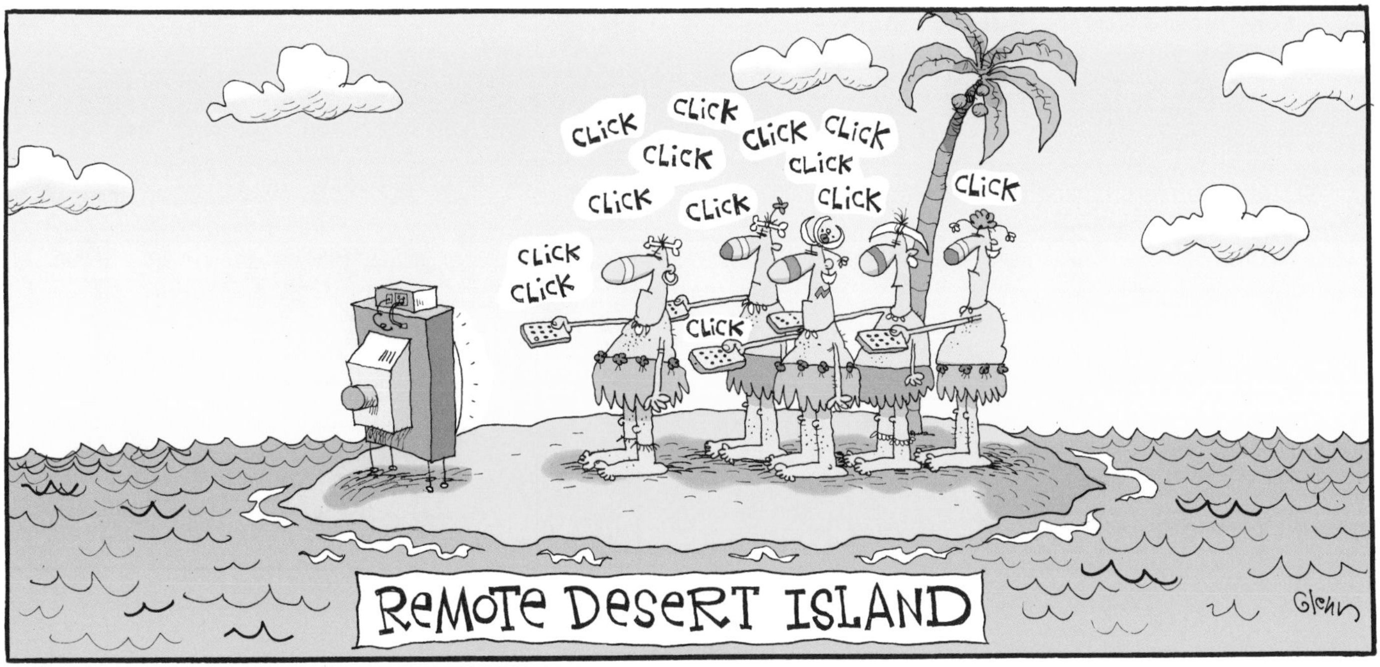
CLICK CLICK CLICK CLICK CLICK CLICK CLICK CLICK CLICK CLICK CLICK CLICK CLICK
REMOTE DESERT ISLAND
Glenn

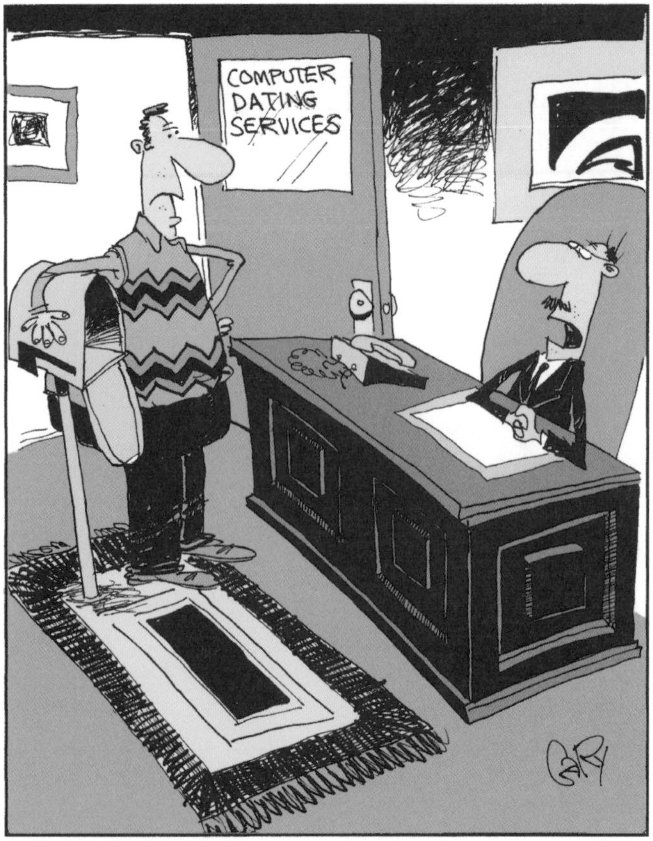
COMPUTER
DATING
SERVICES

"I suppose there could be a glitch in our computer software. But personally, I think you make a cute couple."

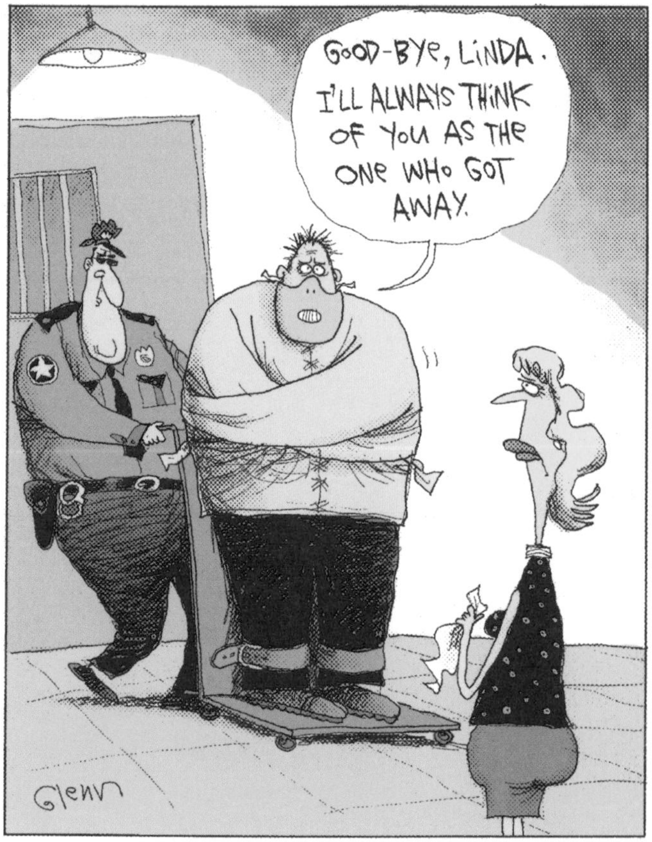
GOOD-BYE, LINDA. I'LL ALWAYS THINK OF YOU AS THE ONE WHO GOT AWAY.

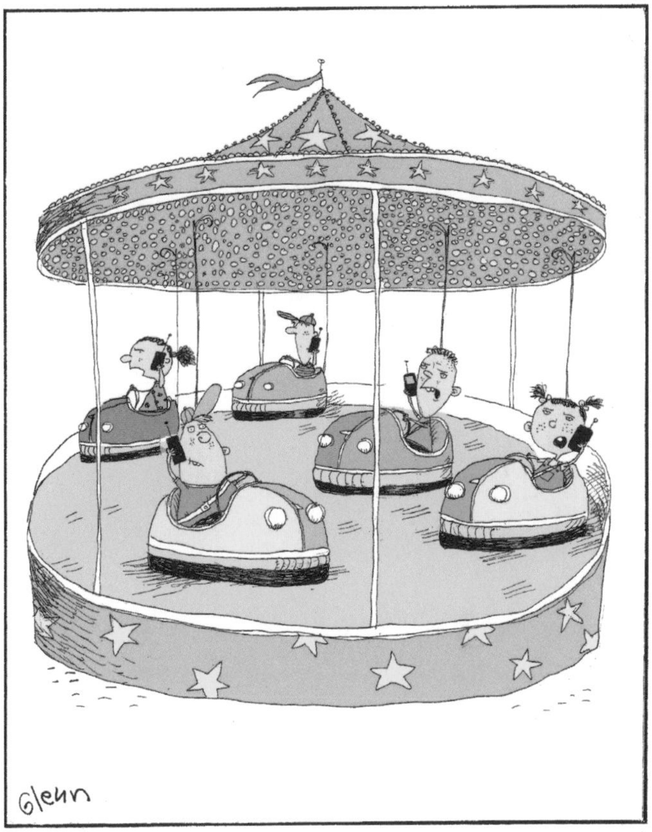
Glenn

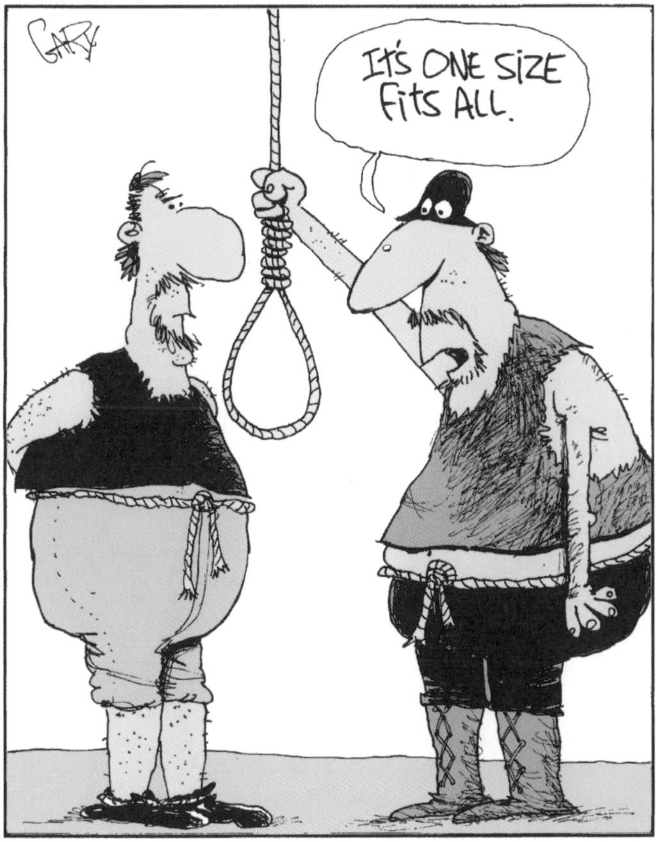
GARY
IT'S ONE SIZE FITS ALL.

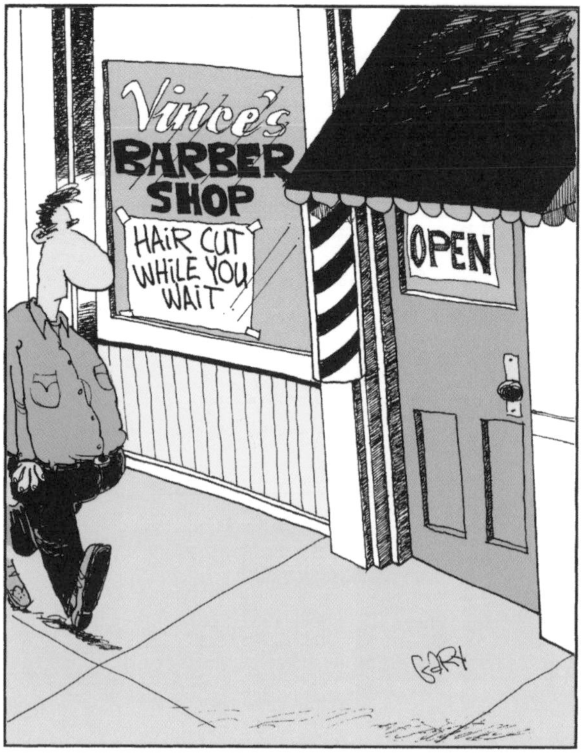
Vince's
BARBER SHOP
HAIR CUT WHILE YOU WAIT
OPEN

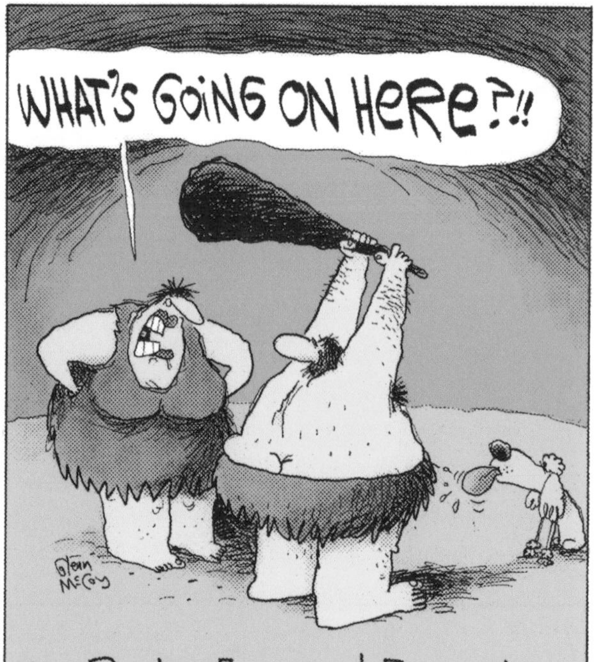
WHAT'S GOING ON HERE?!!

How Poodles Escaped Extinction

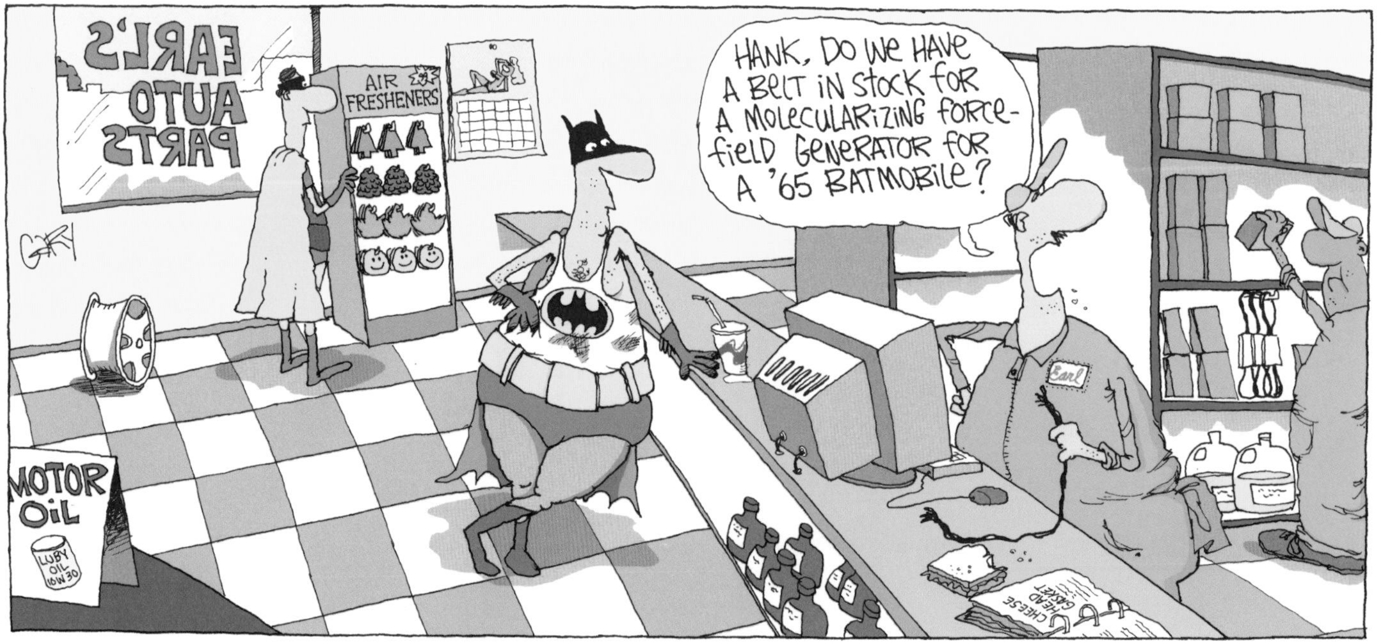
EARL'S AUTO PARTS
AIR FRESHENERS
HANK, DO WE HAVE A BELT IN STOCK FOR A MOLECULARIZING FORCE-FIELD GENERATOR FOR A '65 BATMOBILE?
Earl
MOTOR OIL
LUBY OIL 10W30

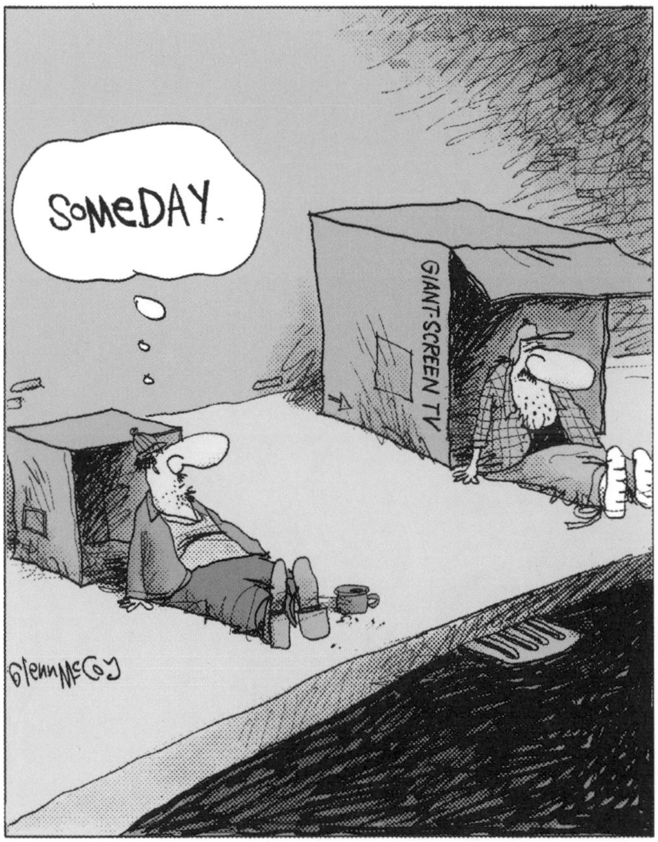
SOMEDAY.
GIANT-SCREEN TV
GLENN McCOY

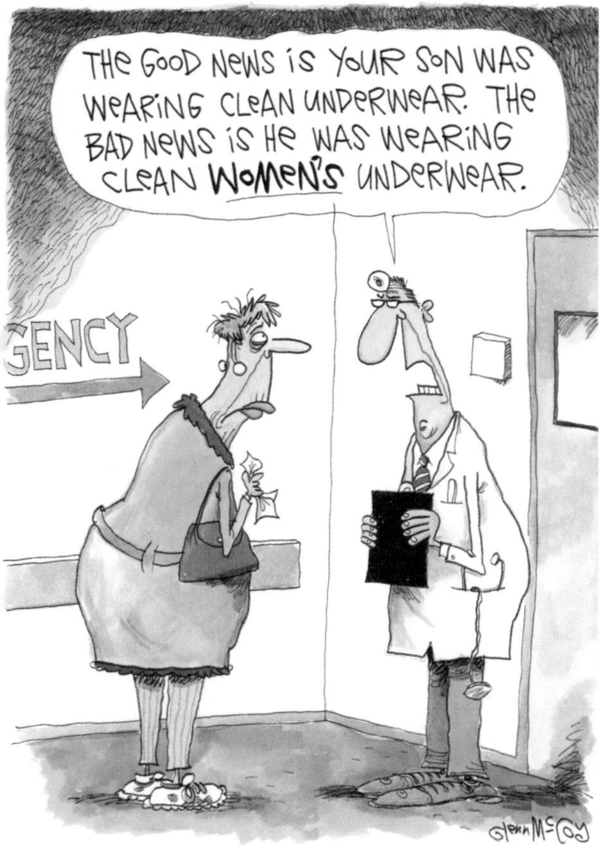
THE GOOD NEWS IS YOUR SON WAS WEARING CLEAN UNDERWEAR. THE BAD NEWS IS HE WAS WEARING CLEAN WOMEN'S UNDERWEAR.
GENCY
GLENN McCOY

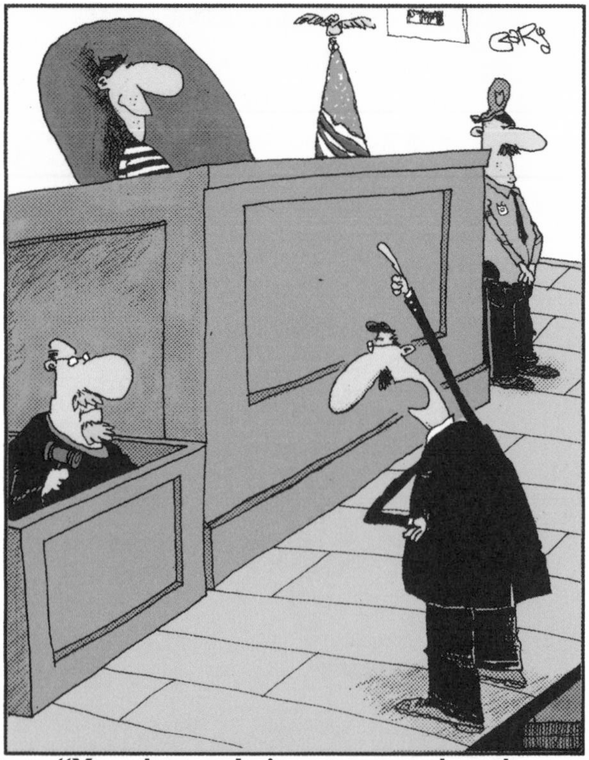

"Your honor, I aim to prove that the defendant is a master of manipulation."

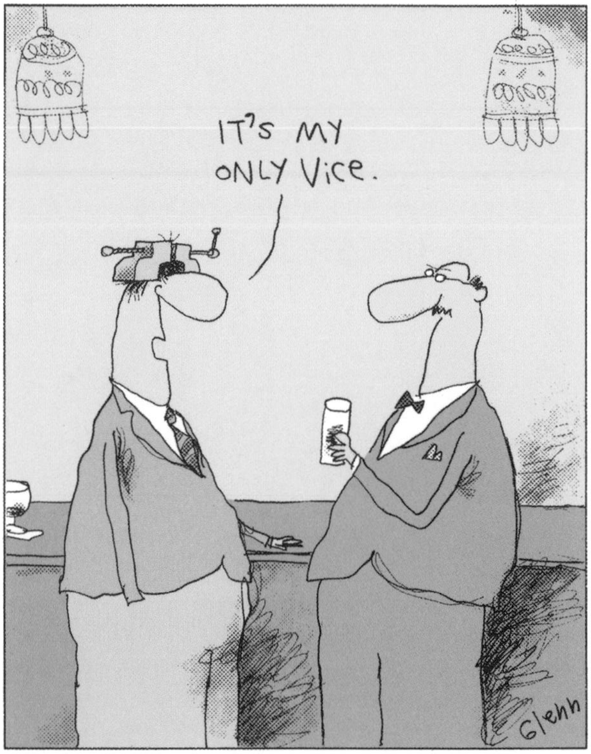
IT'S MY ONLY VICE.

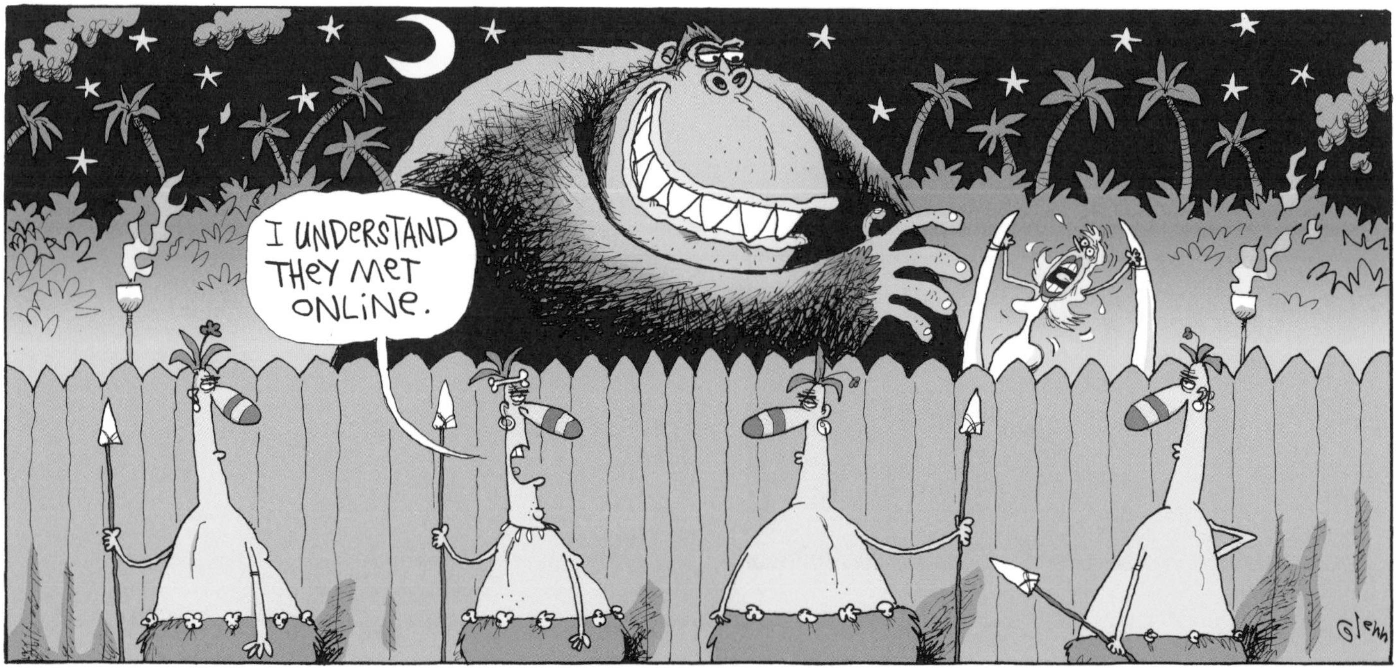
I UNDERSTAND THEY MET ONLINE.

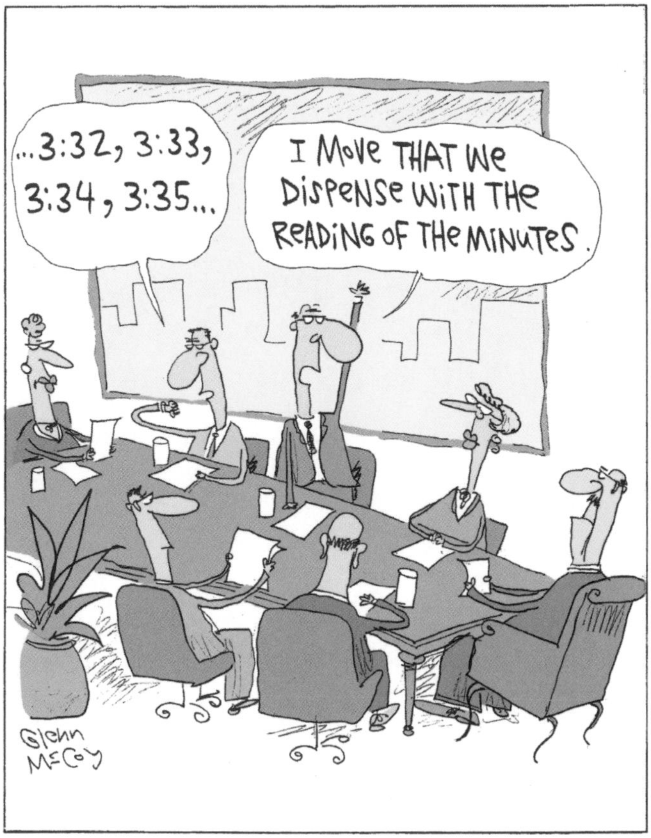
...3:32, 3:33, 3:34, 3:35...
I MOVE THAT WE DISPENSE WITH THE READING OF THE MINUTES.
Glenn McCoy

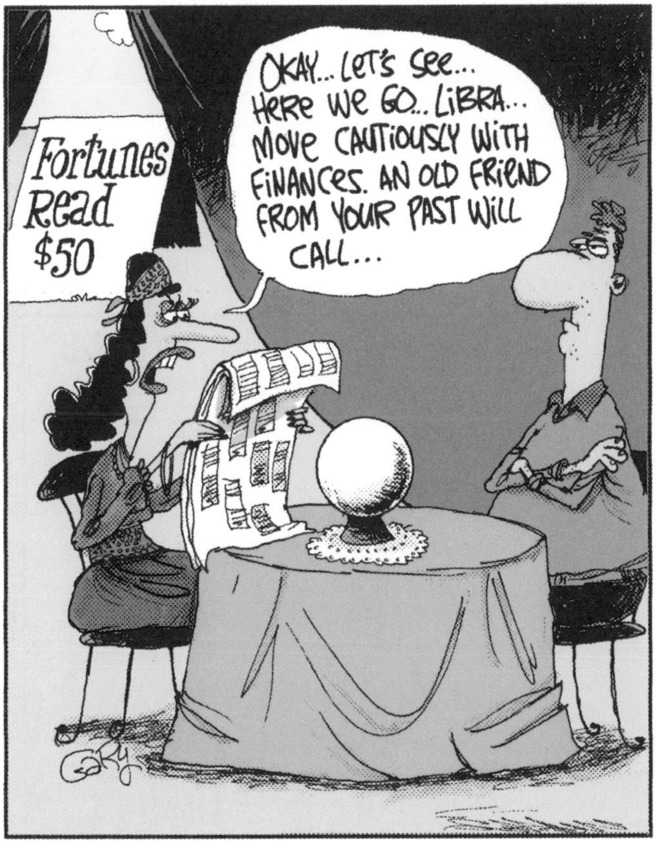
Fortunes Read $50
OKAY... LET'S SEE... HERE WE GO... LIBRA... MOVE CAUTIOUSLY WITH FINANCES. AN OLD FRIEND FROM YOUR PAST WILL CALL...

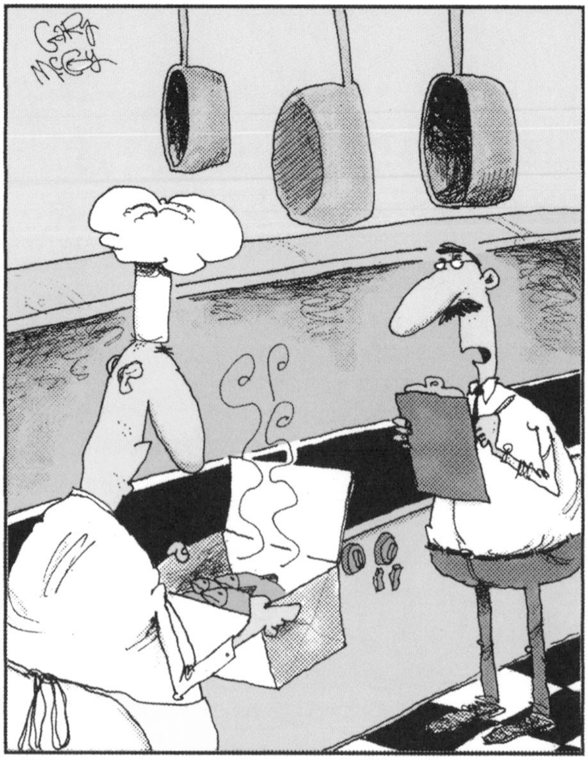
Gary McCoy

"To save money, instead of having our fish flown in, I let it take a Greyhound with just a short stopover in Cleveland."

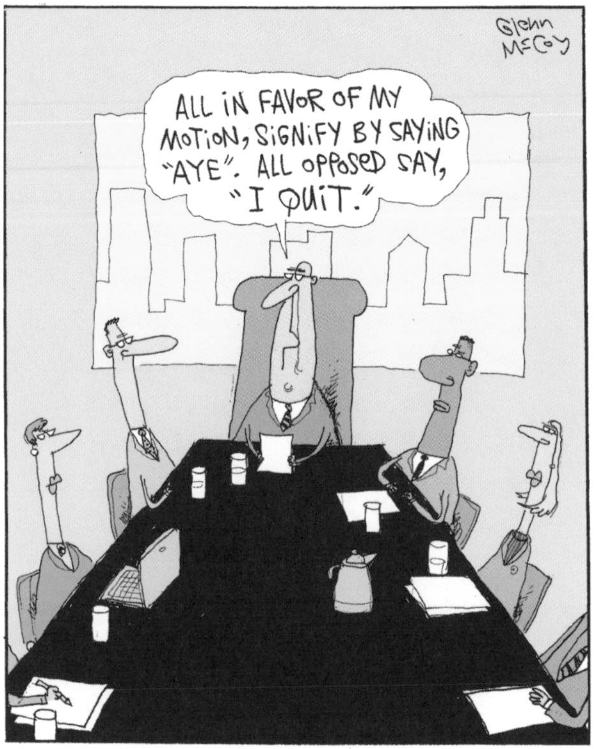
Glenn McCoy
ALL IN FAVOR OF MY MOTION, SIGNIFY BY SAYING "AYE". ALL OPPOSED SAY, "I QUIT."

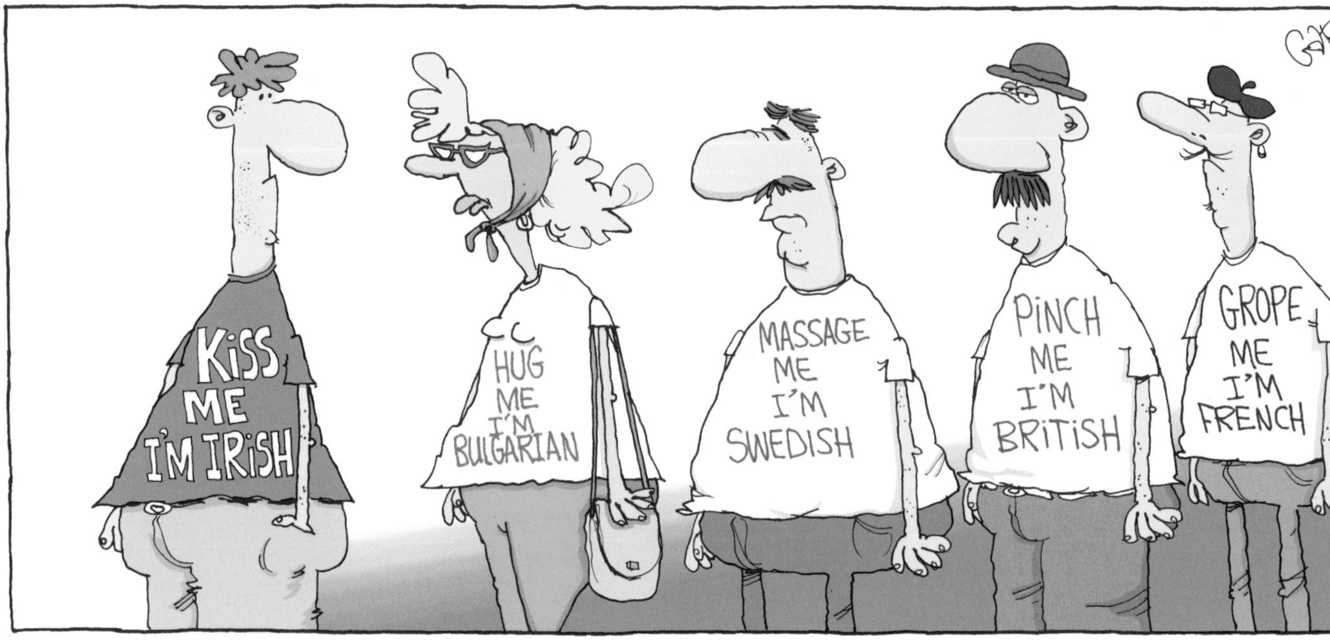
Gary
KISS ME I'M IRISH
HUG ME I'M BULGARIAN
MASSAGE ME I'M SWEDISH
PINCH ME I'M BRITISH
GROPE ME I'M FRENCH

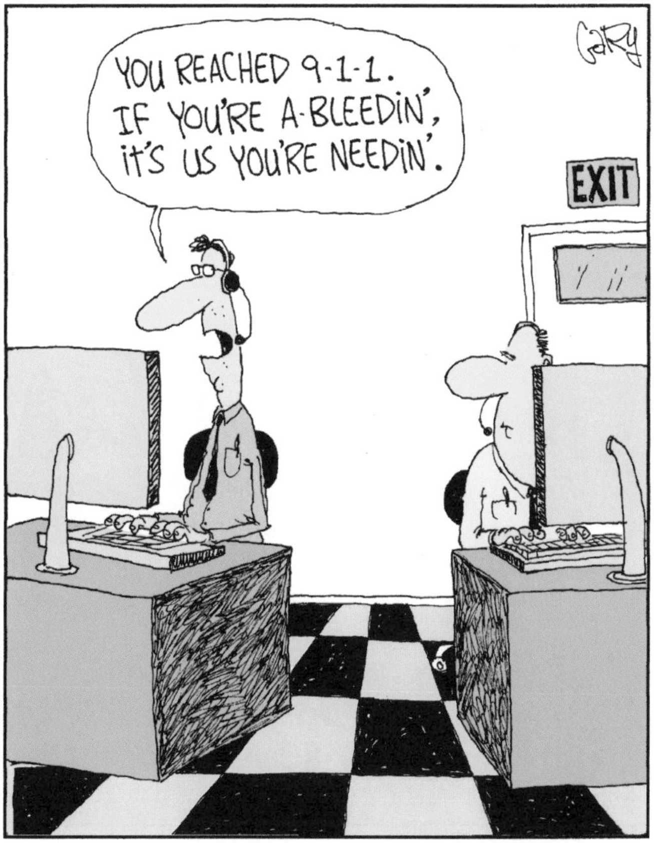
YOU REACHED 9-1-1.
IF YOU'RE A-BLEEDIN',
IT'S US YOU'RE NEEDIN'.
EXIT
GARY

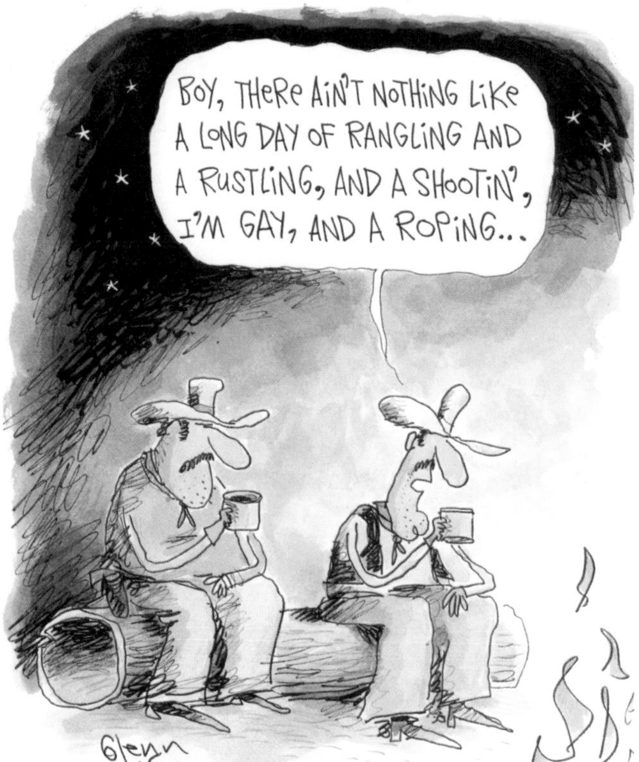
BOY, THERE AIN'T NOTHING LIKE
A LONG DAY OF RANGLING AND
A RUSTLING, AND A SHOOTIN',
I'M GAY, AND A ROPING...
Glenn McCoy

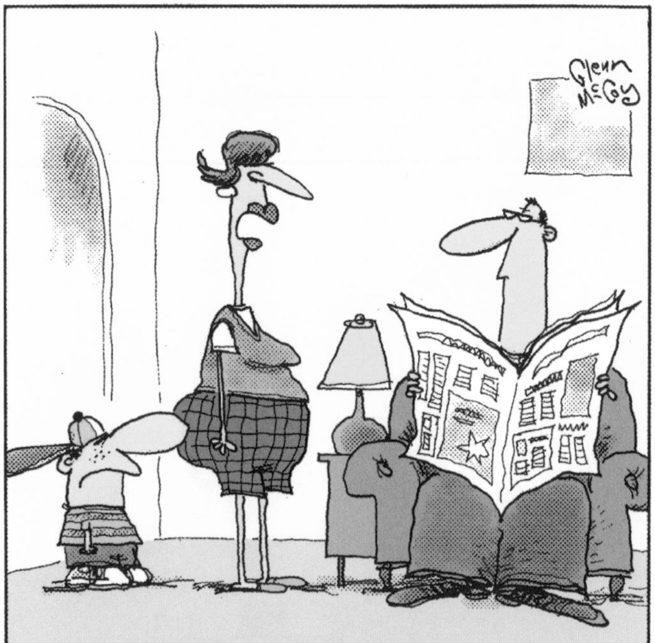
Glenn McCoy

HE WANTS TO KNOW HOW MUCH WE'RE SETTING ASIDE FOR HIS COLLEGE SPRING BREAK TRIP.

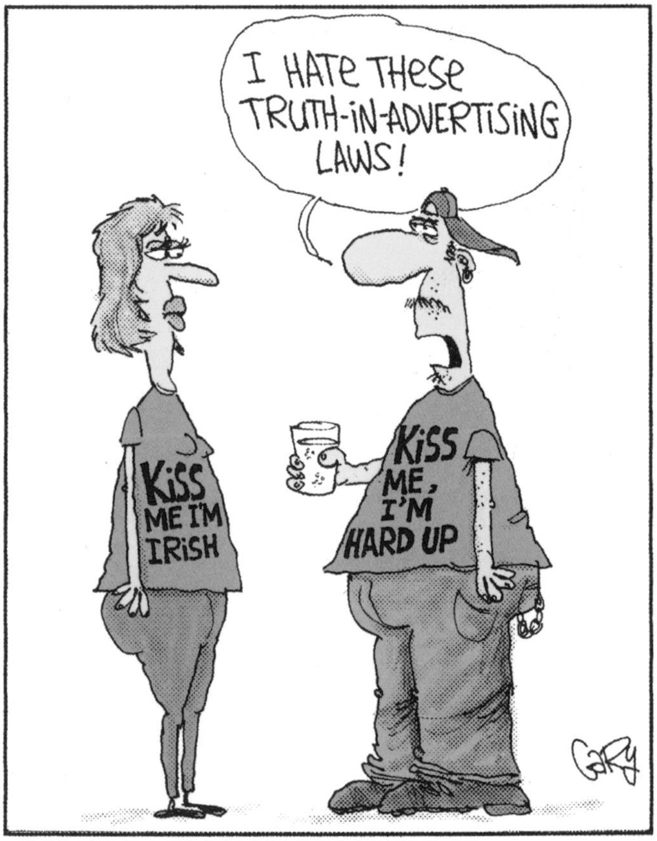
I HATE THESE TRUTH-IN-ADVERTISING LAWS!
KiSS ME I'M IRiSH
KiSS ME, I'M HARD UP
GARY

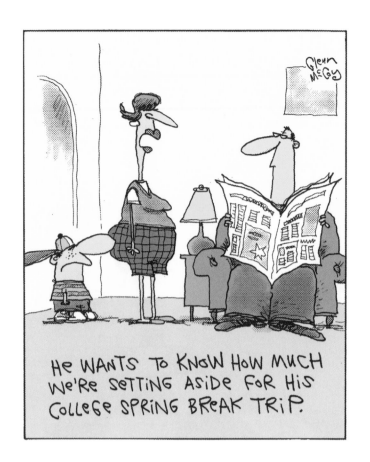

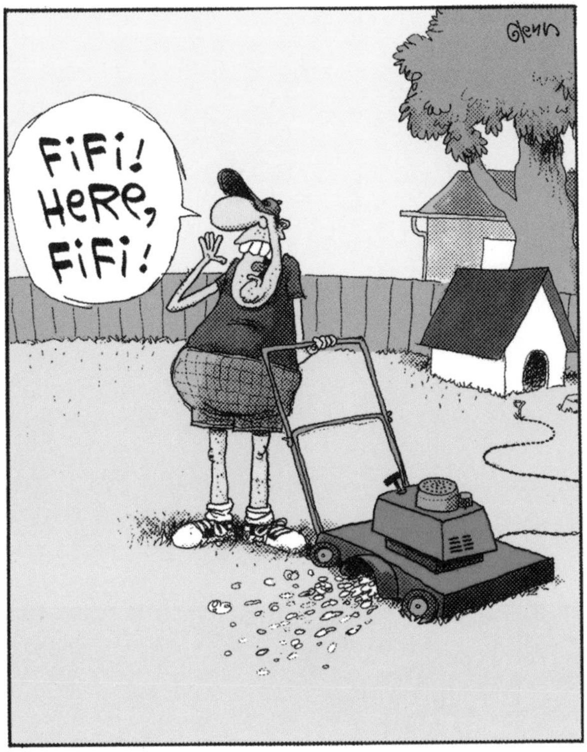
FiFi! HeRe, FiFi!
Glenn

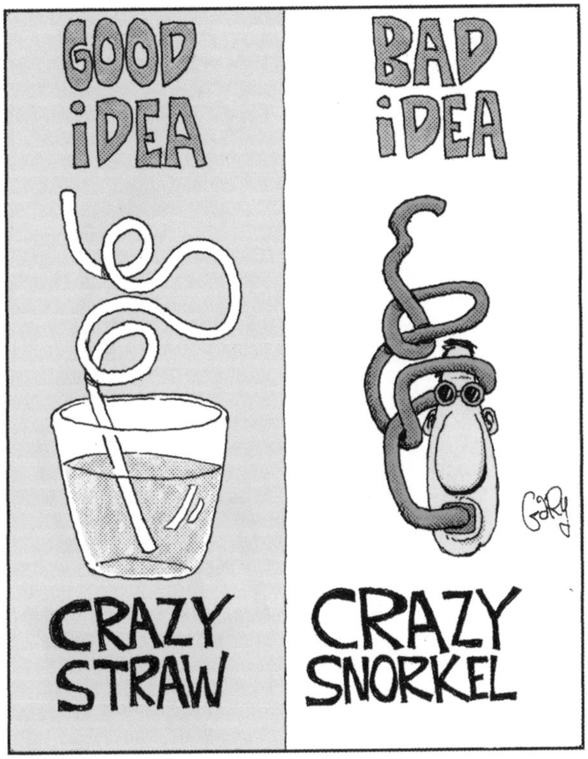
GOOD iDEA
BAD iDEA
CRAZY STRAW
CRAZY SNORKEL

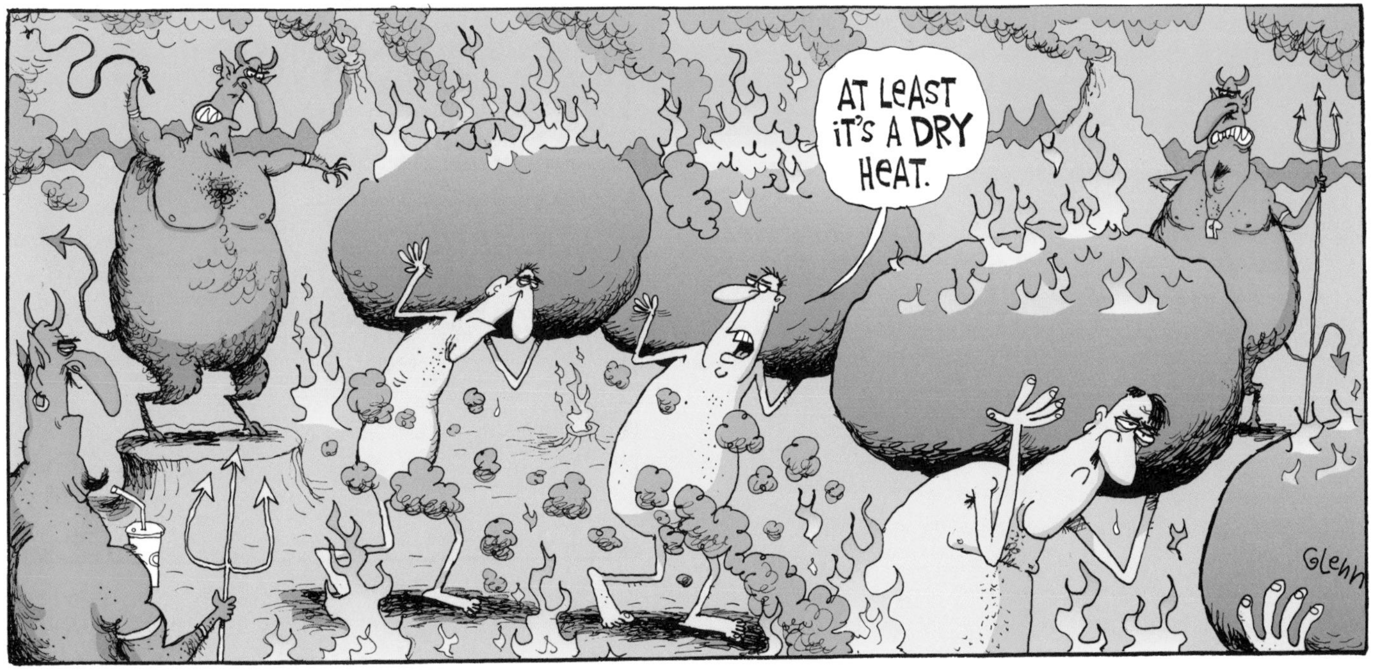
AT LeAST iT'S A DRY HeAT.
Glenn

H. FLY
ATTORNEY
MAKE SURE TO READ THE FINE PRINT.
GARY

CHANGE
Glenn

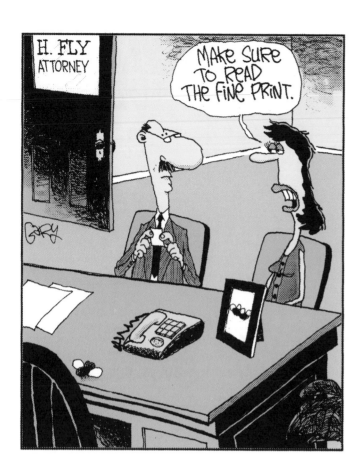

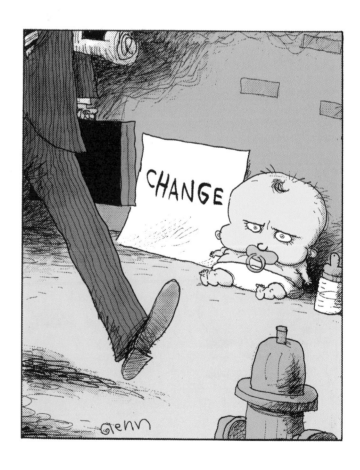

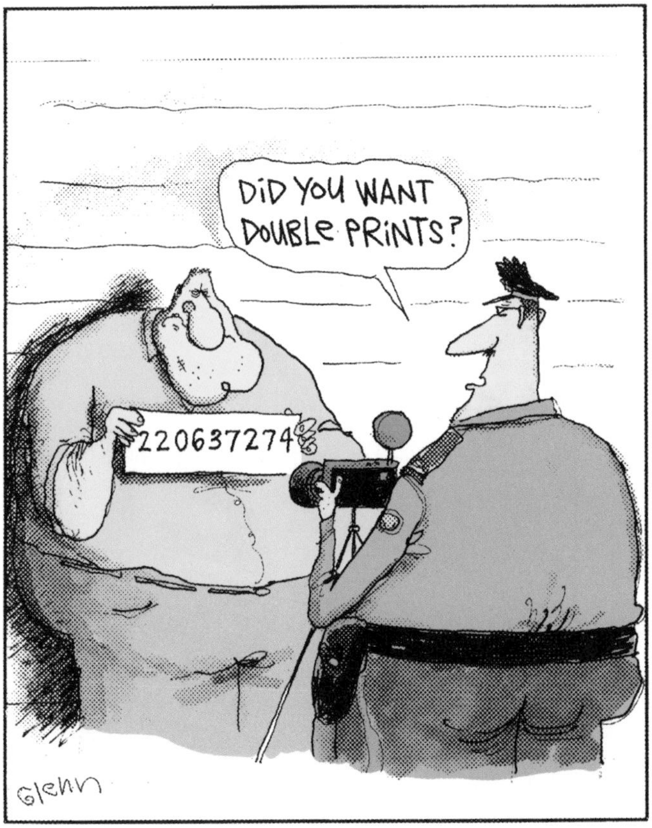
DID YOU WANT DOUBLE PRINTS?
220637274
Glenn

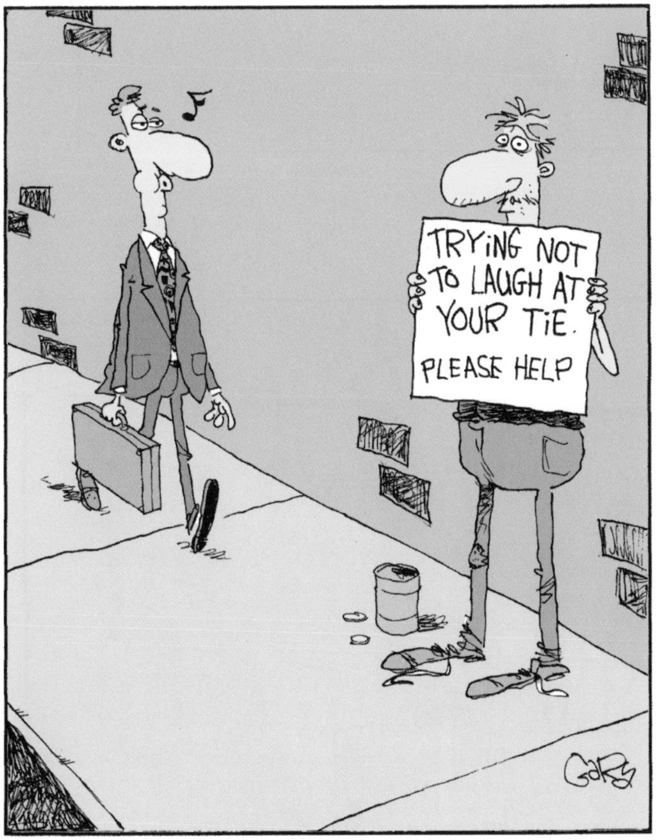
TRYING NOT TO LAUGH AT YOUR TIE.
PLEASE HELP
Gary

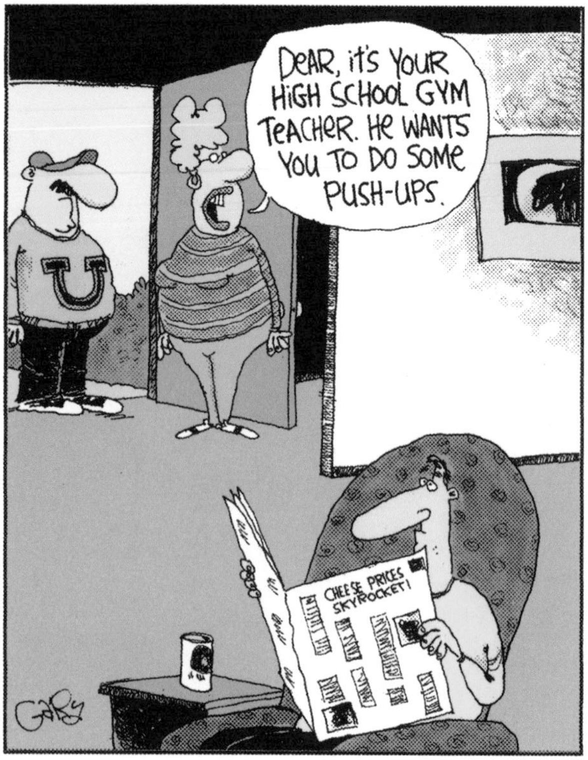
DeAR, it's YOUR HiGH SCHOOL GYM TeACHeR. He WANTS YOU TO DO SOME PUSH-UPS.
U
CHEESE PRICES SKYROCKET!
GARY

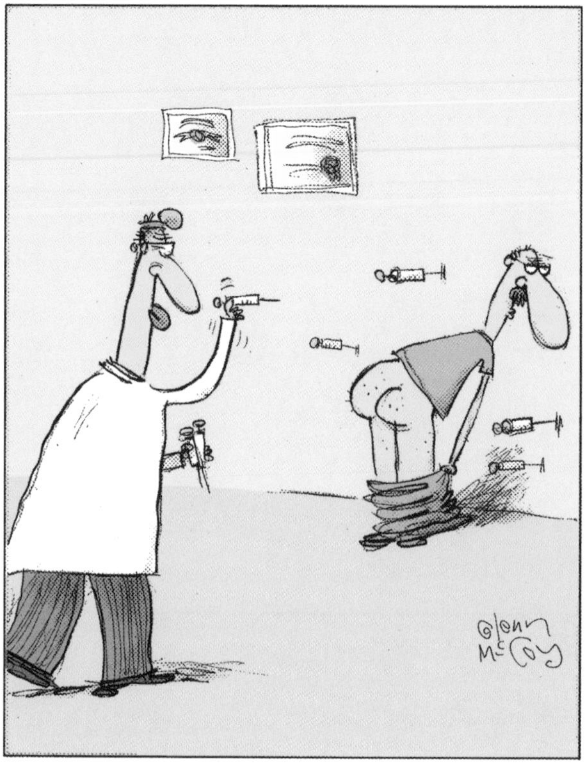
Glenn McCoy

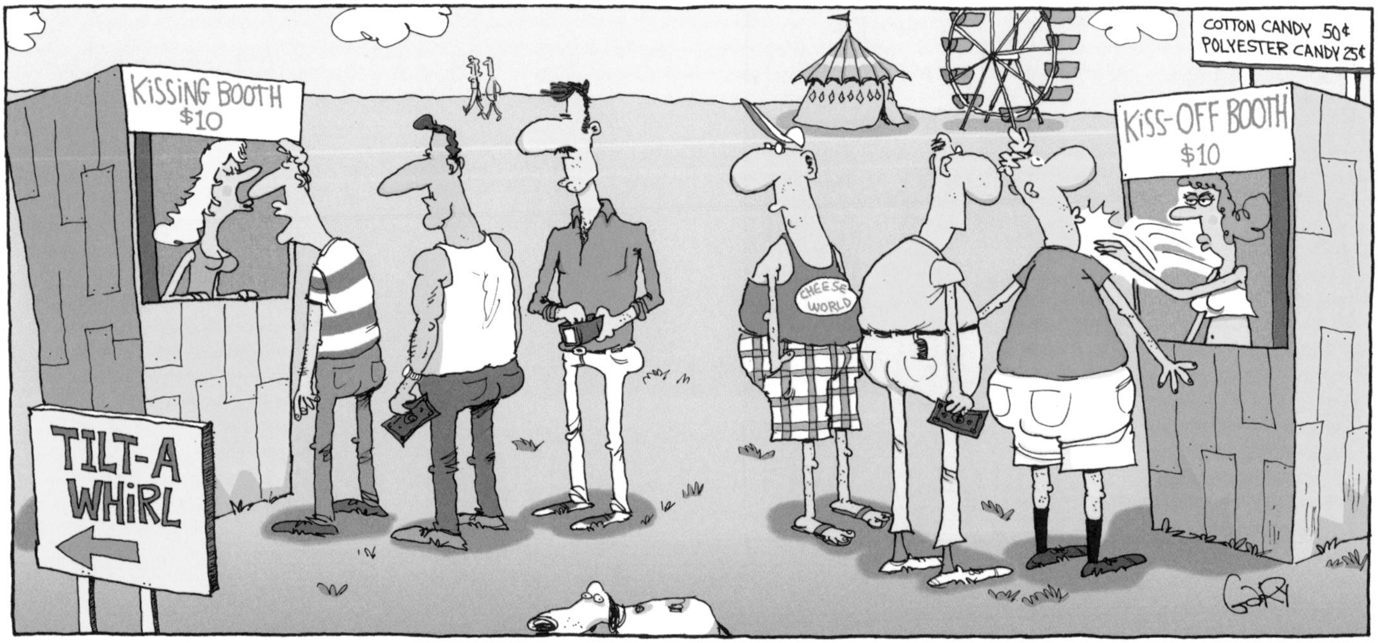
KiSSiNG BOOTH $10
COTTON CANDY 50¢
POLYESTER CANDY 25¢
KiSS-OFF BOOTH $10
CHEESE WORLD
TILT-A WHiRL
GARY

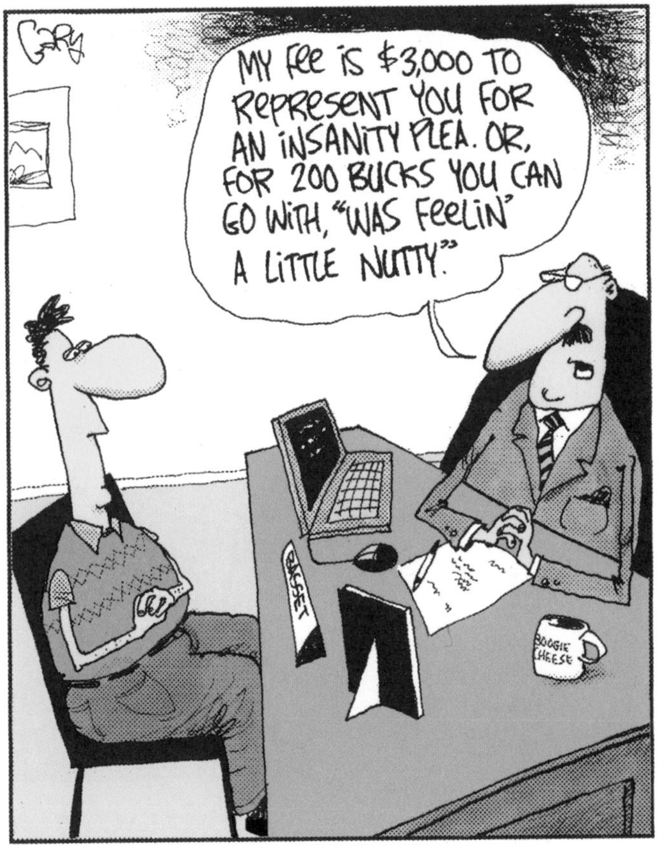
MY FEE IS $3,000 TO REPRESENT YOU FOR AN INSANITY PLEA. OR, FOR 200 BUCKS YOU CAN GO WITH, "WAS FEELIN' A LITTLE NUTTY."

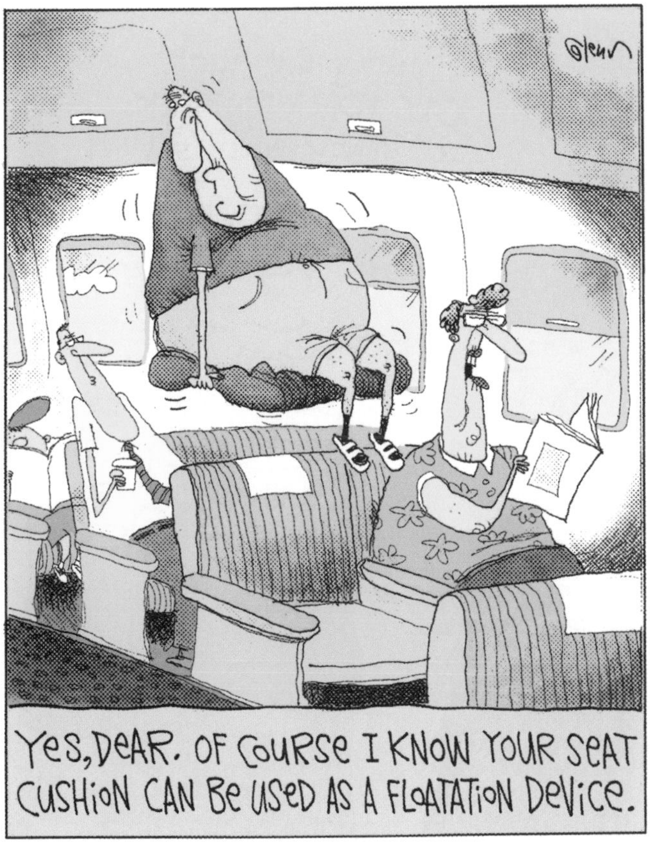

YES, DEAR. OF COURSE I KNOW YOUR SEAT CUSHION CAN BE USED AS A FLOATATION DEVICE.

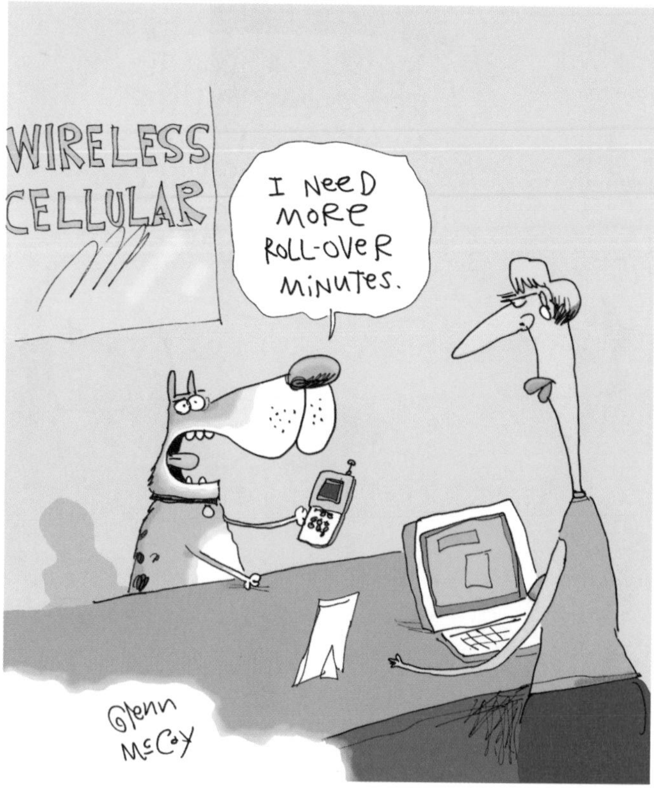
WIRELESS CELLULAR
I NeeD MORe ROLL-OVER MiNUTeS.
Glenn McCoy

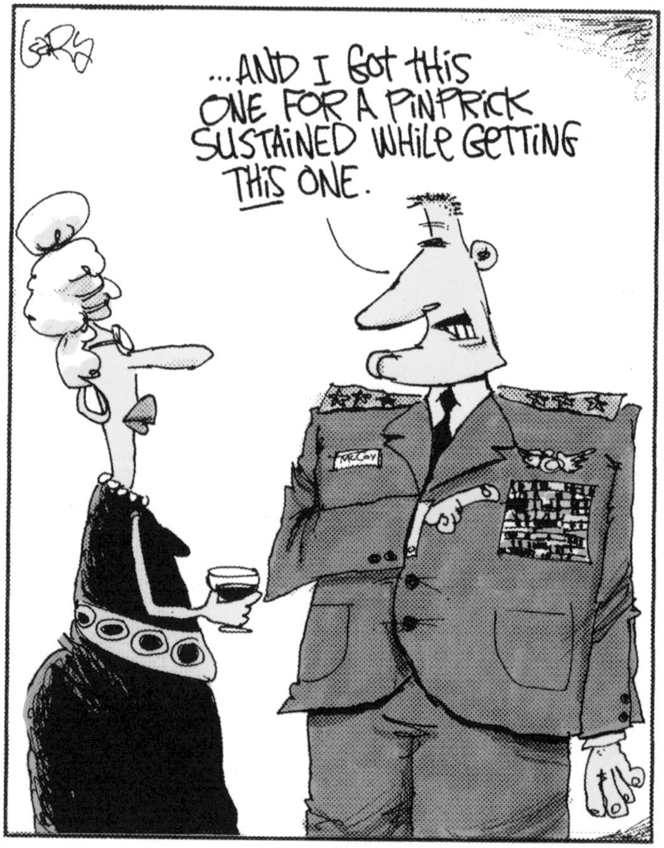
GARY
...AND I GOT THIS ONE FOR A PINPRICK SUSTAINED WHILE GETTING THIS ONE.
McCoy

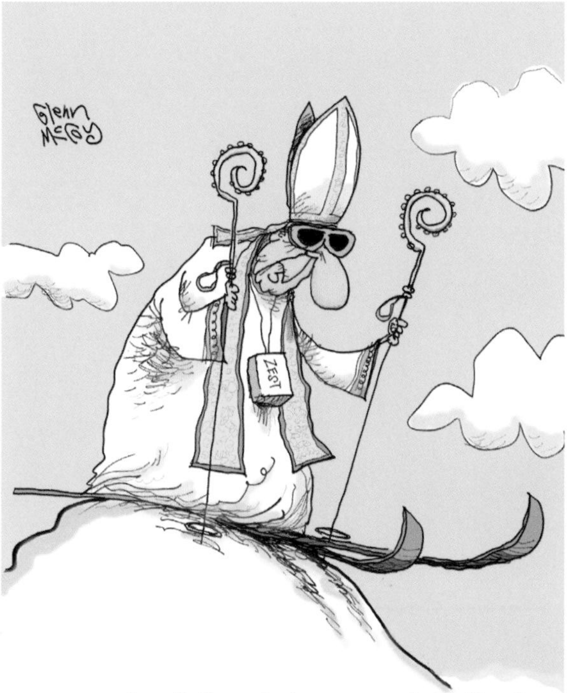
ZEST
Glenn McCoy

SOAP ON A ROPE ON A POPE ON A SLOPE.

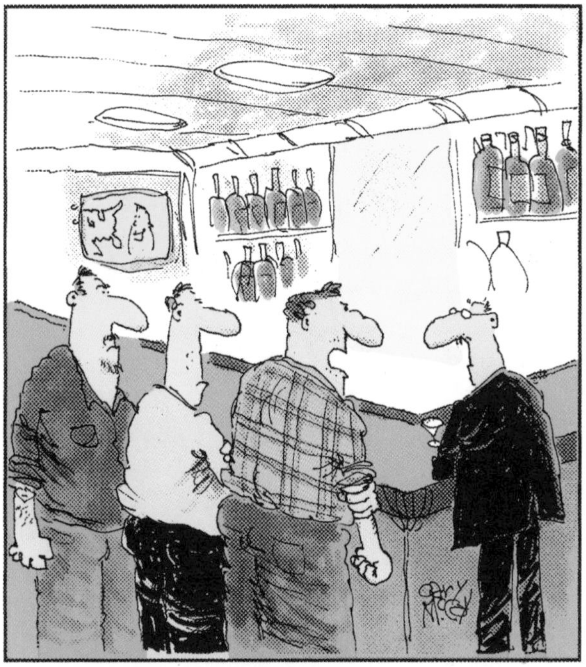

"We heard that you specialize in breast-reduction surgery. Care to step outside for a minute?"

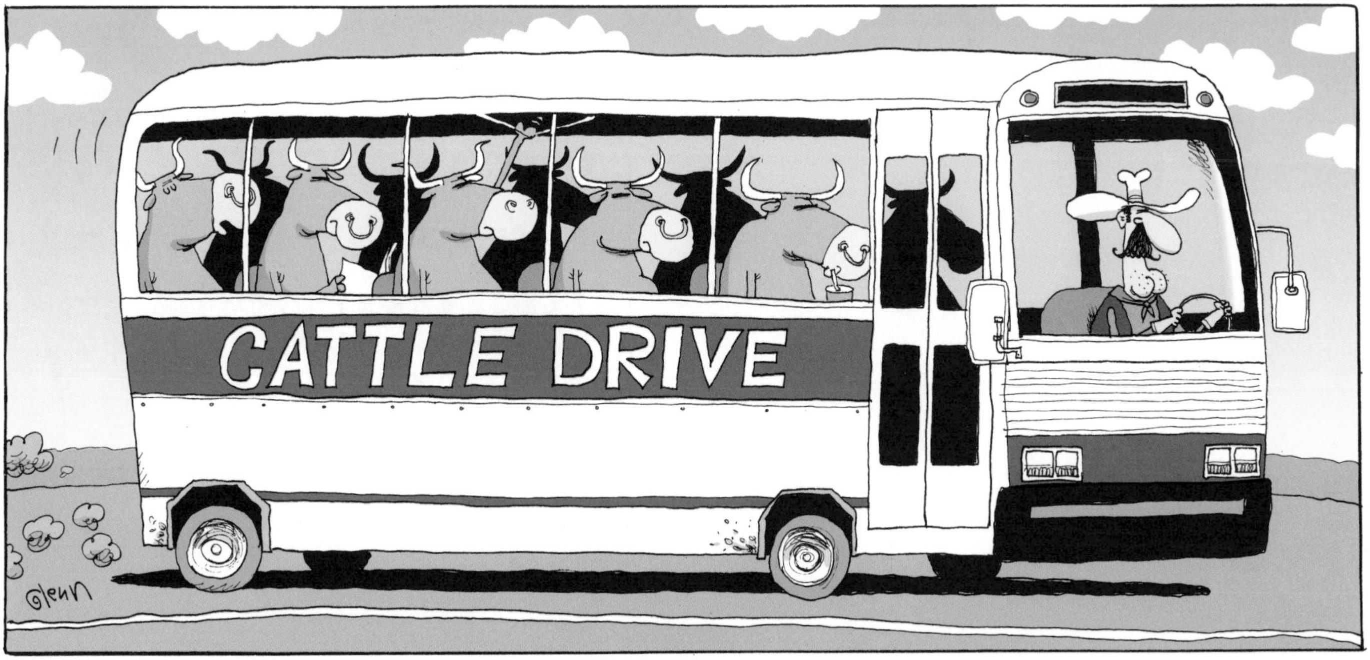
CATTLE DRIVE
Glenn

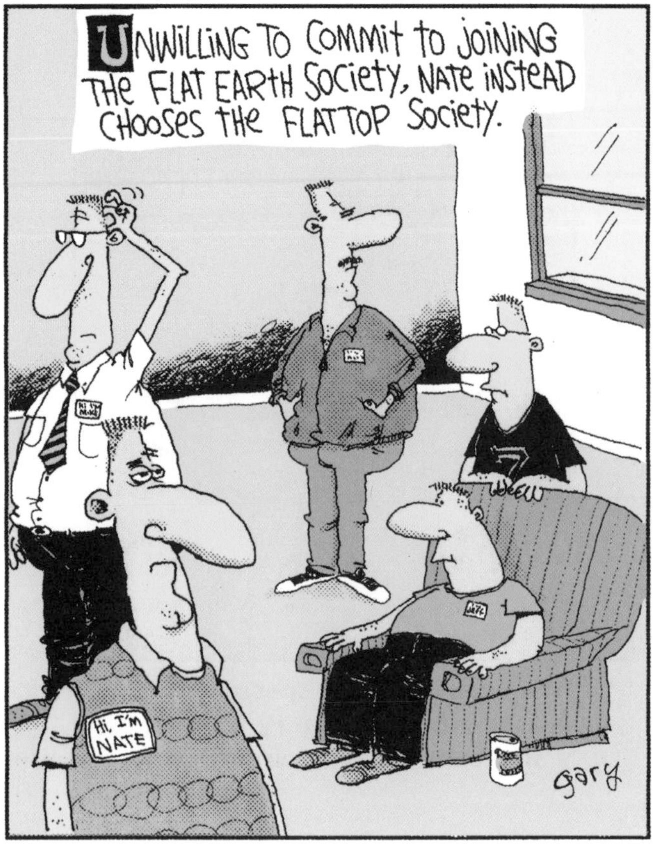
UNWILLING TO COMMIT TO JOINING THE FLAT EARTH SOCIETY, NATE INSTEAD CHOOSES THE FLATTOP SOCIETY.
HI, I'M NATE
gary

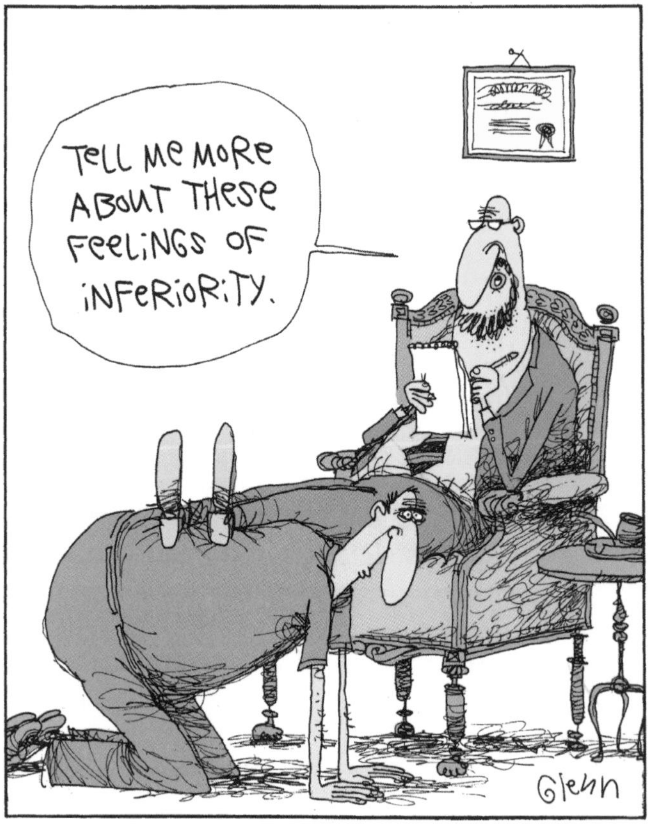
TELL ME MORE ABOUT THESE FEELINGS OF INFERIORITY.
Glenn

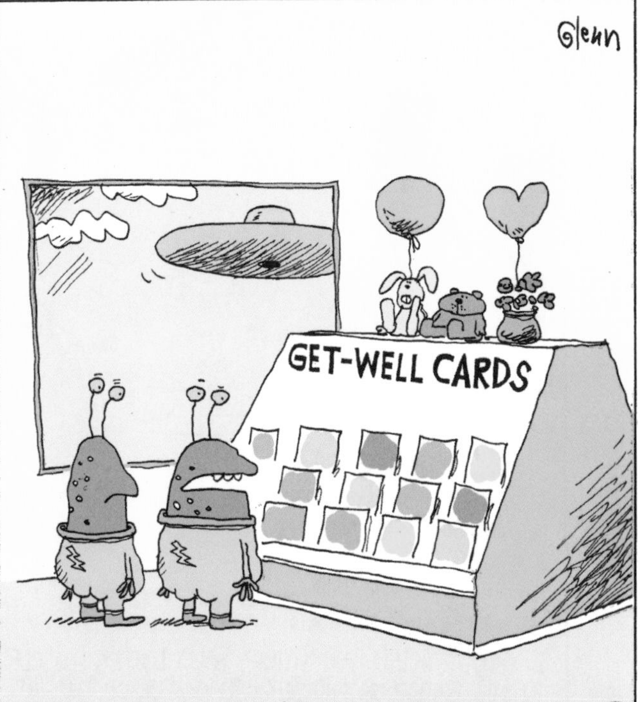
Glenn
GET-WELL CARDS

THEIR MEDICINE IS APPARENTLY FAR MORE ADVANCED THAN OURS.

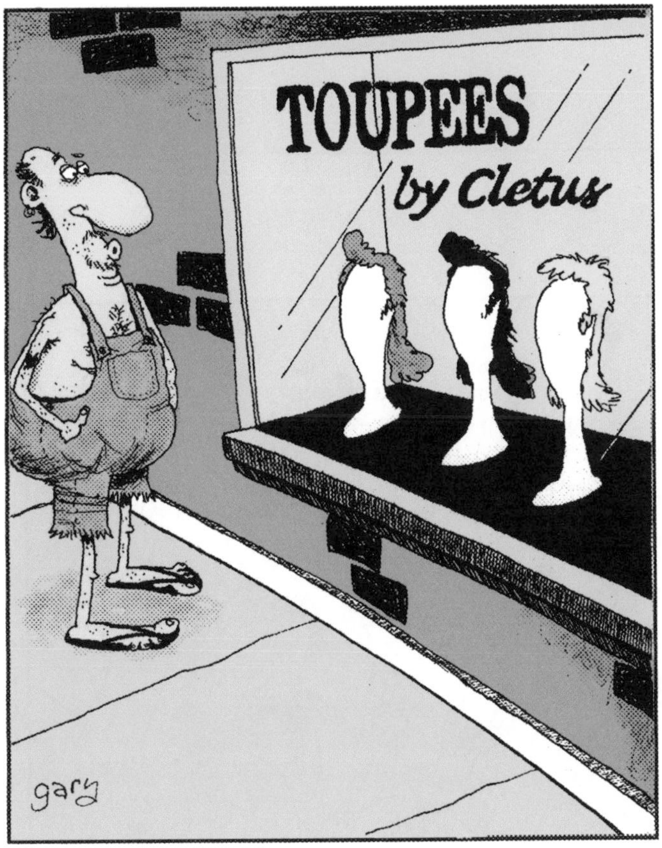
TOUPEES
by Cletus
gary

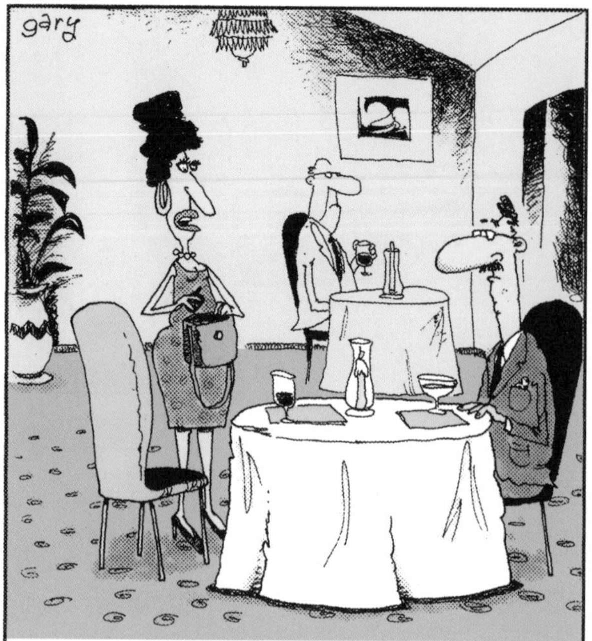

"I JUST CALLED THE SITTER. BILLY LOCKED HIMSELF IN THE BATHROOM AND SUZIE THREW UP ON THE CAT. NOW – WHAT SOUNDS GOOD FOR DESSERT?"

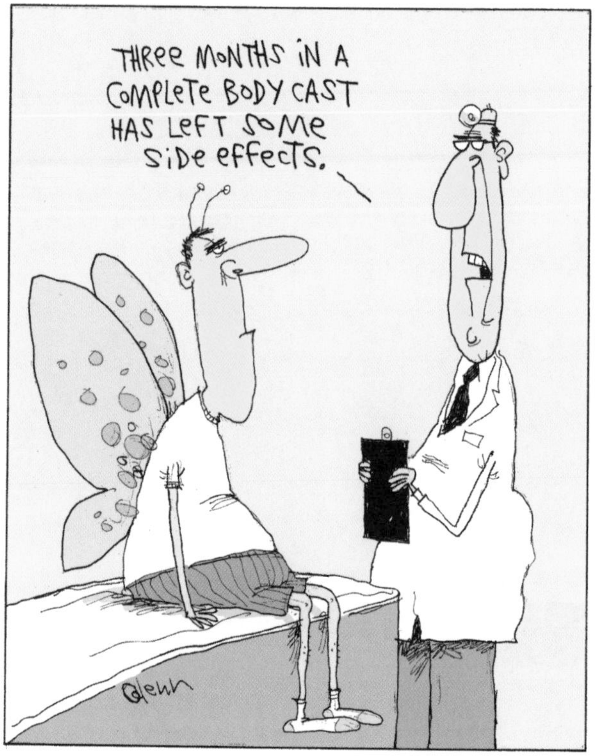
THREE MONTHS IN A COMPLETE BODY CAST HAS LEFT SOME SIDE EFFECTS.

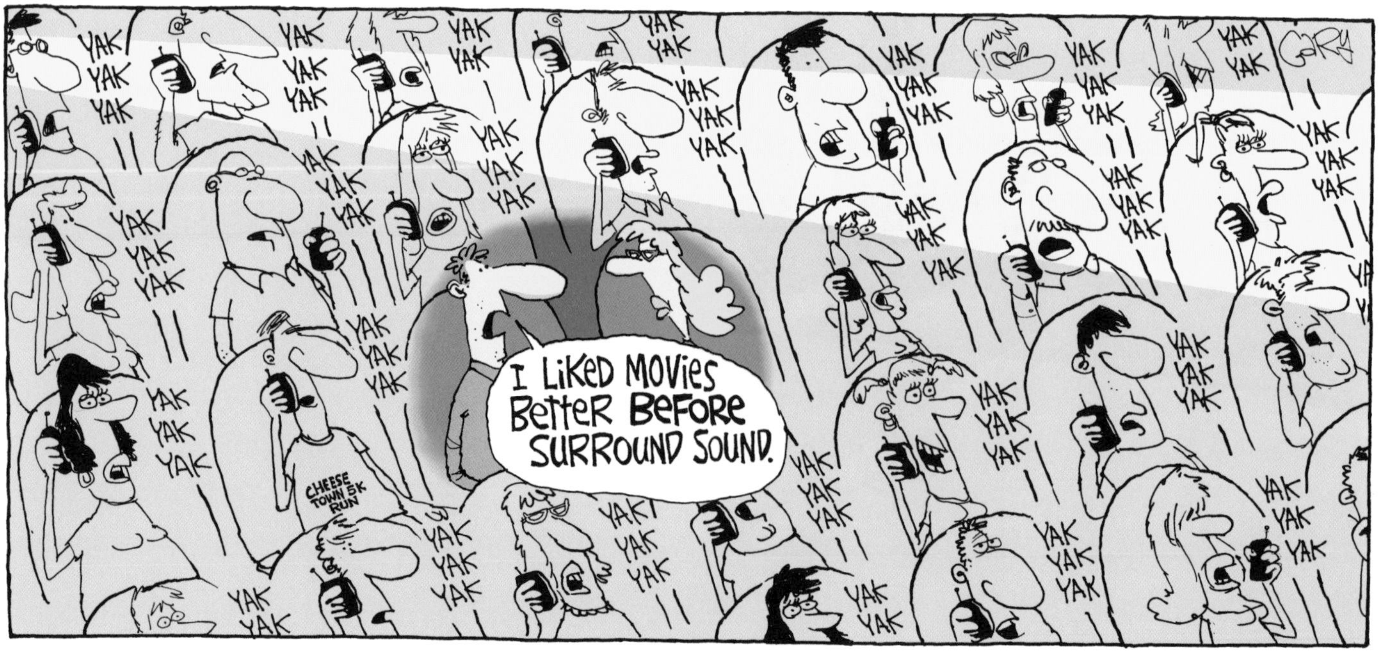
I LIKED MOVIES BETTER BEFORE SURROUND SOUND.
CHEESE TOWN 5K RUN

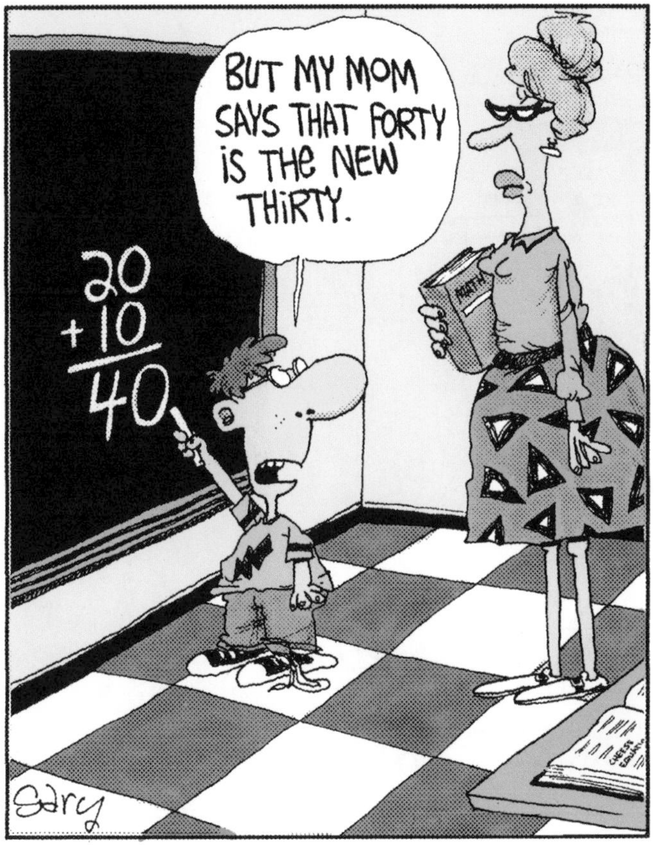
BUT MY MOM SAYS THAT FORTY IS THE NEW THIRTY.
20
+10
40
MATH
Gary

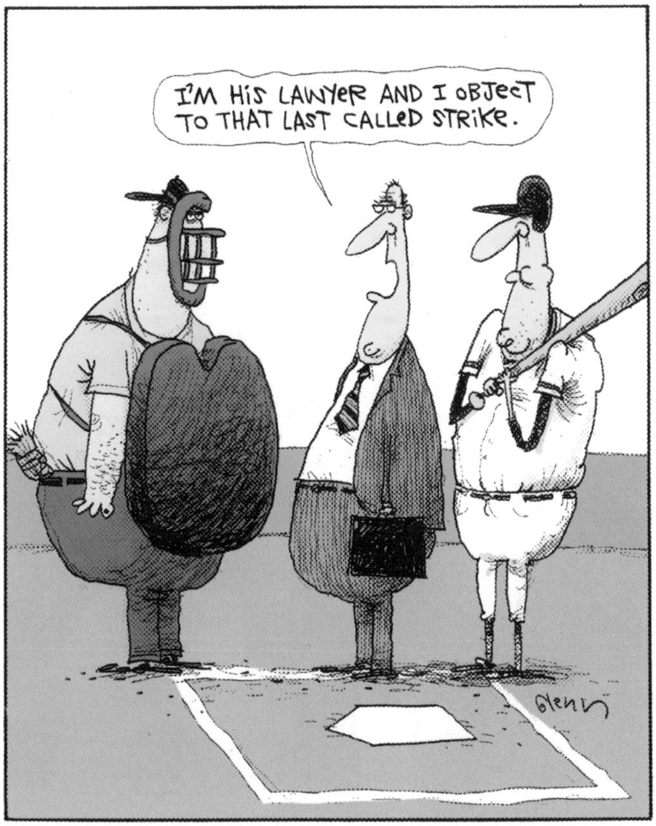
I'M HIS LAWYER AND I OBJECT TO THAT LAST CALLED STRIKE.
Glenn

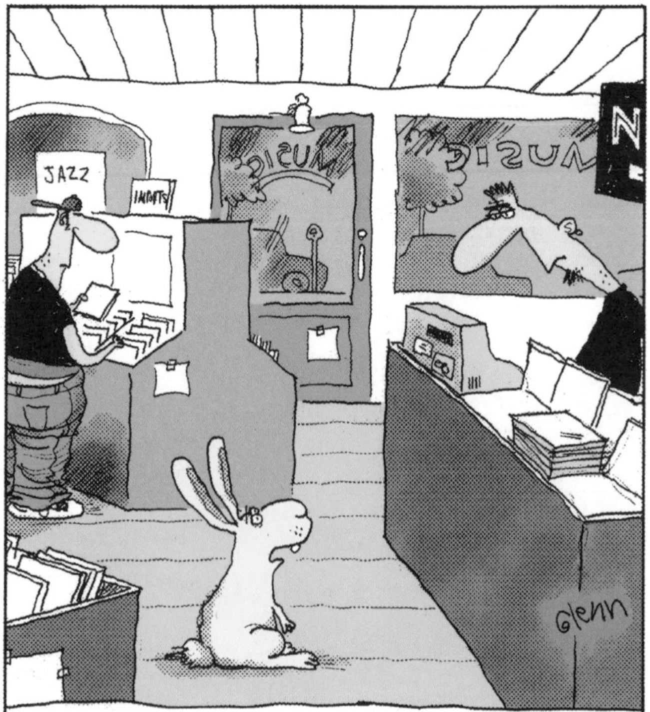
JAZZ
MUSIC
Glenn

WHERE'S YOUR HIP-HOP?

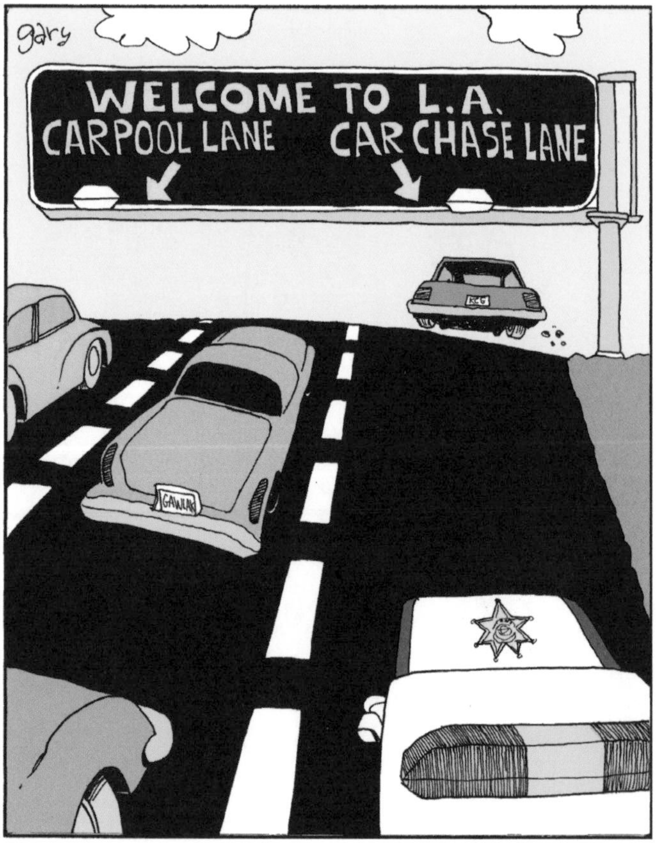
gary
WELCOME TO L.A.
CARPOOL LANE
CAR CHASE LANE

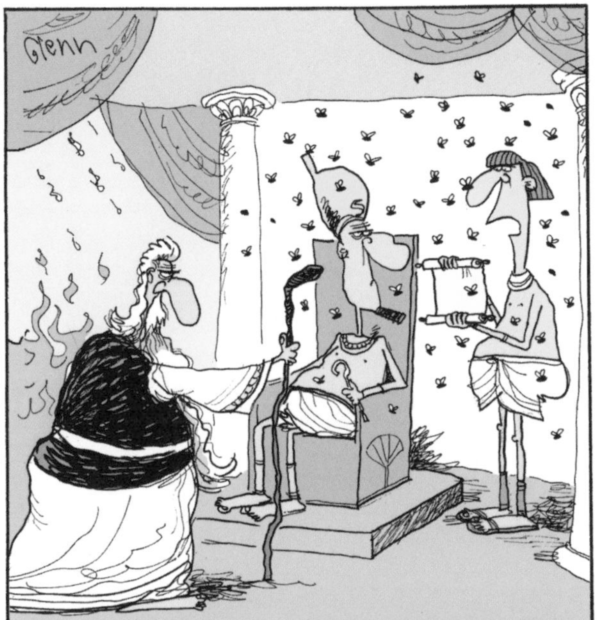
Glenn

BAD NEWS. OUR LOCUST-AND-BURNING-HAIL INSURANCE HAS LAPSED.

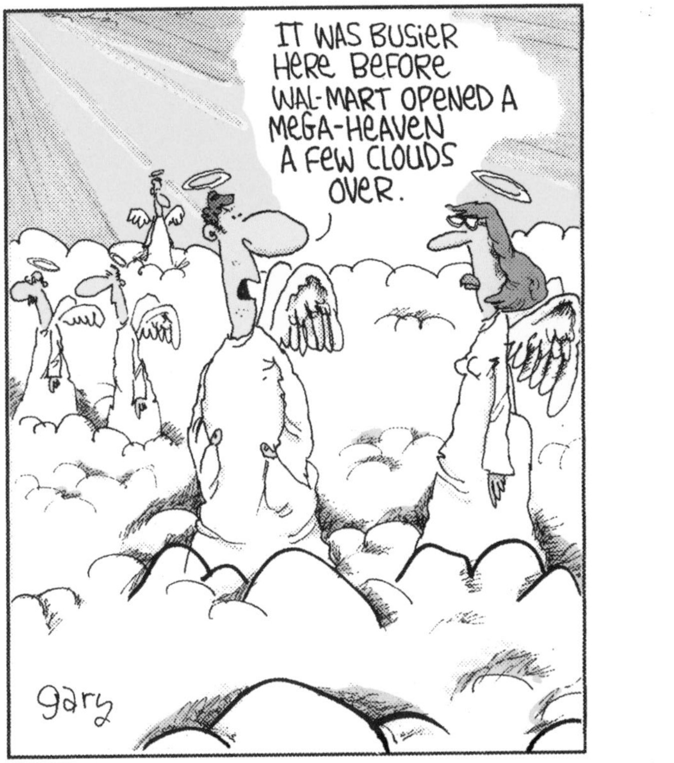
IT WAS BUSIER HERE BEFORE WAL-MART OPENED A MEGA-HEAVEN A FEW CLOUDS OVER.
gary

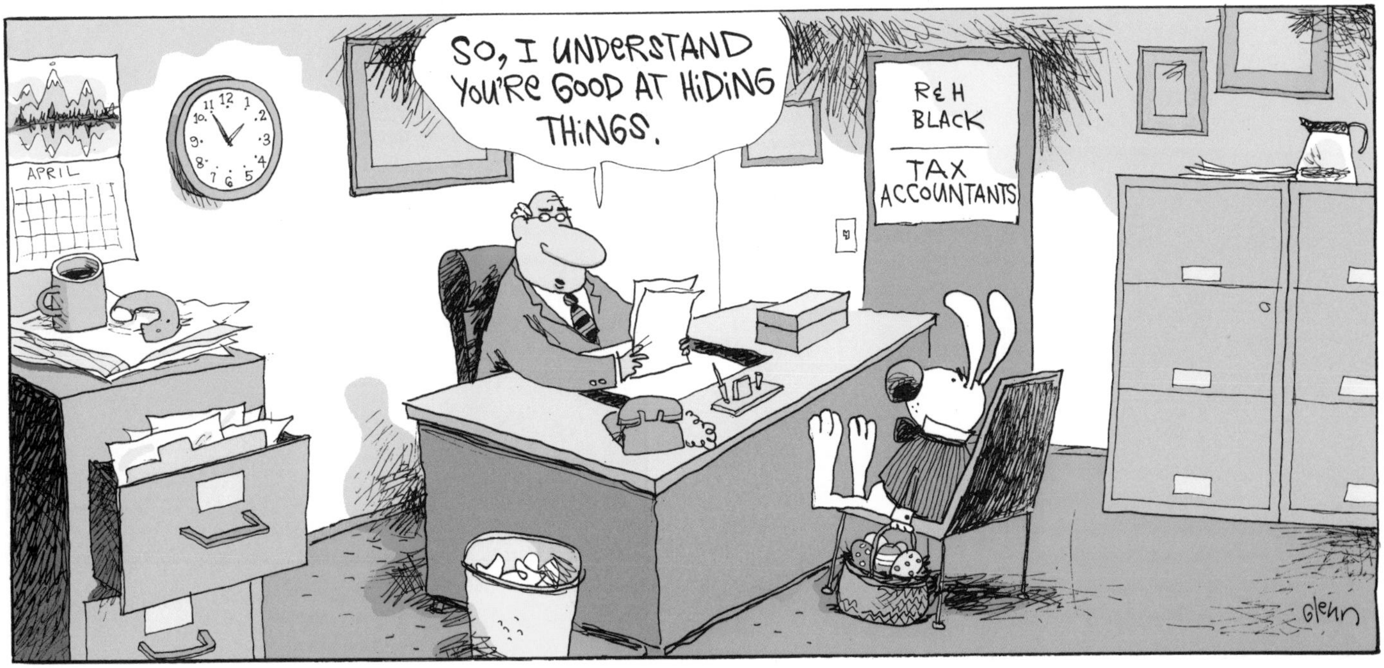
SO, I UNDERSTAND YOU'RE GOOD AT HIDING THINGS.
APRIL
R&H BLACK
TAX ACCOUNTANTS
Glenn

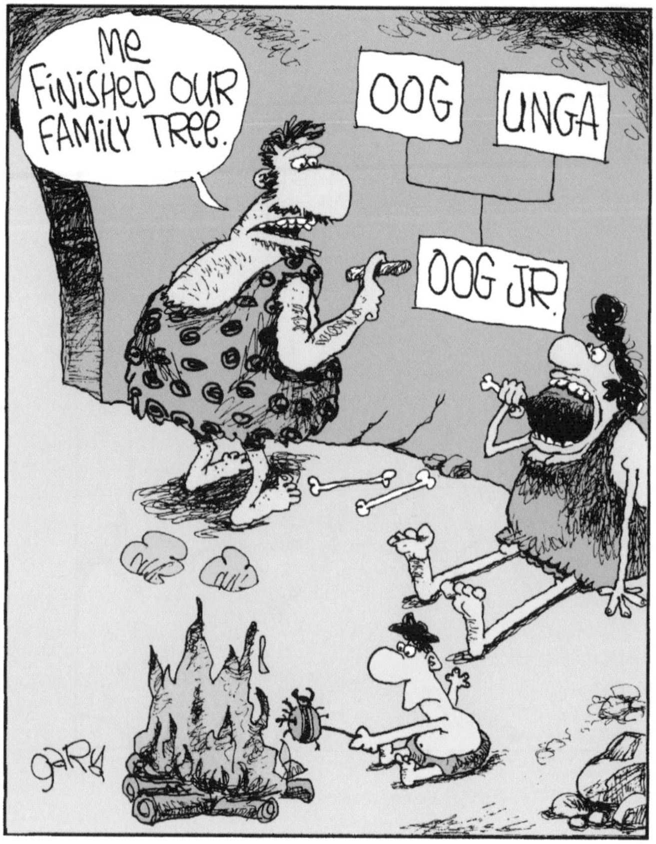
ME FINISHED OUR FAMILY TREE.
OOG
UNGA
OOG JR.

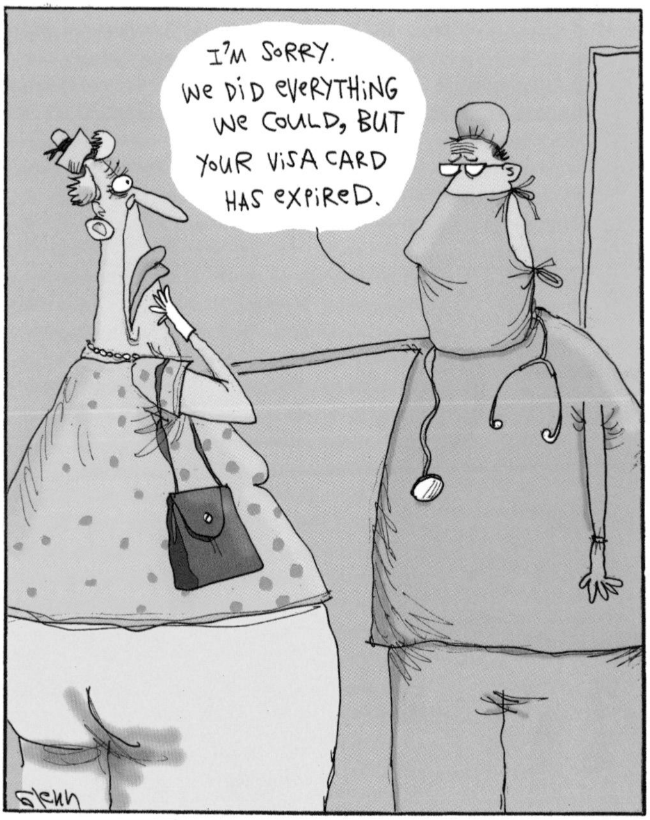
I'M SORRY. WE DID EVERYTHING WE COULD, BUT YOUR VISA CARD HAS EXPIRED.

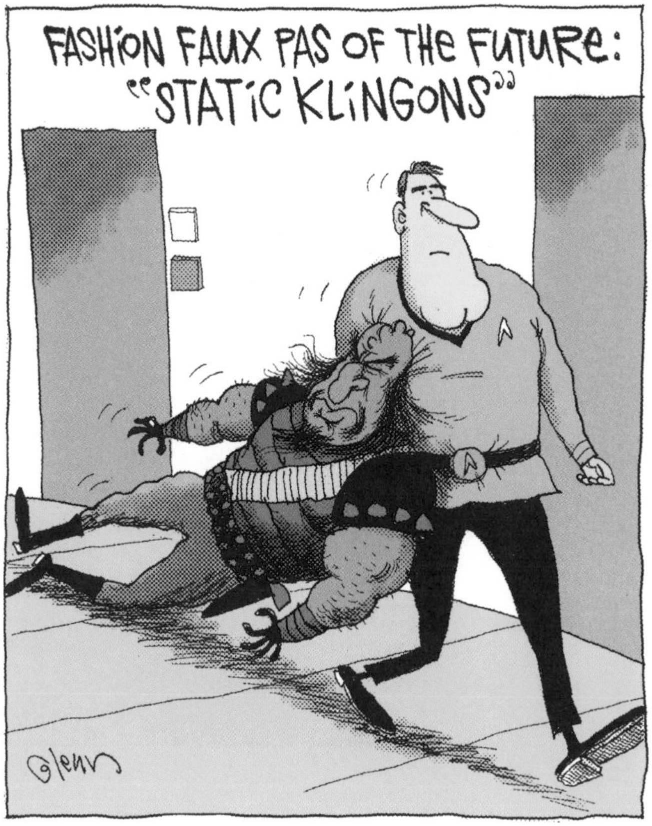
FASHION FAUX PAS OF THE FUTURE:
"STATIC KLINGONS"
Glenn

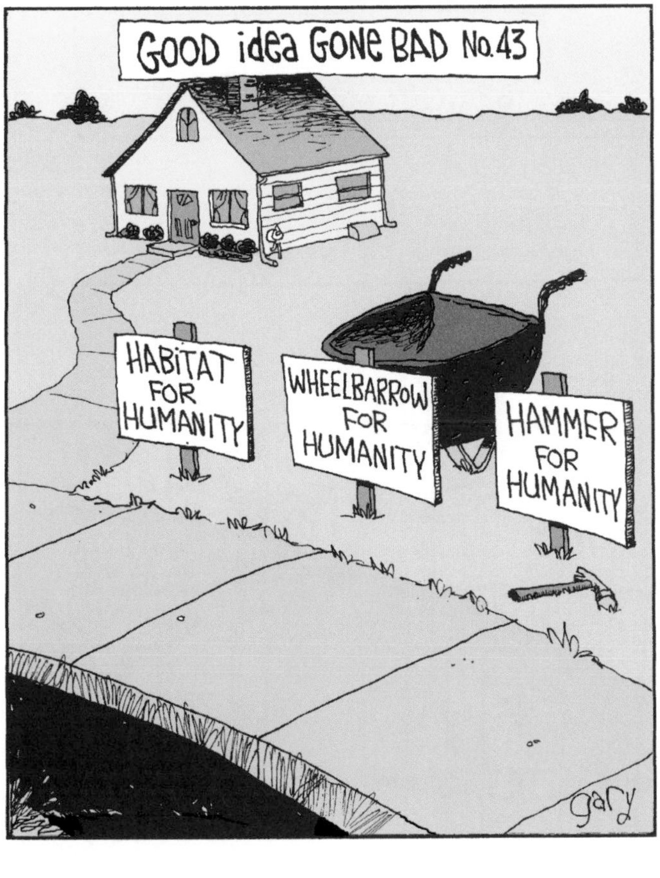
GOOD idea GONE BAD No.43
HABITAT FOR HUMANITY
WHEELBARROW FOR HUMANITY
HAMMER FOR HUMANITY
gary

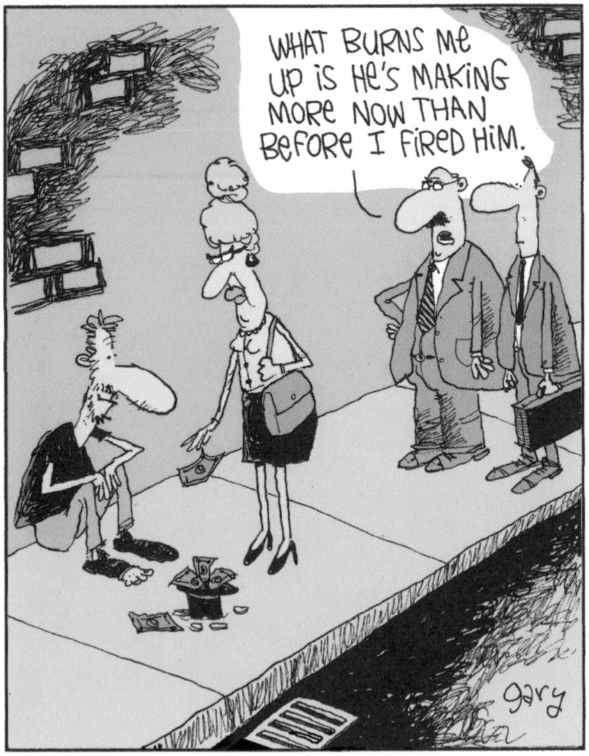
WHAT BURNS ME UP IS HE'S MAKING MORE NOW THAN BEFORE I FIRED HIM.
gary

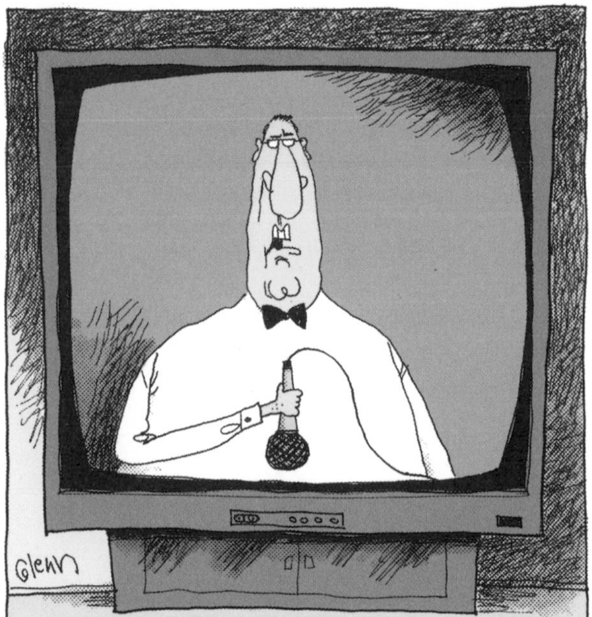
Glenn

"We are experiencing technical difficulties."

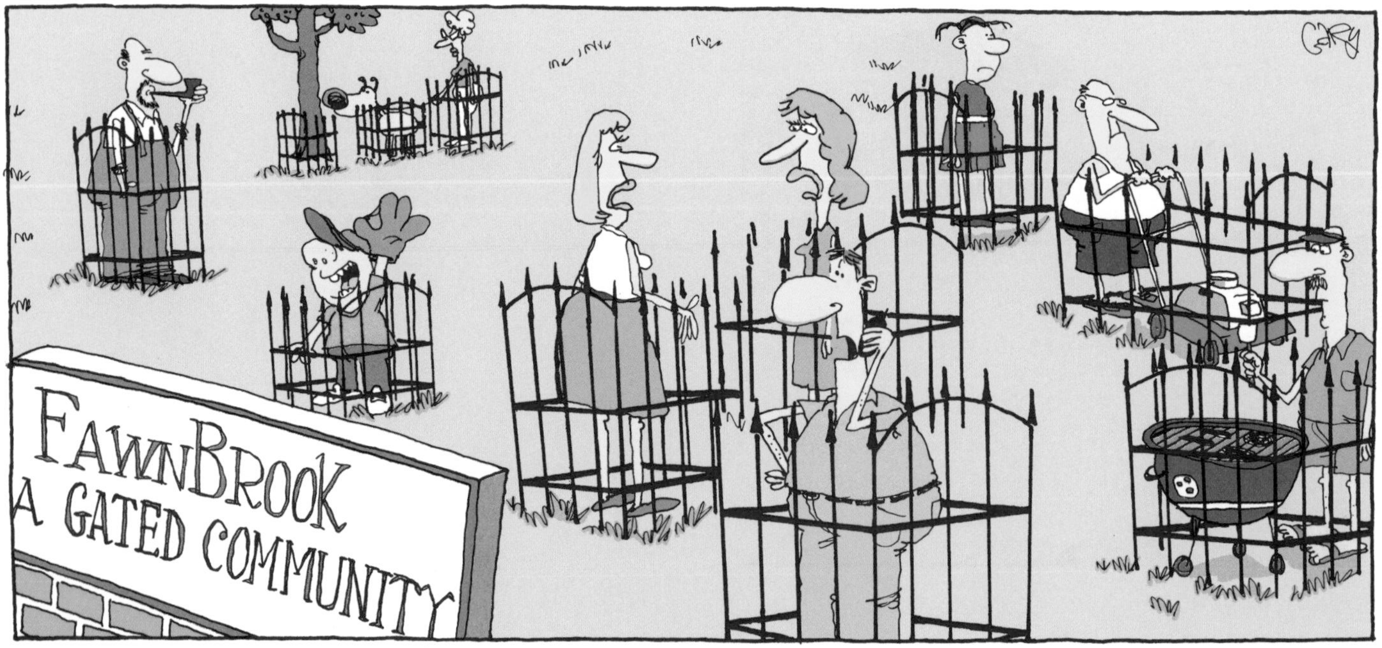
Gary
FAWNBROOK
A GATED COMMUNITY

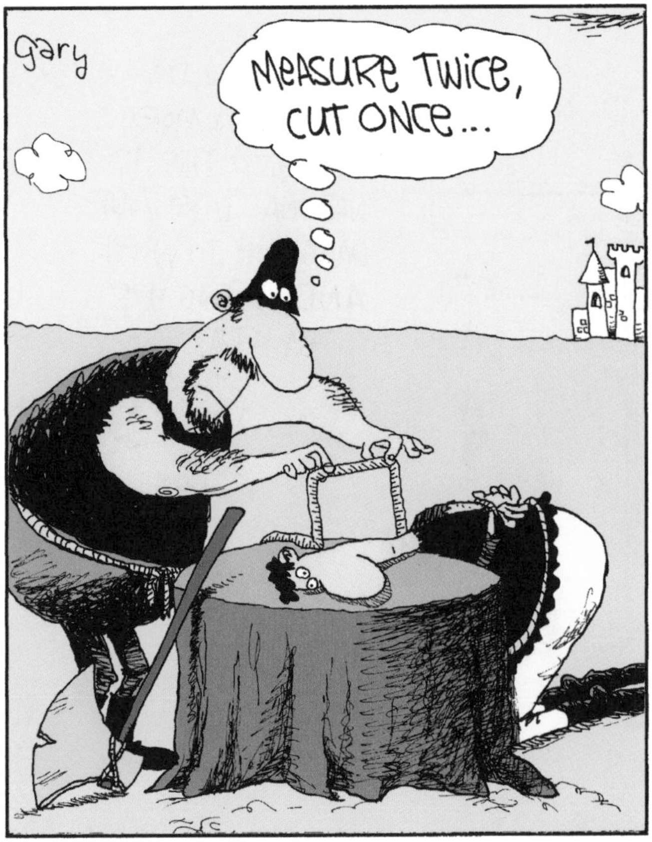
gary
Measure twice, cut once...

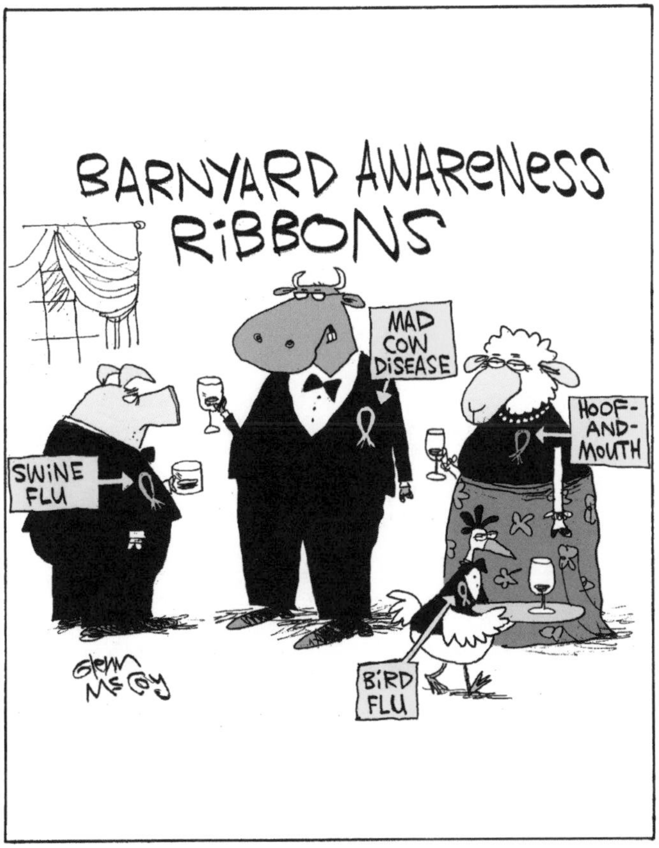
BARNYARD AWARENESS RIBBONS
MAD COW DISEASE
SWINE FLU
HOOF-AND-MOUTH
BIRD FLU
Glenn McCoy

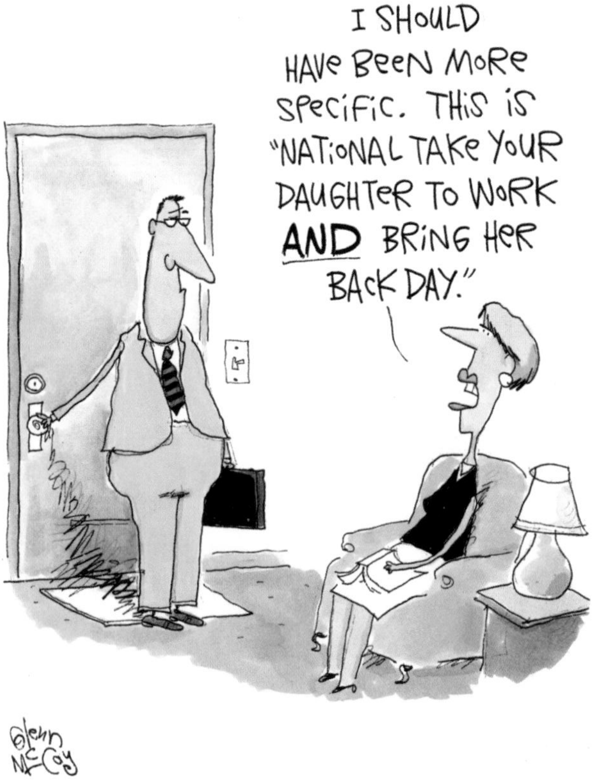
I SHOULD HAVE BEEN MORE SPECIFIC. THIS IS "NATIONAL TAKE YOUR DAUGHTER TO WORK AND BRING HER BACK DAY."
Glenn McCoy

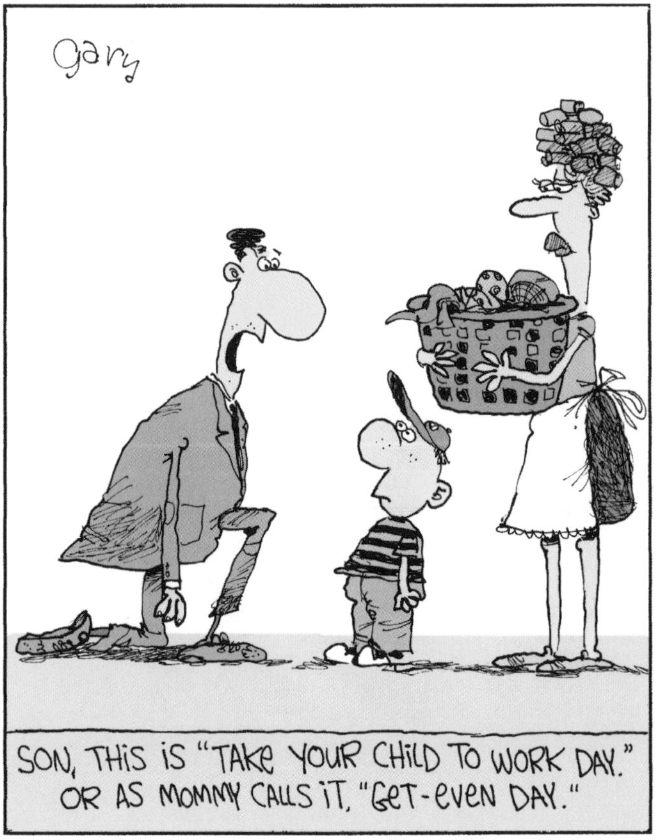
gary
SON, THIS IS "TAKE YOUR CHILD TO WORK DAY." OR AS MOMMY CALLS IT, "GET-EVEN DAY."

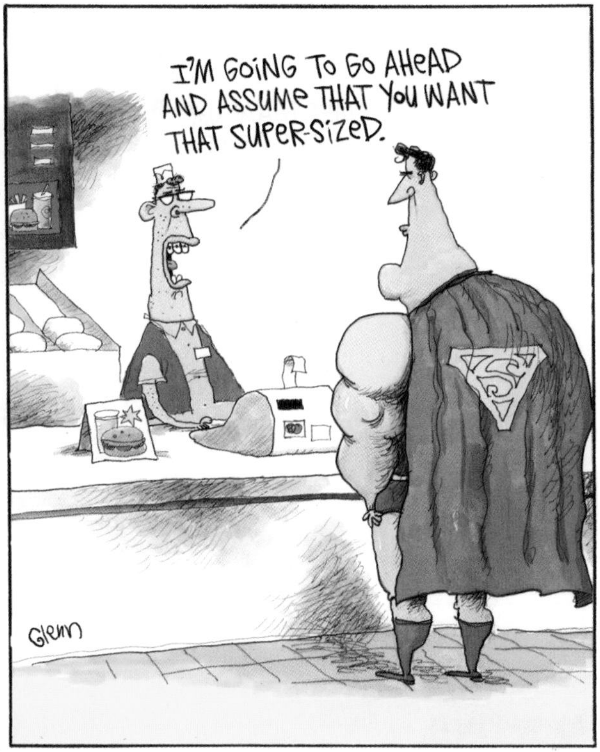
I'M GOING TO GO AHEAD AND ASSUME THAT YOU WANT THAT SUPER-SIZED.
Glenn

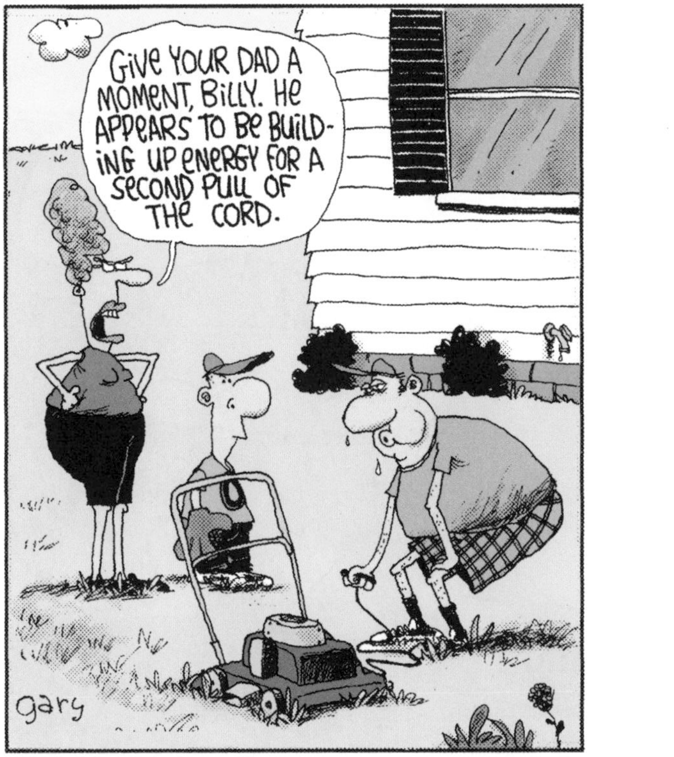
GIVE YOUR DAD A MOMENT, BILLY. HE APPEARS TO BE BUILDING UP ENERGY FOR A SECOND PULL OF THE CORD.
gary

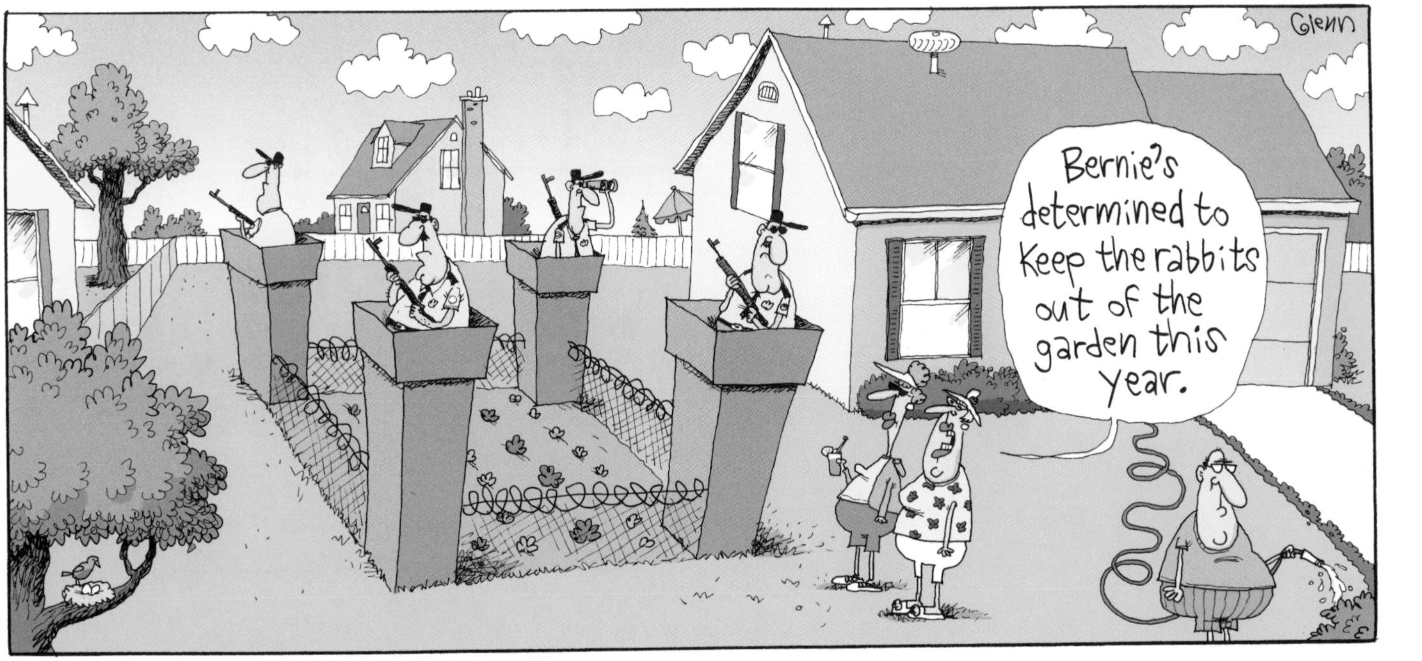
Glenn
Bernie's determined to keep the rabbits out of the garden this year.

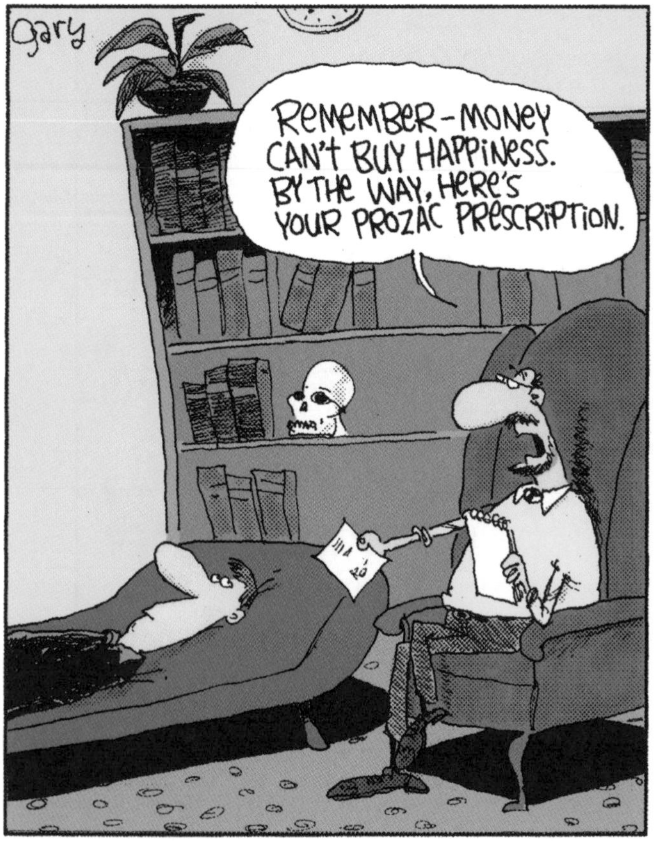
Gary
REMEMBER-MONEY CAN'T BUY HAPPINESS. BY THE WAY, HERE'S YOUR PROZAC PRESCRIPTION.

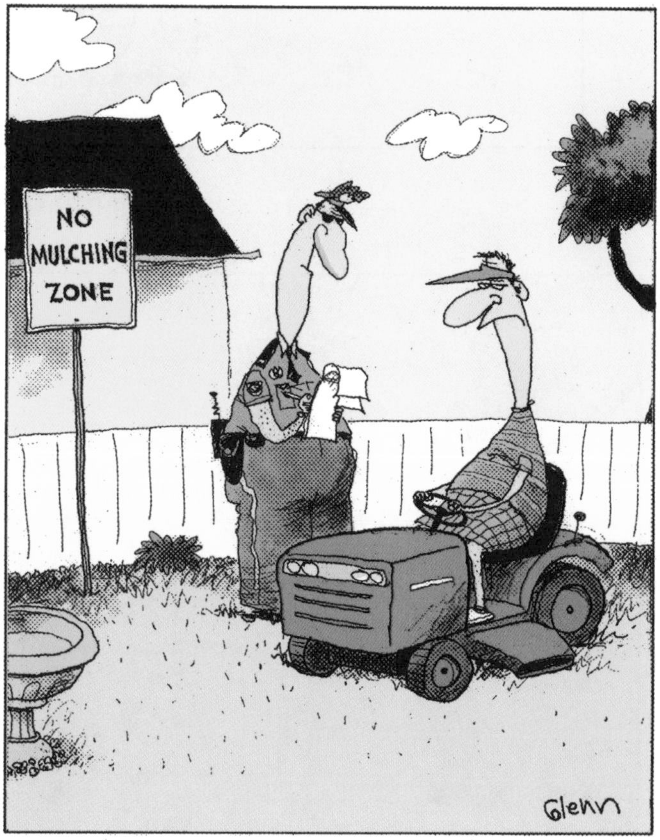
NO MULCHING ZONE
Glenn

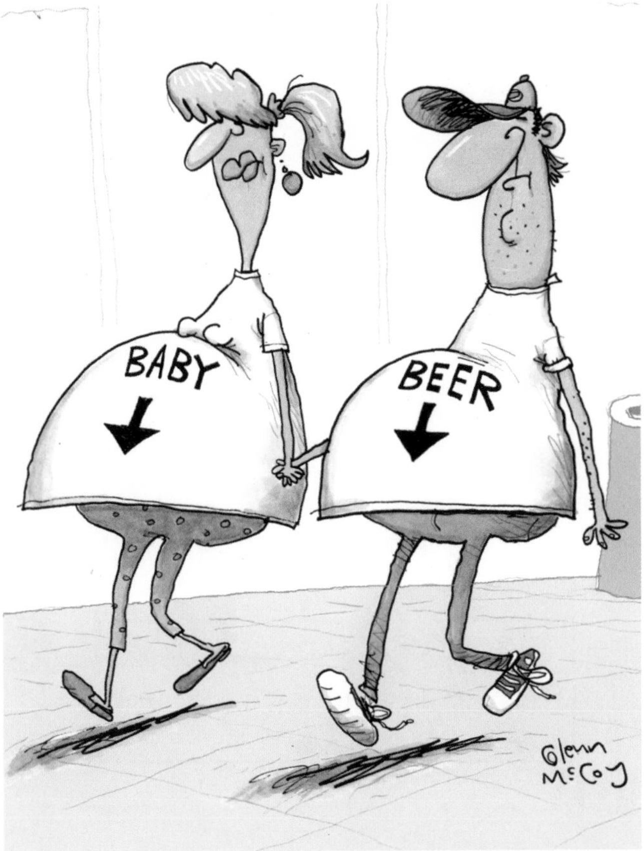
BABY
BEER
Glenn McCoy

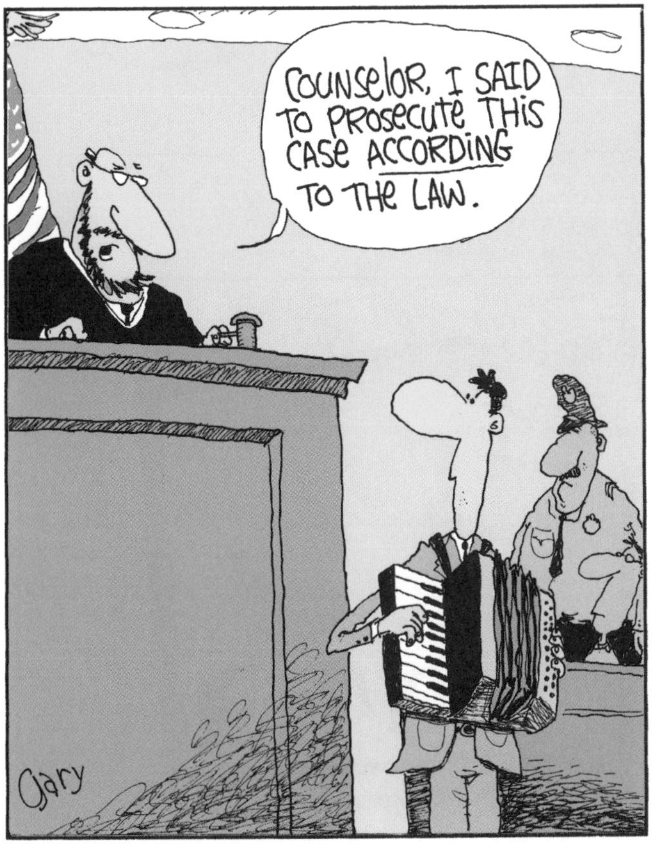
COUNSELOR, I SAID TO PROSECUTE THIS CASE ACCORDING TO THE LAW.
Gary

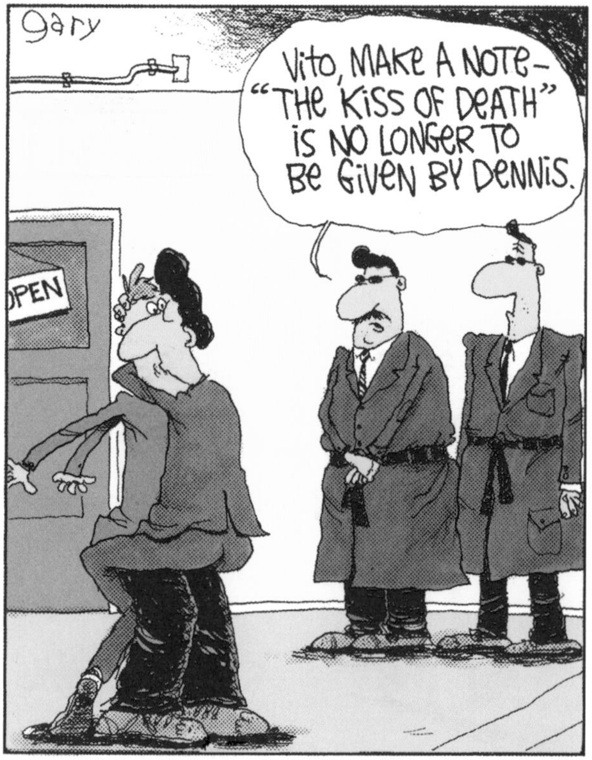
gary
Vito, MAKE A NOTE– "THE KISS OF DEATH" is NO LONGER TO Be GiVEN BY DENNiS.
OPEN

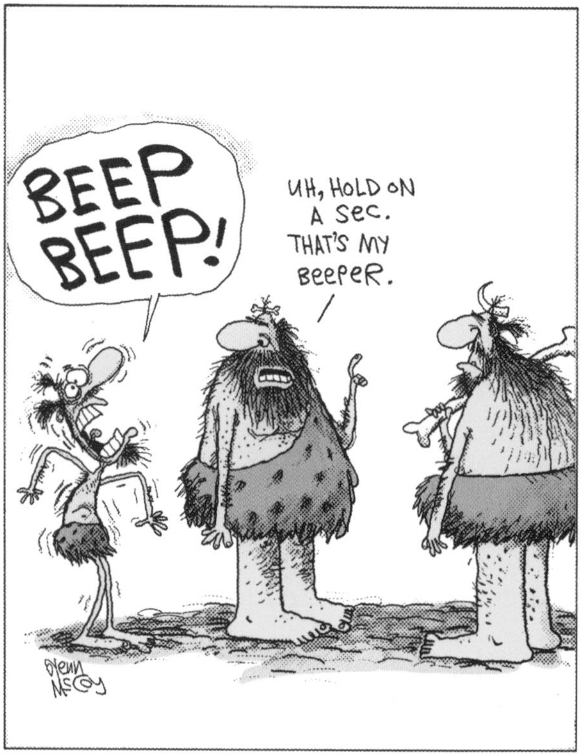
BEEP BEEP!
UH, HOLD ON A Sec. THAT'S MY BeePeR.

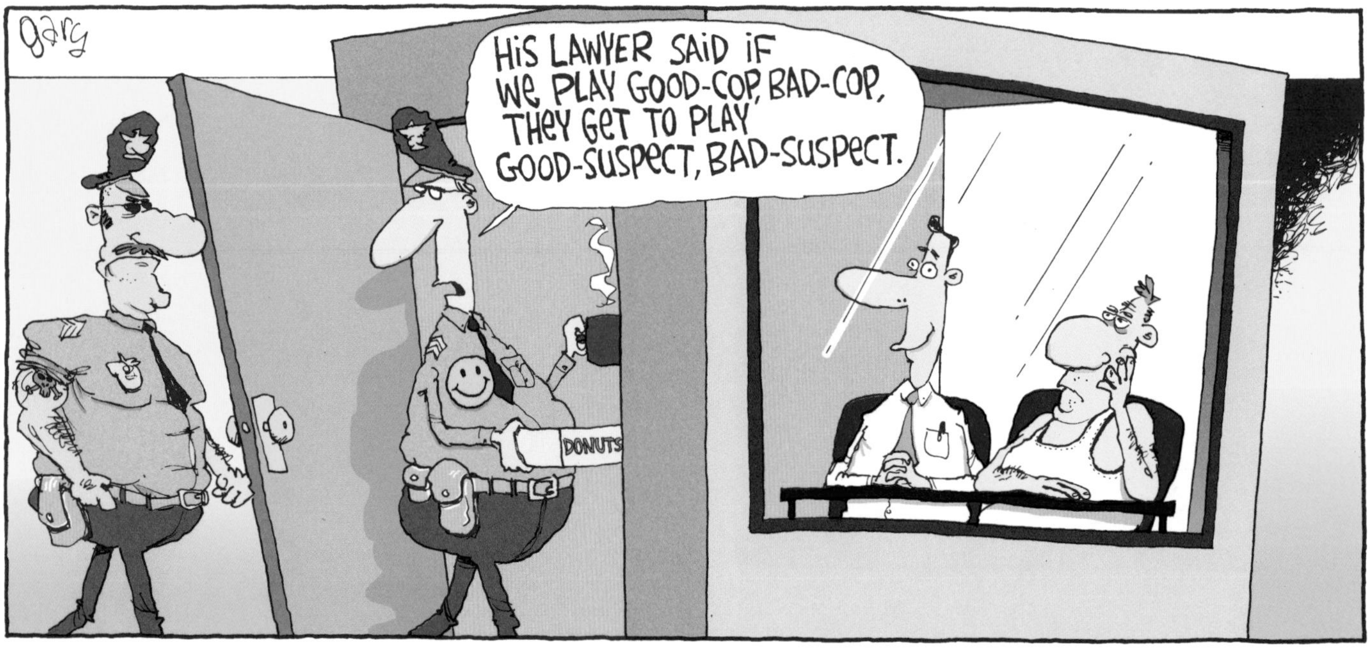
gary
His LAWYER SAID iF We PLAY GOOD-COP, BAD-COP, THEY GET TO PLAY GOOD-SUSPECT, BAD-SUSPECT.
DONUTS

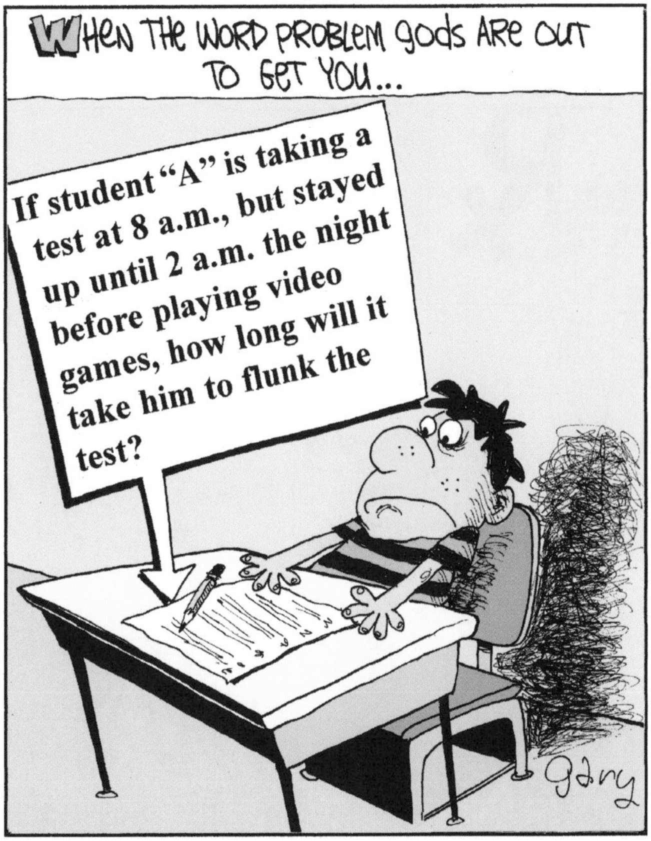
WHEN THE WORD PROBLEM GODS ARE OUT TO GET YOU...
If student "A" is taking a test at 8 a.m., but stayed up until 2 a.m. the night before playing video games, how long will it take him to flunk the test?
Gary

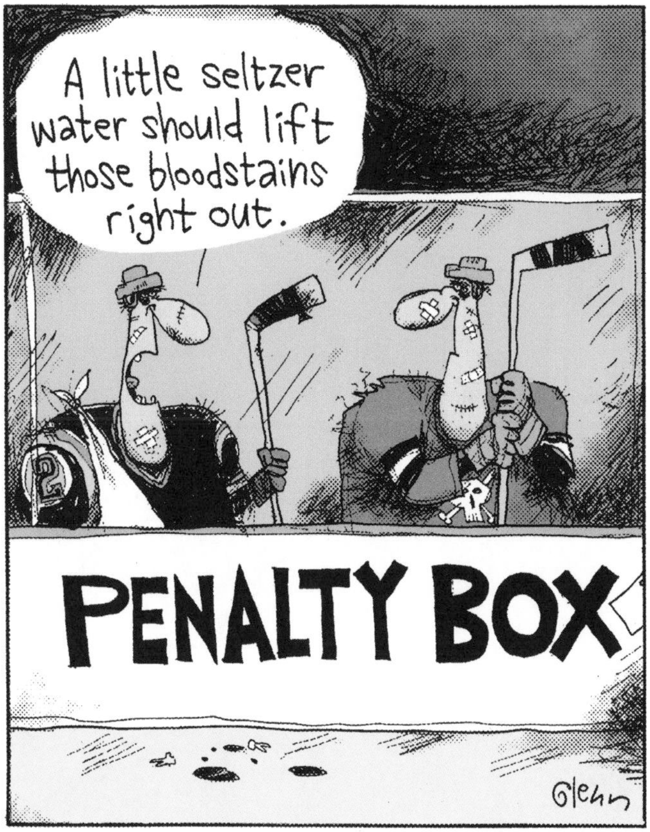
A little seltzer water should lift those bloodstains right out.
PENALTY BOX
Glenn

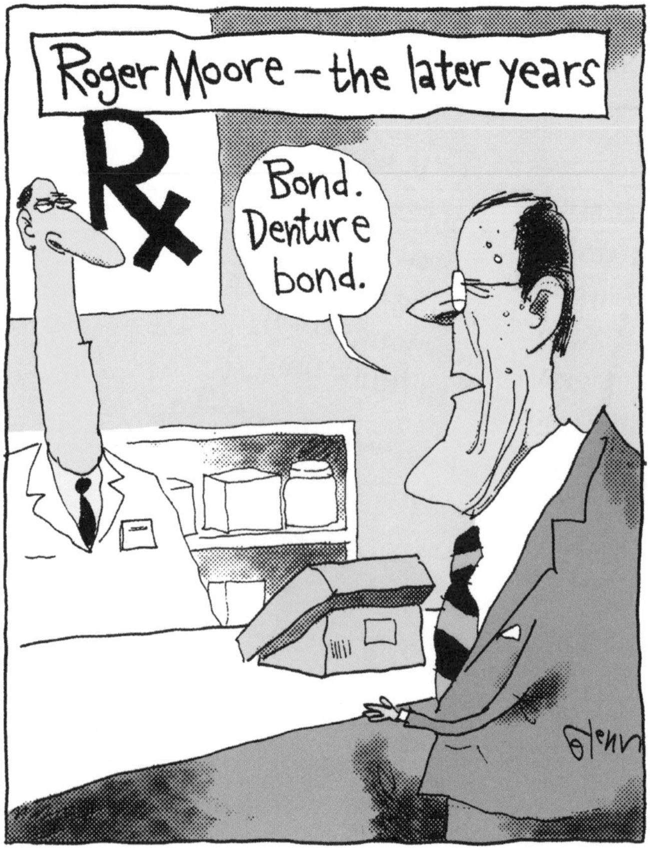
Roger Moore – the later years
Rx
Bond. Denture bond.
Glenn

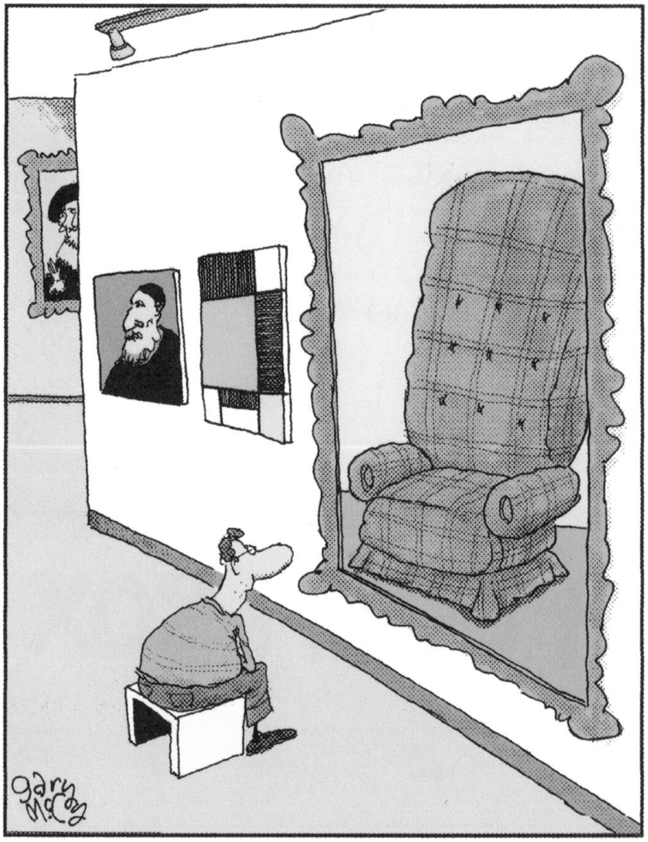
gary McCoy

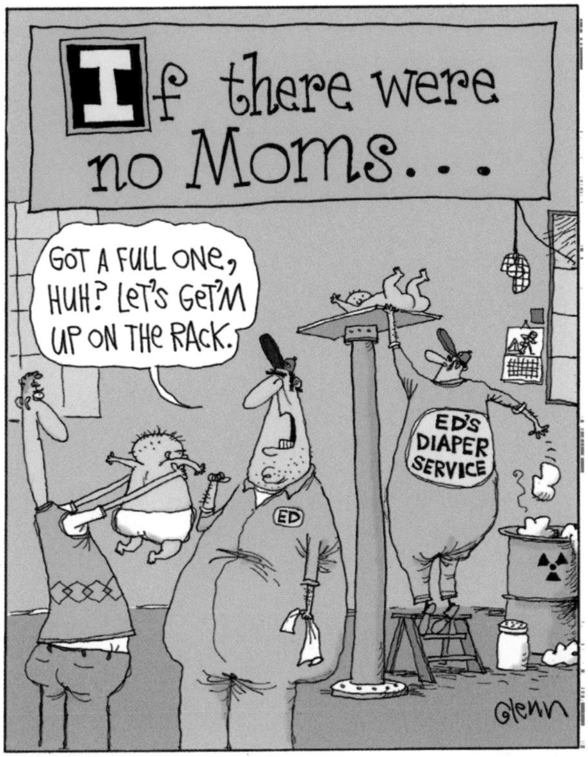
If there were no Moms. . .
GOT A FULL ONE, HUH? LET'S GET'M UP ON THE RACK.
ED'S DIAPER SERVICE
ED
Glenn

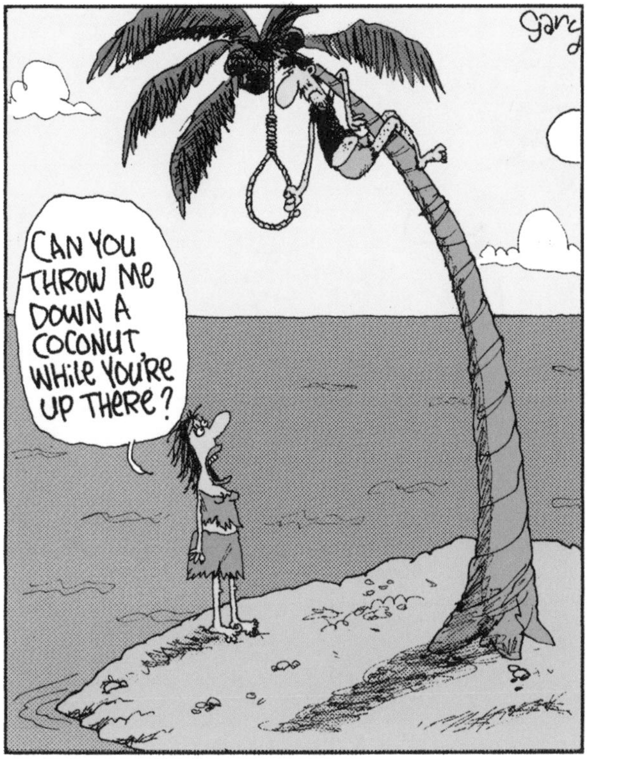
CAN YOU THROW ME DOWN A COCONUT WHILE YOU'RE UP THERE?
Gary

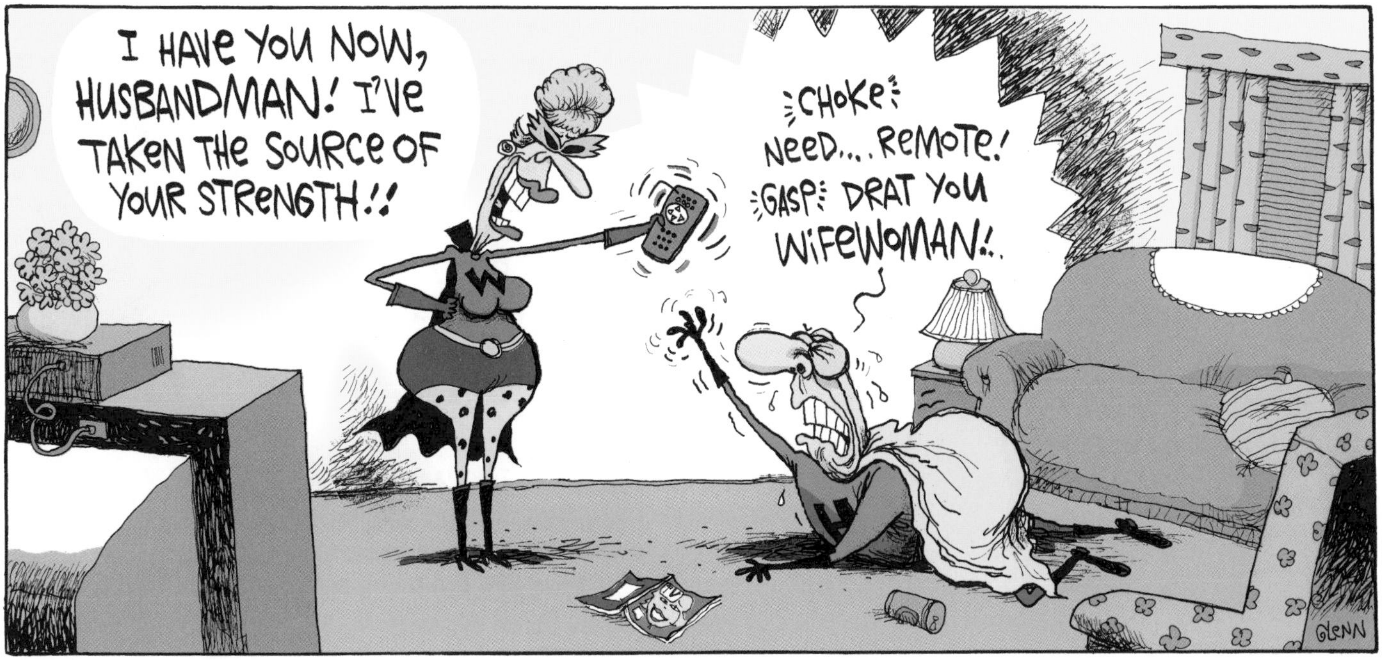
I HAVE YOU NOW, HUSBANDMAN! I'VE TAKEN THE SOURCE OF YOUR STRENGTH!!
CHOKE NEED.... REMOTE! GASP DRAT YOU WIFEWOMAN!..
GLENN

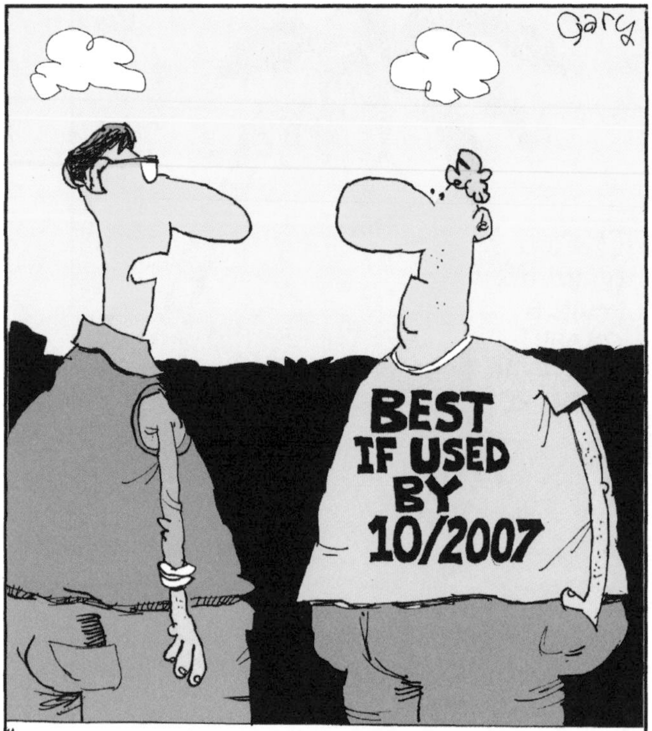
BEST
IF USED
BY
10/2007

"EARL, I KNOW YOU HAVE A PROBLEM WITH GIRLS TAKING ADVANTAGE OF YOU, BUT I DON'T THINK THIS IS THE BEST WAY TO DEAL WITH IT."

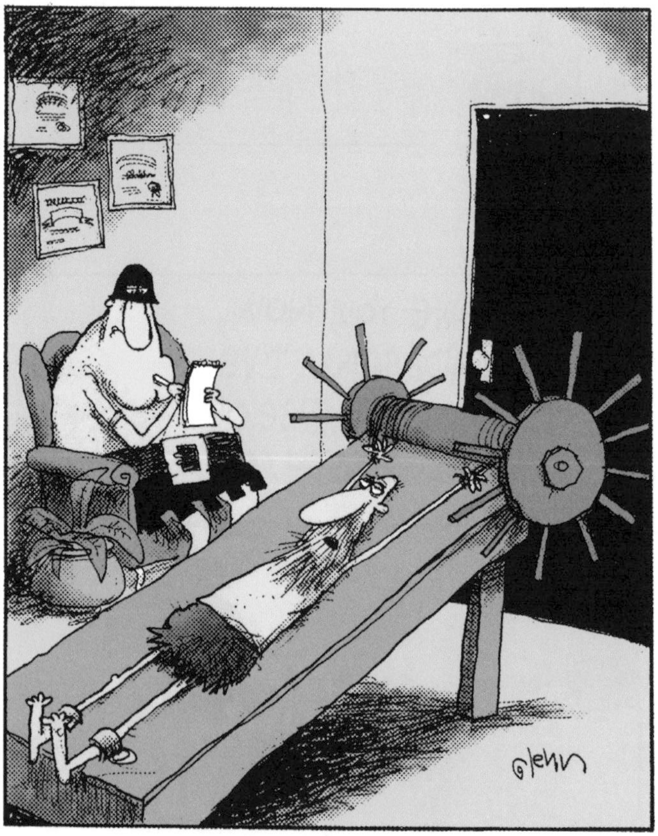

"I feel like I'm being pulled at from both ends."

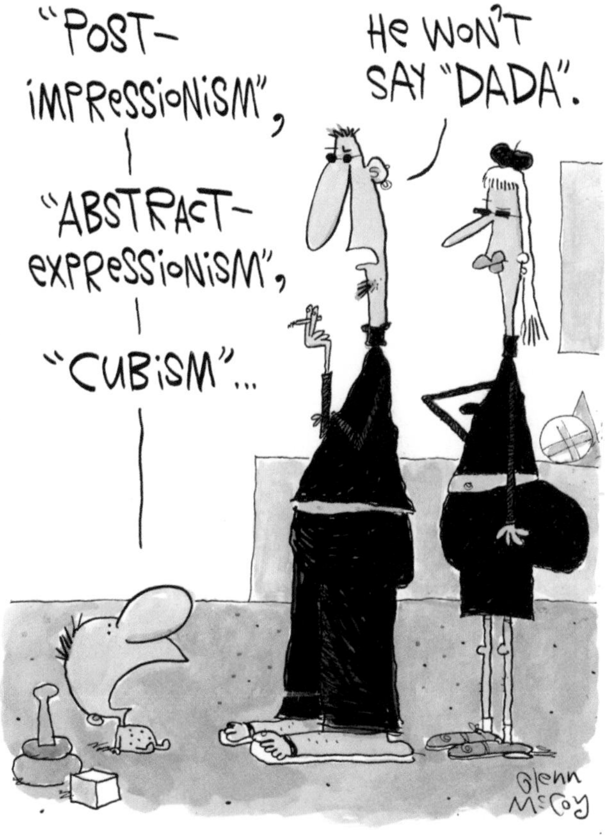
"POST-impressionism",
"ABSTRACT-expressionism",
"CUBISM"...
He WON'T SAY "DADA".
Glenn McCoy

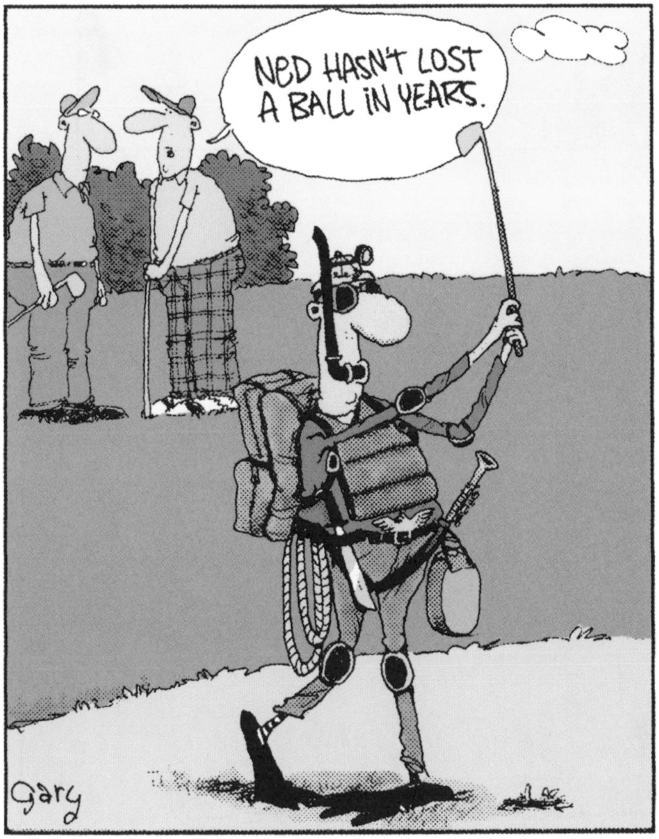
NED HASN'T LOST A BALL IN YEARS.
gary

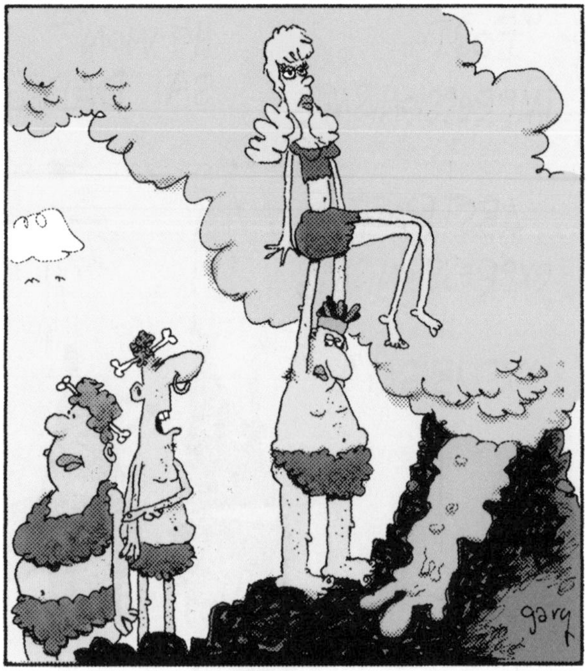
gary

"Chief, do we really want to sacrifice the only babe on the island, especially when Eunice here is available?"

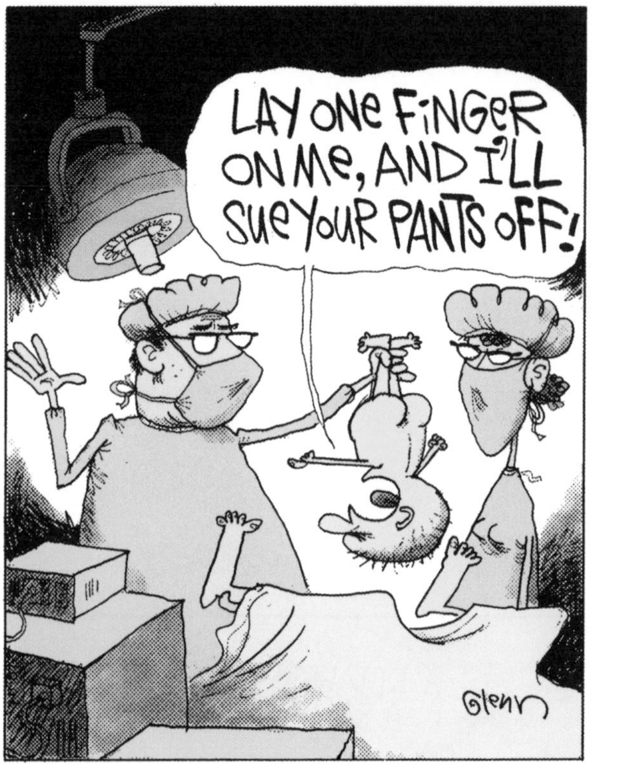
LAY ONE FINGER ON ME, AND I'LL SUE YOUR PANTS OFF!
Glenn

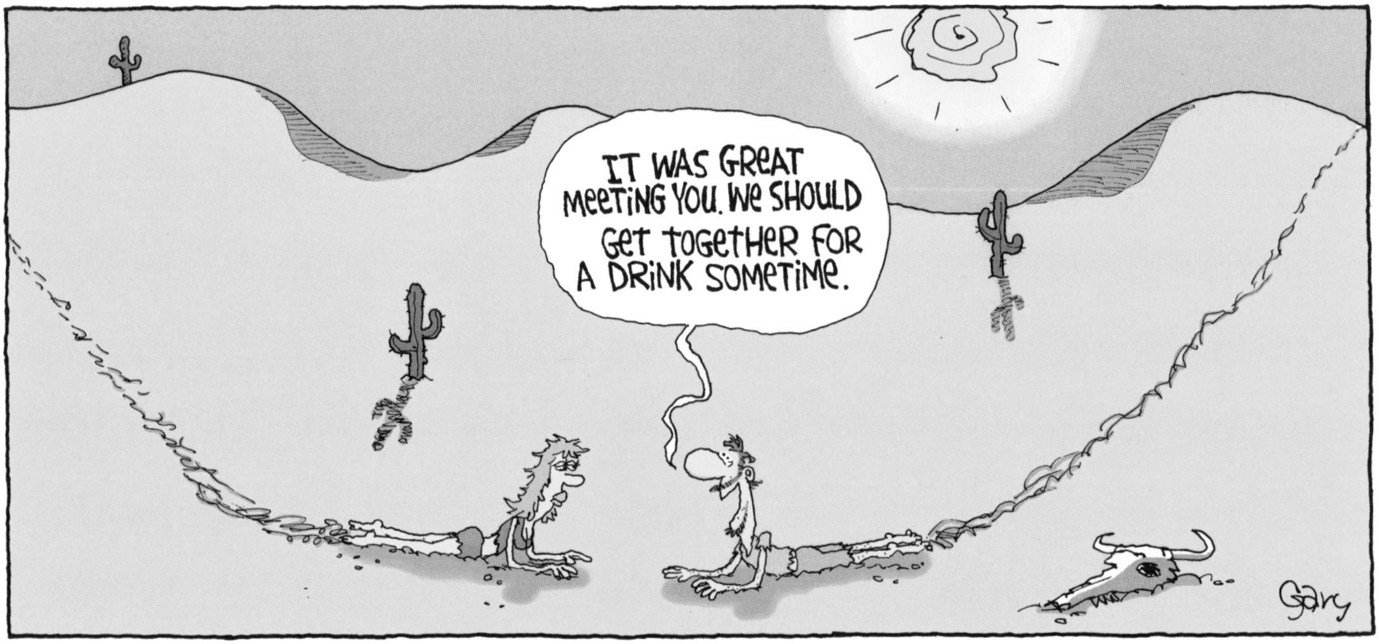
IT WAS GREAT MEETING YOU. WE SHOULD GET TOGETHER FOR A DRINK SOMETIME.
Gary

THIS DISCOVERY COULD ANSWER A LOT OF QUESTIONS ON HOW THE PYRAMIDS CAME TO BE!
ONE PYRAMID
THIS END UP
gary

DON KING ON A BAD HAIR DAY
Glenn

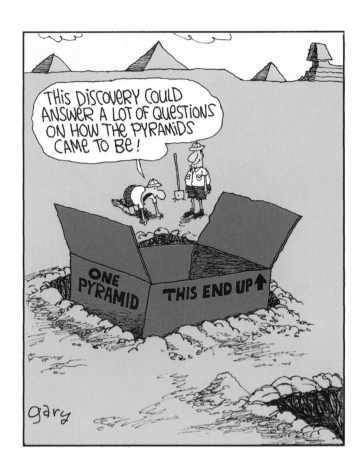

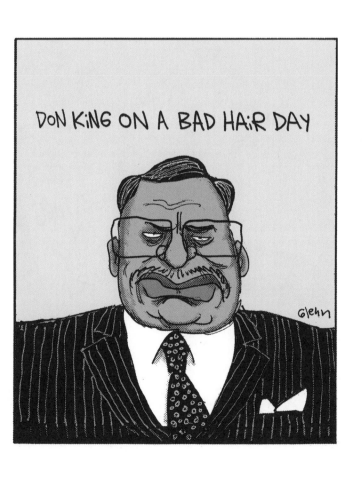

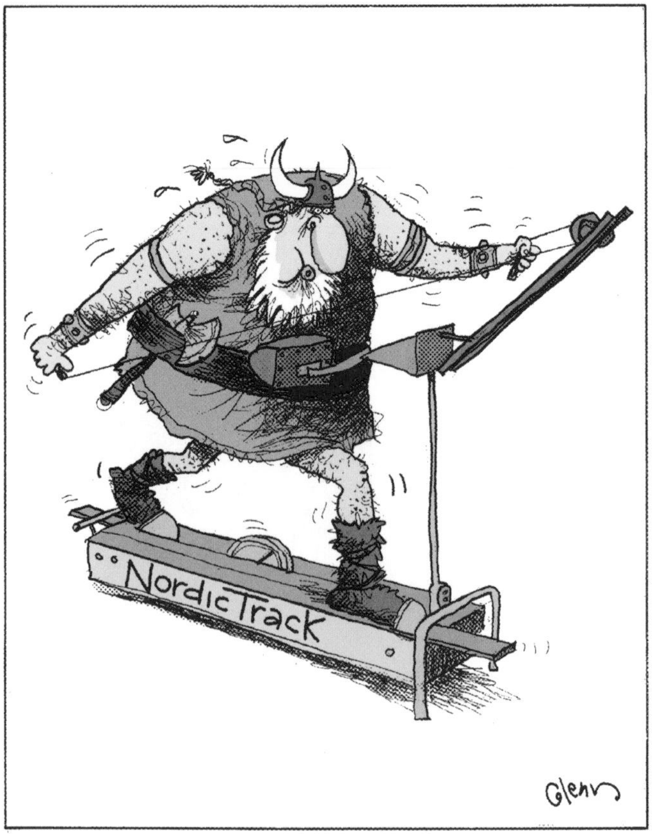
NordicTrack
Glenn

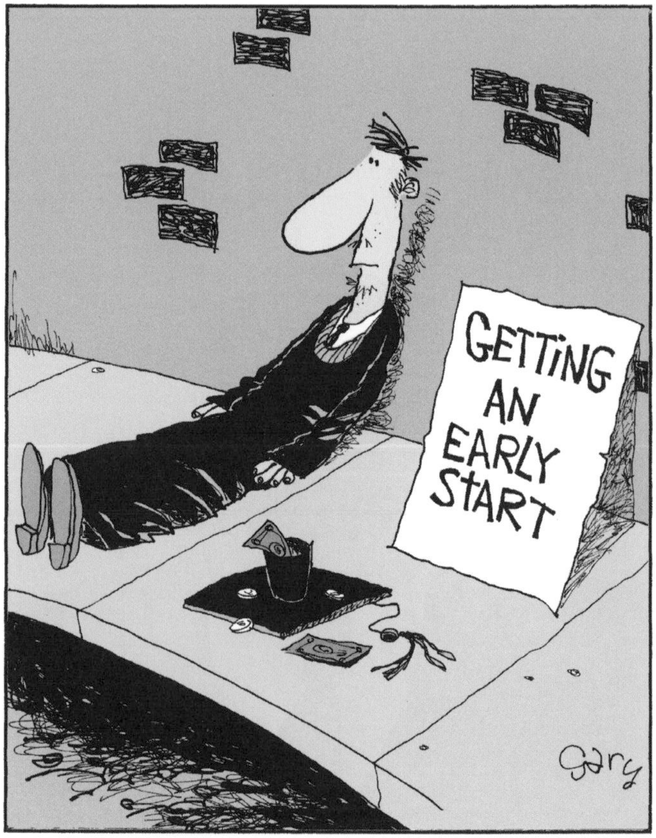
GETTING AN EARLY START
Gary

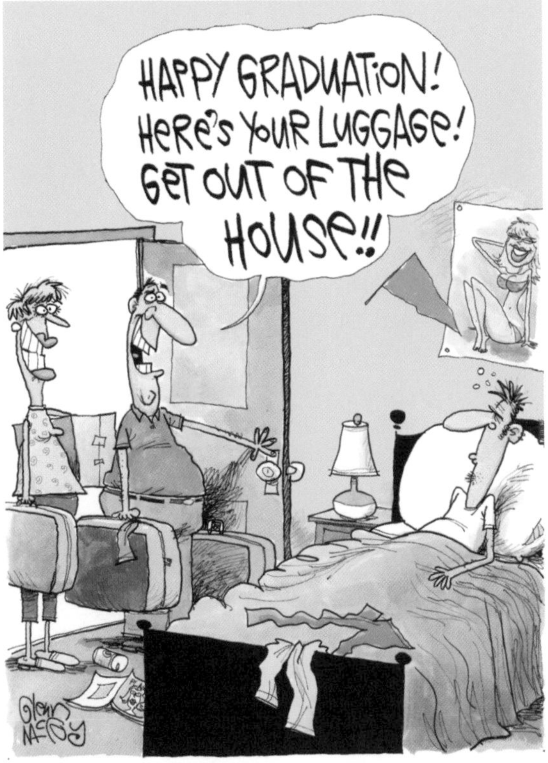
HAPPY GRADUATION! HERE'S YOUR LUGGAGE! GET OUT OF THE HOUSE!!
Glenn McCoy

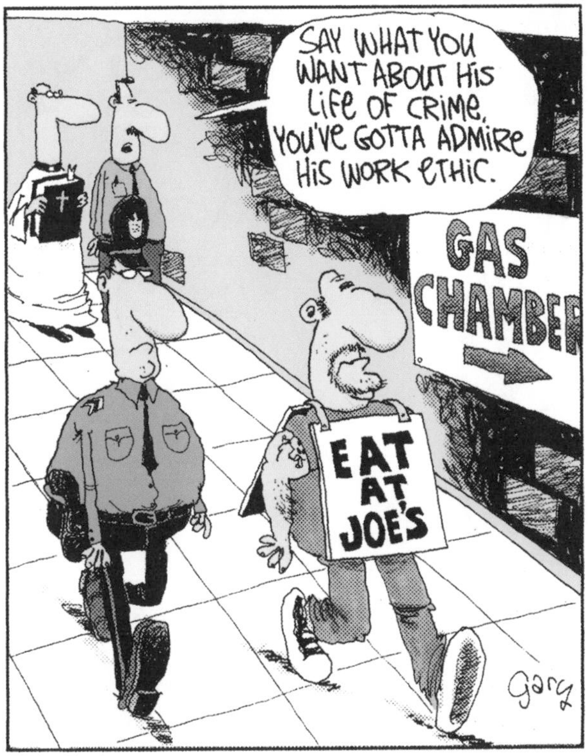
SAY WHAT YOU WANT ABOUT HIS LIFE OF CRIME, YOU'VE GOTTA ADMIRE HIS WORK ETHIC.
GAS CHAMBER
EAT AT JOE'S
gary

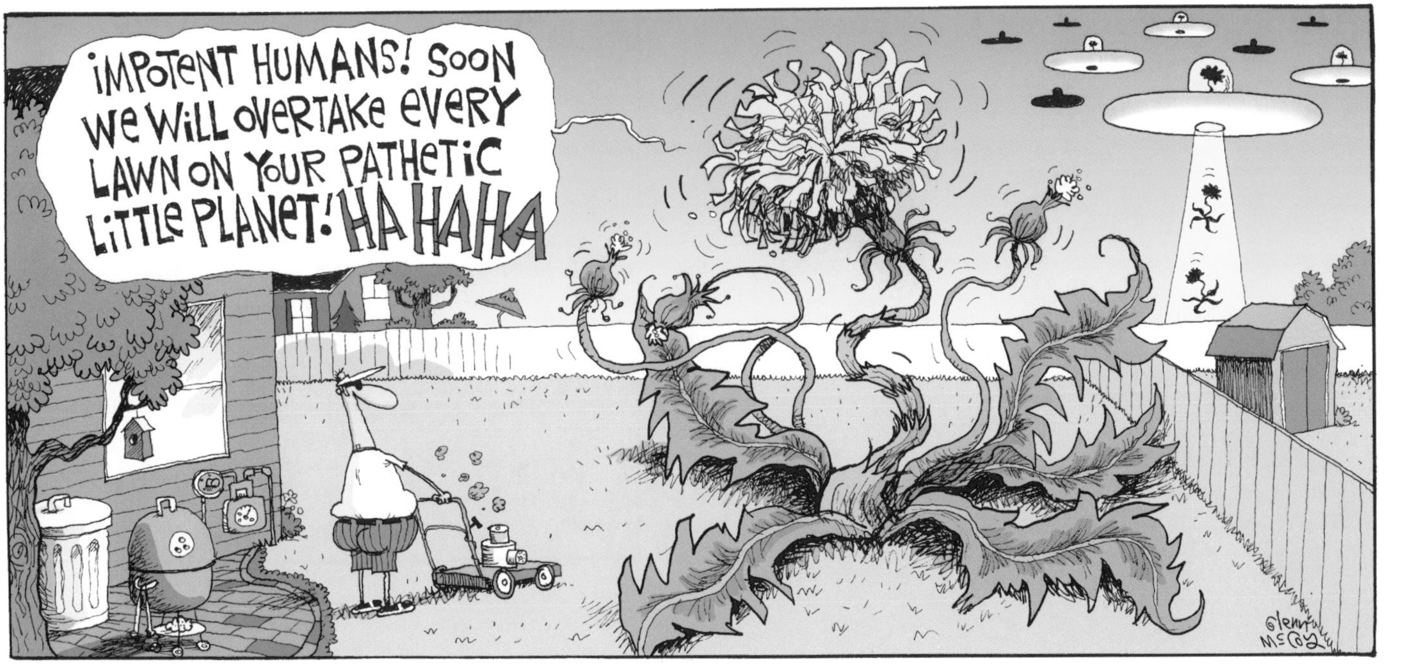
IMPOTENT HUMANS! SOON WE WILL OVERTAKE EVERY LAWN ON YOUR PATHETIC LITTLE PLANET! HA HAHA
Glenn McCoy

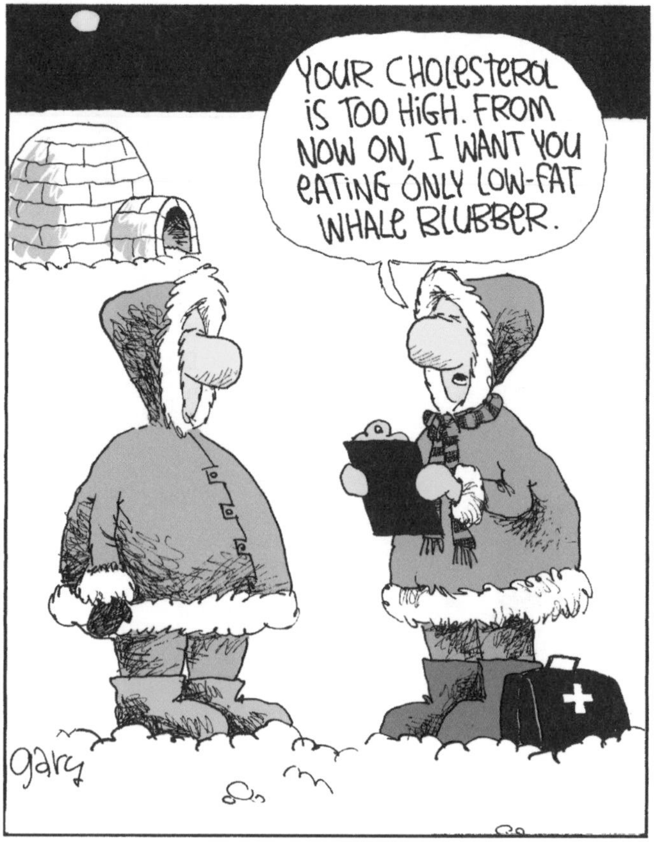
YOUR CHOLESTEROL IS TOO HIGH. FROM NOW ON, I WANT YOU EATING ONLY LOW-FAT WHALE BLUBBER.
gary

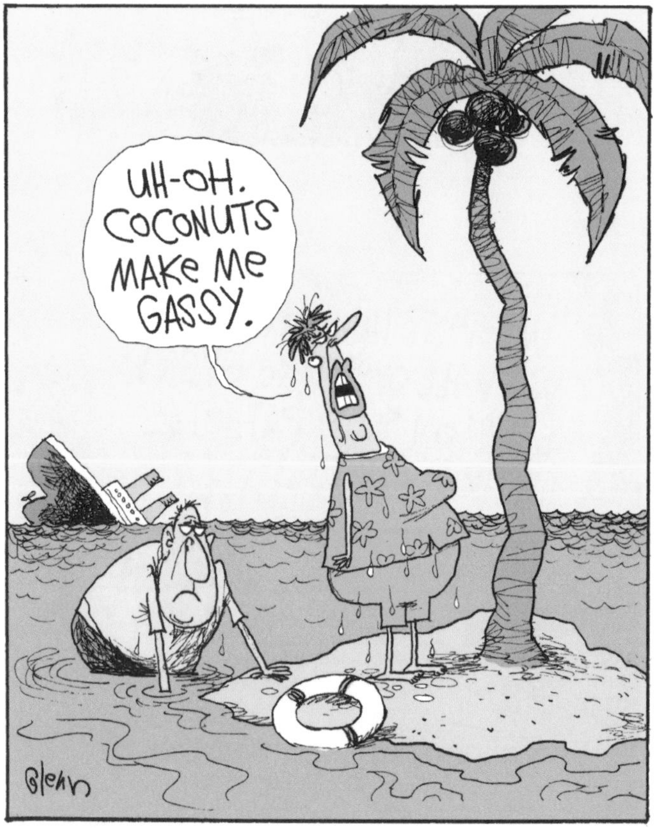
UH-OH. COCONUTS MAKE ME GASSY.
Glenn

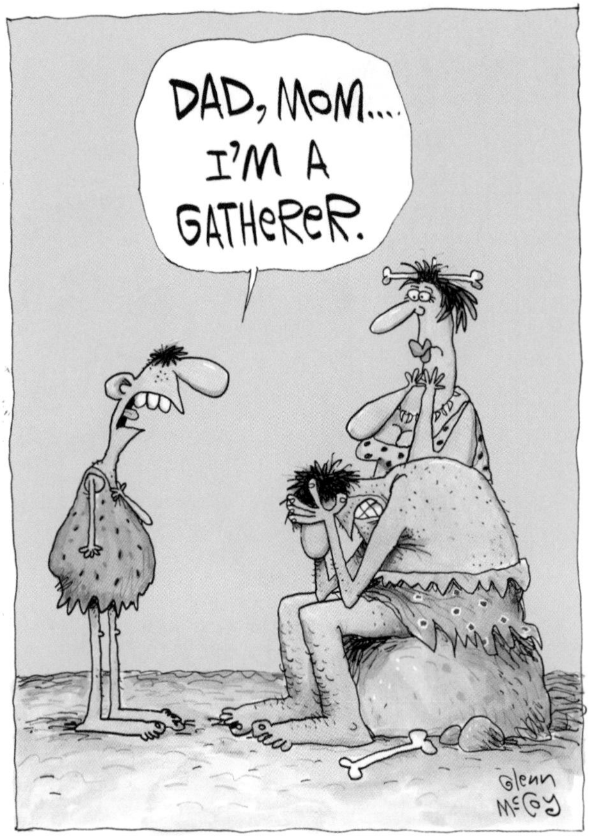
DAD, MOM.... I'M A GATHERER.
Glenn McCoy

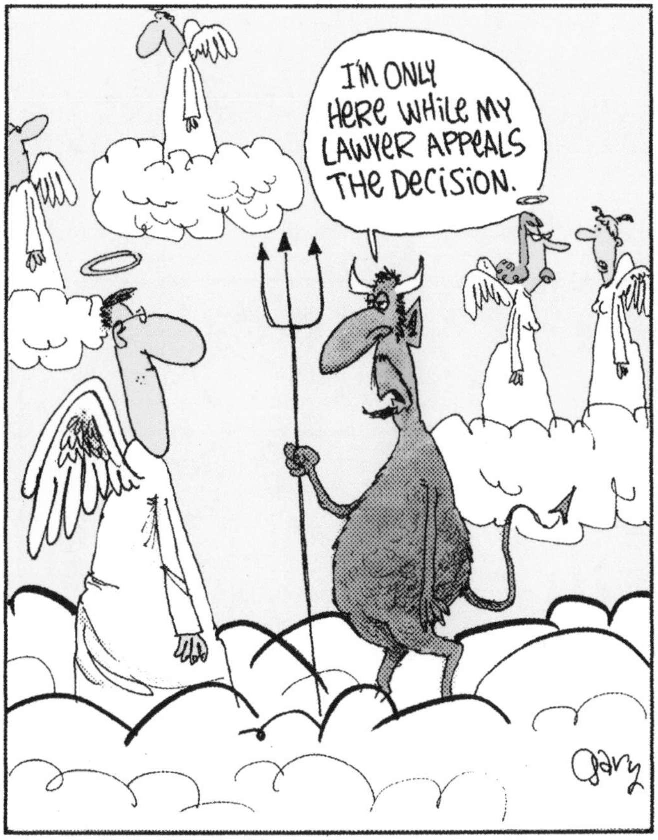
I'M ONLY HERE WHILE MY LAWYER APPEALS THE DECISION.
Gary

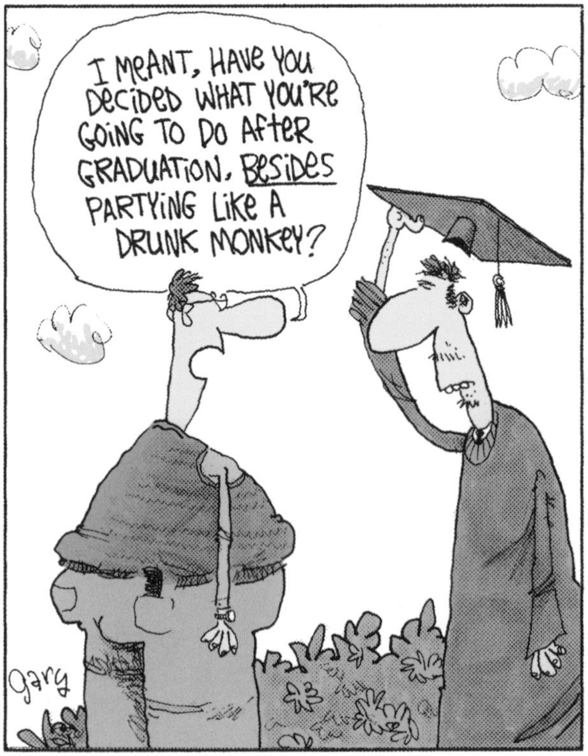
I MEANT, HAVE YOU DECIDED WHAT YOU'RE GOING TO DO AFTER GRADUATION, BESIDES PARTYING LIKE A DRUNK MONKEY?
gary

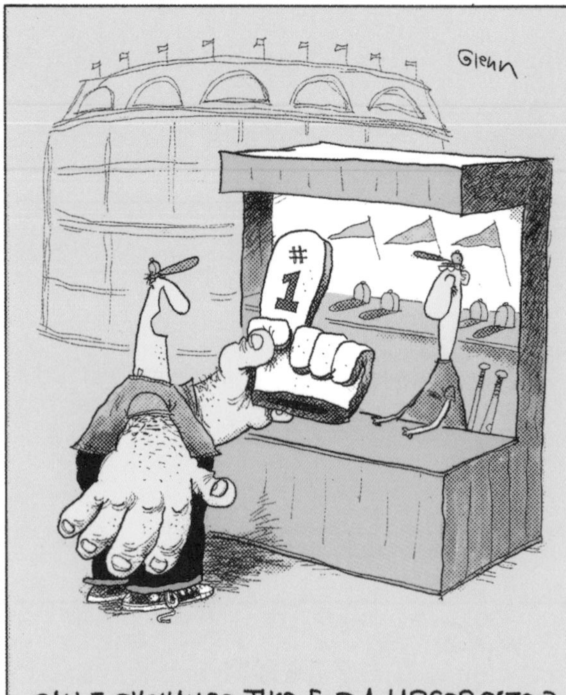
Glenn
#1

CAN I EXCHANGE THIS FOR A LARGER SIZE?

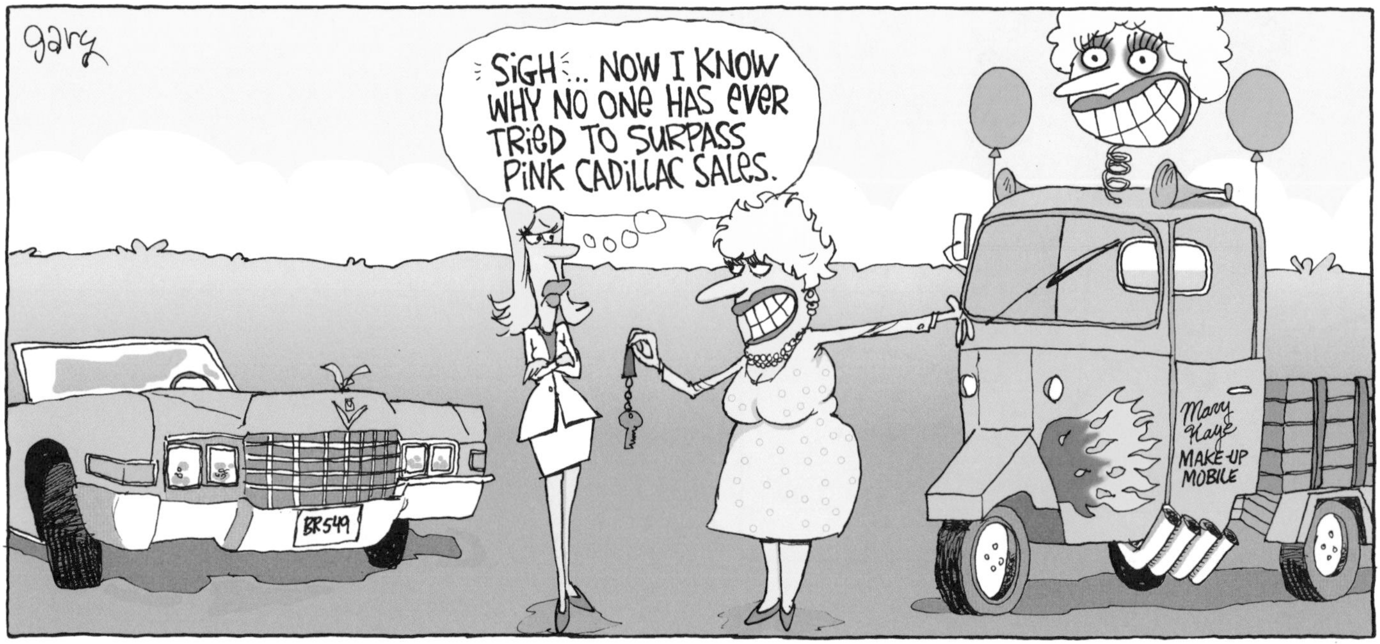
gary
SIGH... NOW I KNOW WHY NO ONE HAS EVER TRIED TO SURPASS PINK CADILLAC SALES.
BR549
Mary Kaye MAKE-UP MOBILE

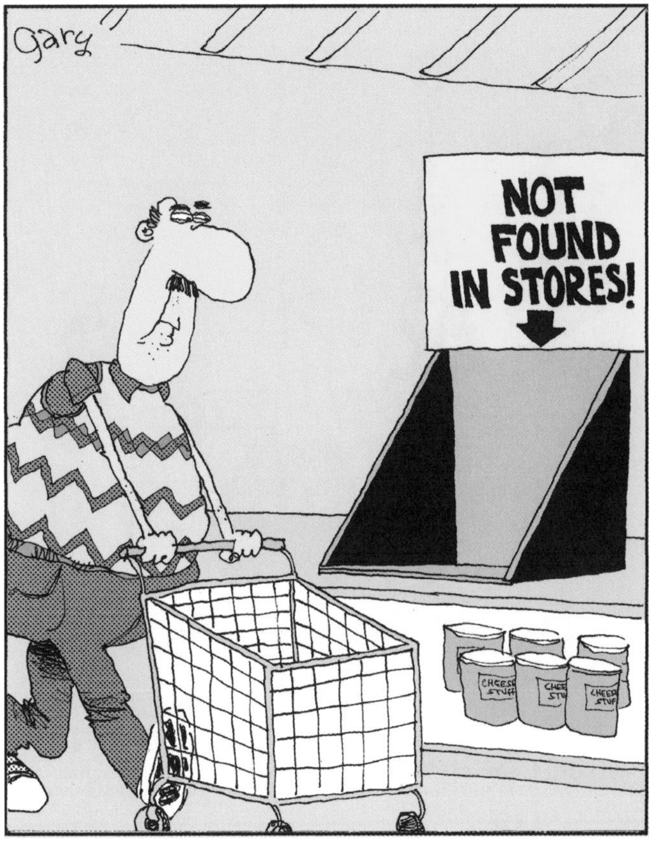
Gary
NOT FOUND IN STORES!
CHEESE STUFF

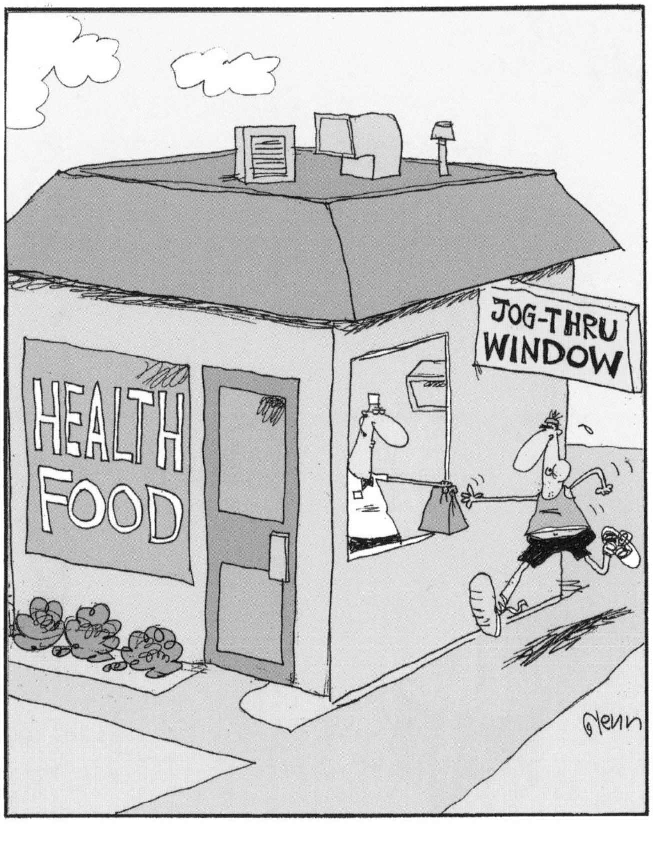
JOG-THRU WINDOW
HEALTH FOOD
Glenn

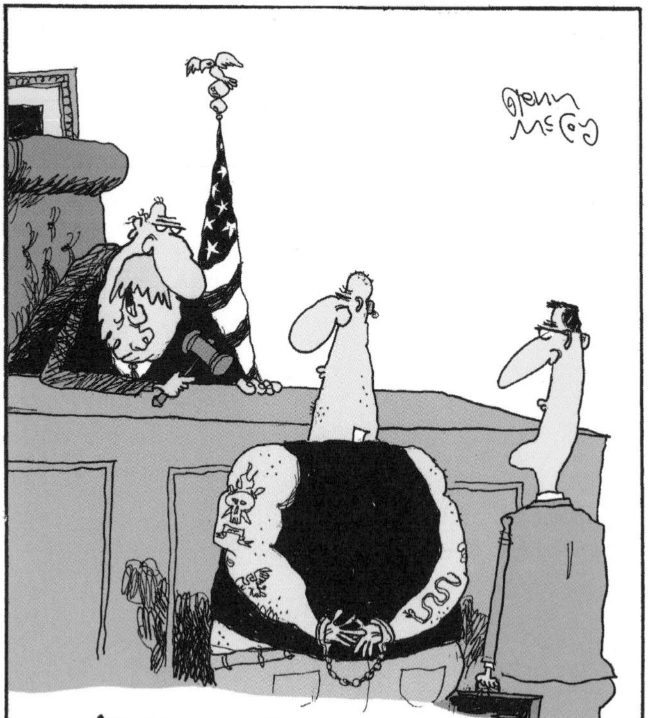
Glenn McCoy

I DON'T CARE WHAT JUDGE JUDY ALLOWS. YOU WILL REFER TO ME BY MY <u>LAST</u> NAME!

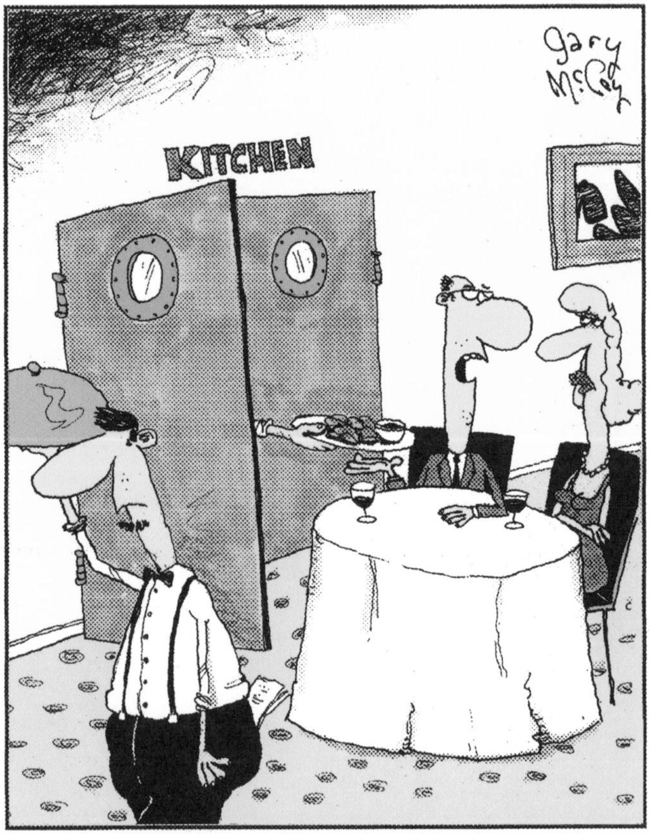
Gary McCoy
KITCHEN

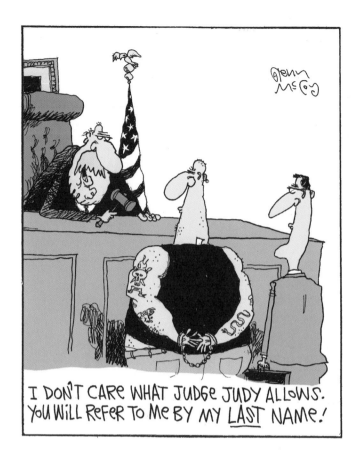

"Well, you may think the maitre d' slighted me by giving us this table. But I happen to see no downside to getting our ravioli quicker, thereby fresher than anyone else's."

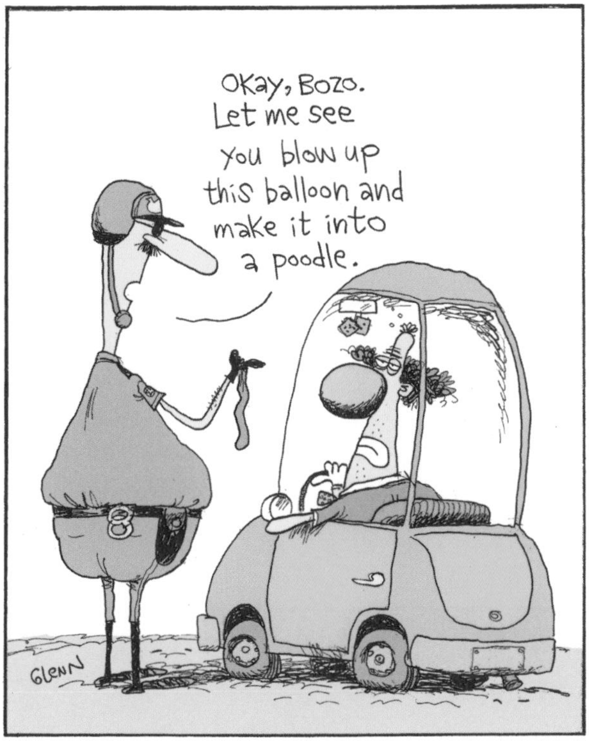
Okay, Bozo. Let me see you blow up this balloon and make it into a poodle.
GLENN

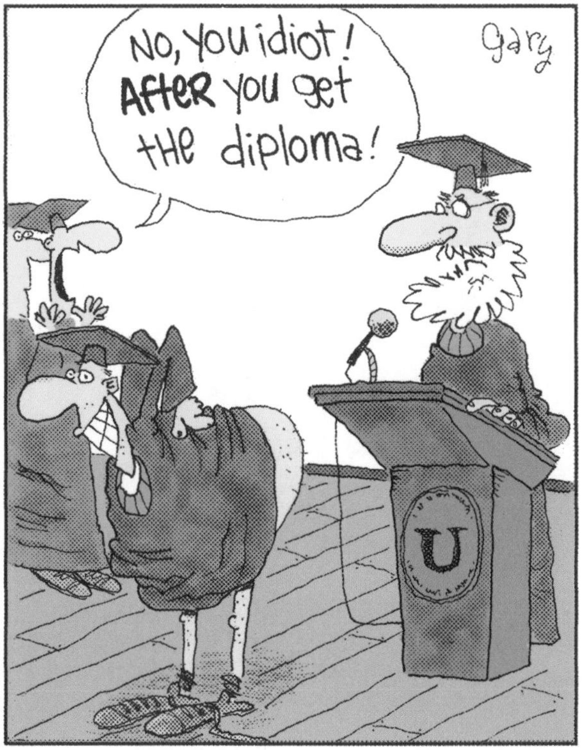
No, you idiot! **After** you get the diploma!
gary
U

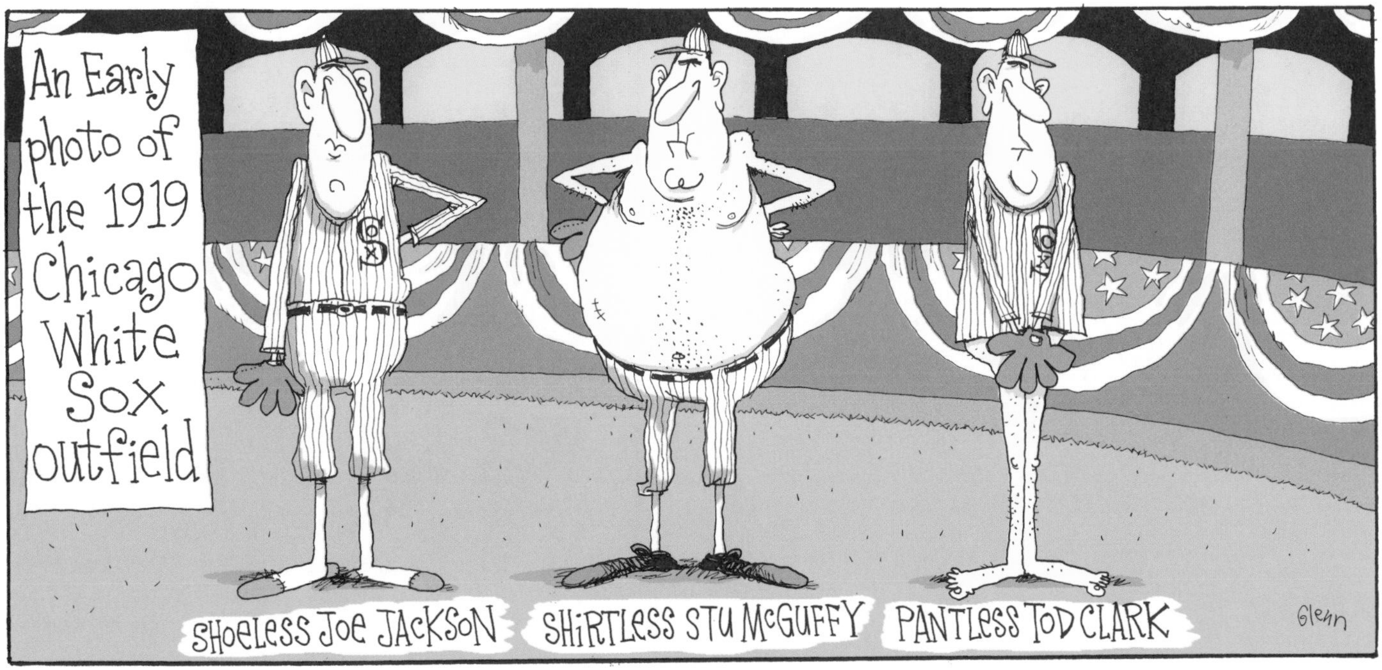
An Early photo of the 1919 Chicago White Sox outfield
SHOELESS JOE JACKSON
SHIRTLESS STU McGUFFY
PANTLESS TOD CLARK
Glenn

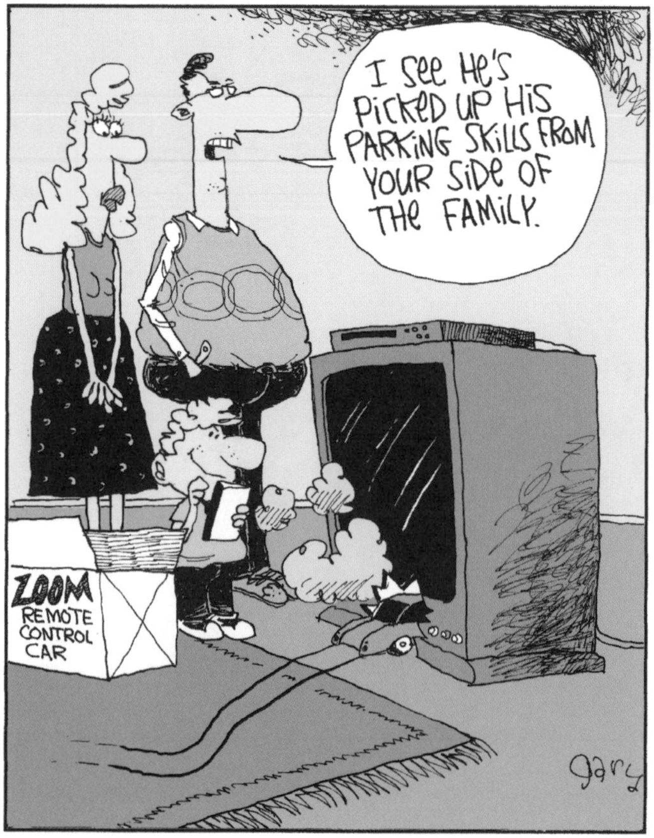
I SEE HE'S PICKED UP HIS PARKING SKILLS FROM YOUR SIDE OF THE FAMILY.
ZOOM REMOTE CONTROL CAR
gary

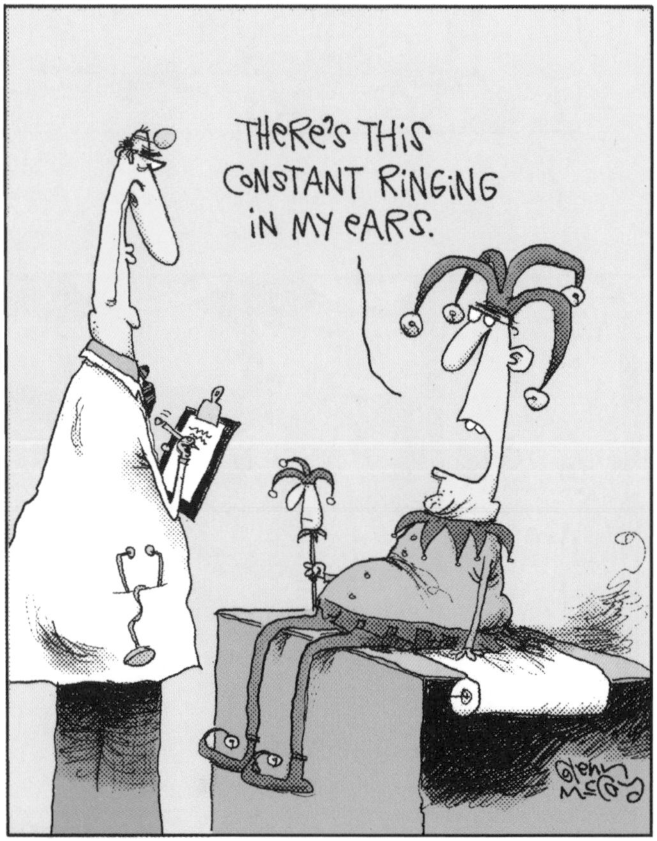
THERE'S THIS CONSTANT RINGING IN MY EARS.
Glenn McCoy

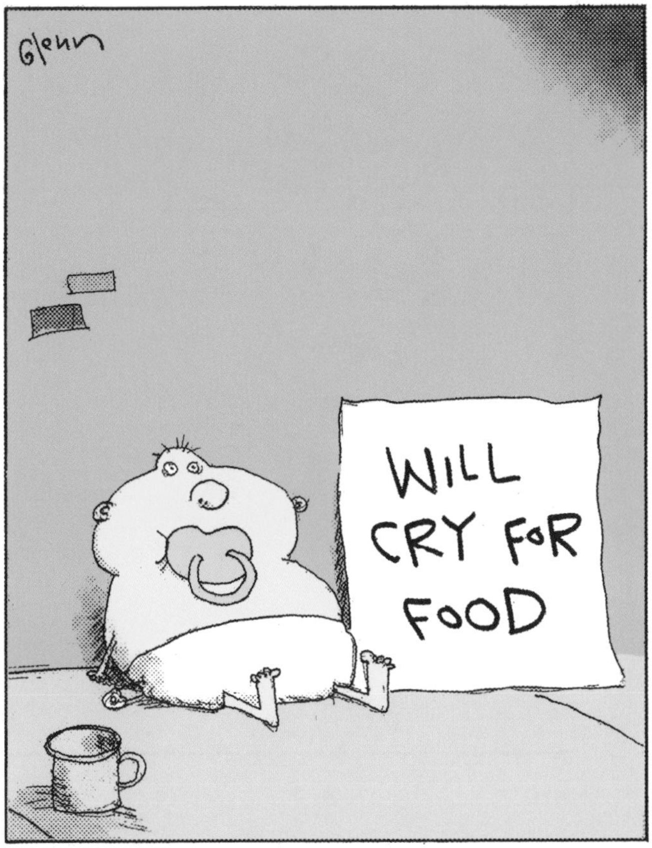
Glenn
WILL CRY FOR FOOD

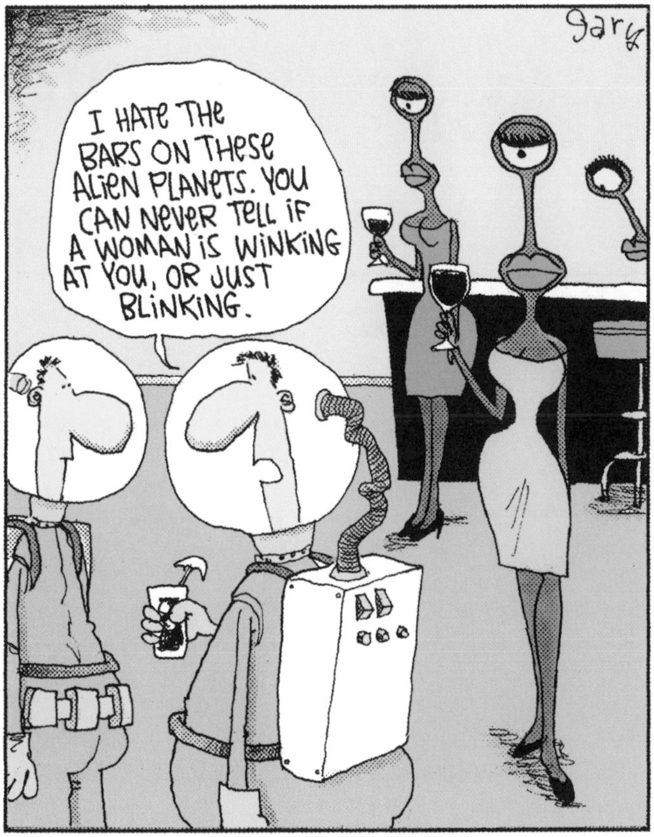
gary
I HATE THE BARS ON THESE ALIEN PLANETS. YOU CAN NEVER TELL IF A WOMAN IS WINKING AT YOU, OR JUST BLINKING.

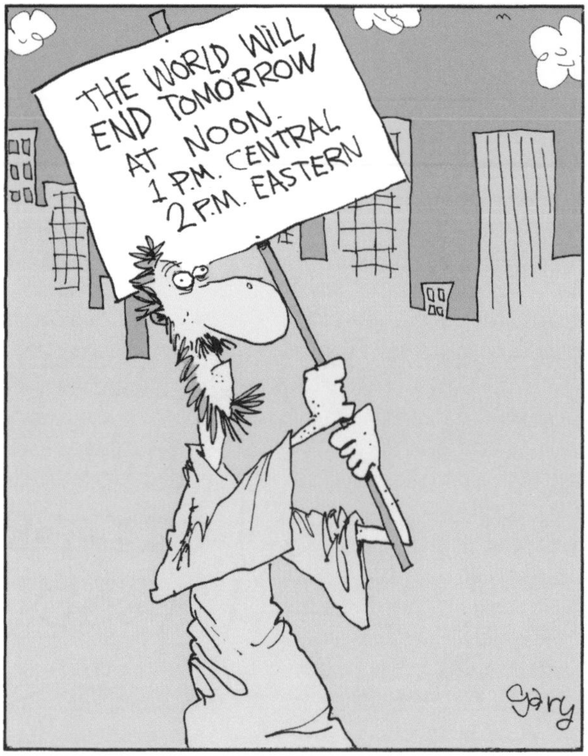
THE WORLD WILL END TOMORROW AT NOON. 1 P.M. CENTRAL 2 P.M. EASTERN
gary

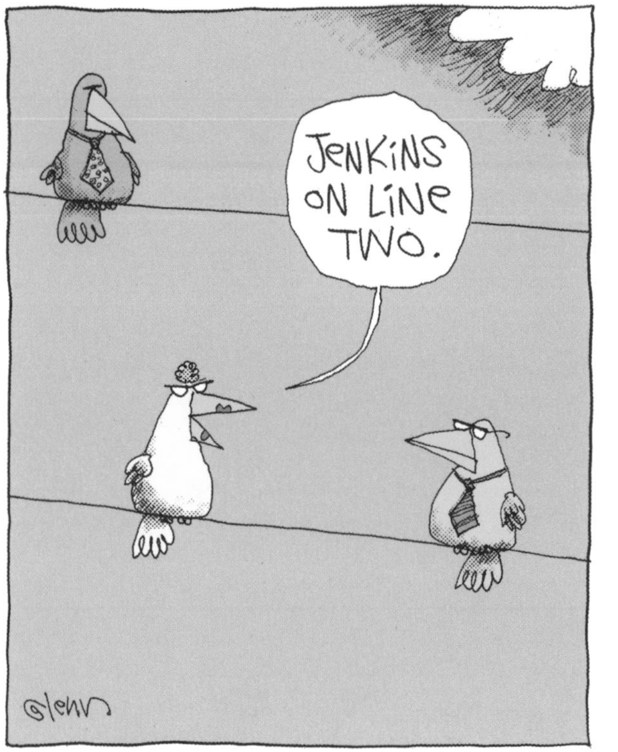
JENKINS ON LINE TWO.
Glenn

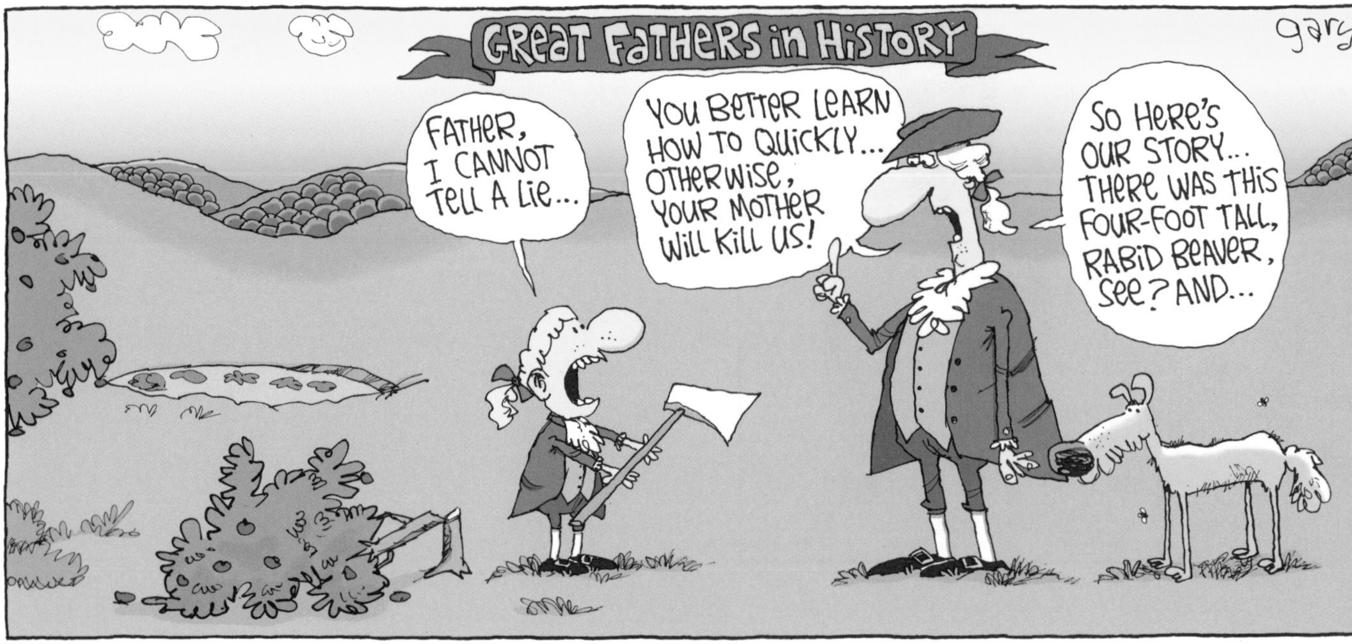
GREAT FATHERS IN HISTORY
gary
FATHER, I CANNOT TELL A LIE...
YOU BETTER LEARN HOW TO QUICKLY... OTHERWISE, YOUR MOTHER WILL KILL US!
SO HERE'S OUR STORY... THERE WAS THIS FOUR-FOOT TALL, RABID BEAVER, SEE? AND...

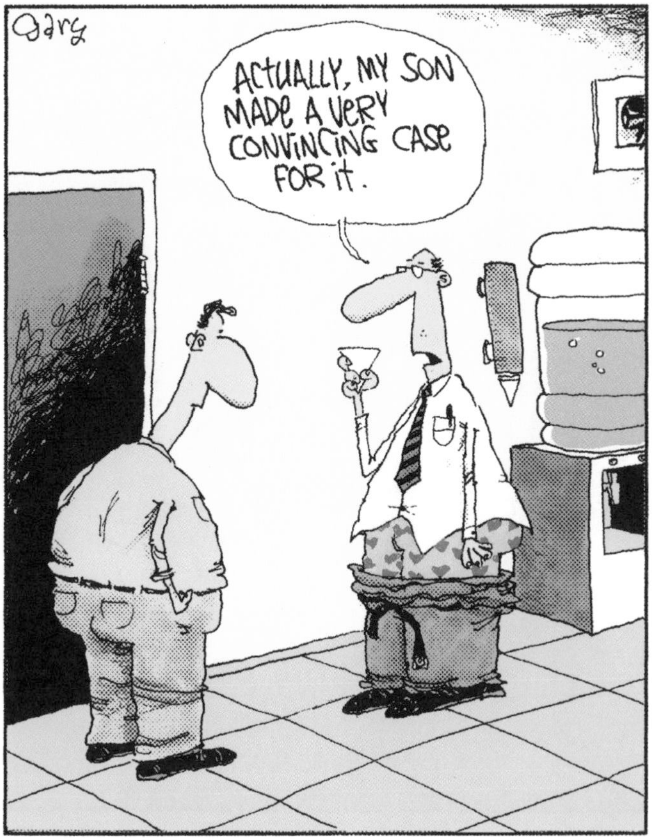
ACTUALLY, MY SON MADE A VERY CONVINCING CASE FOR IT.

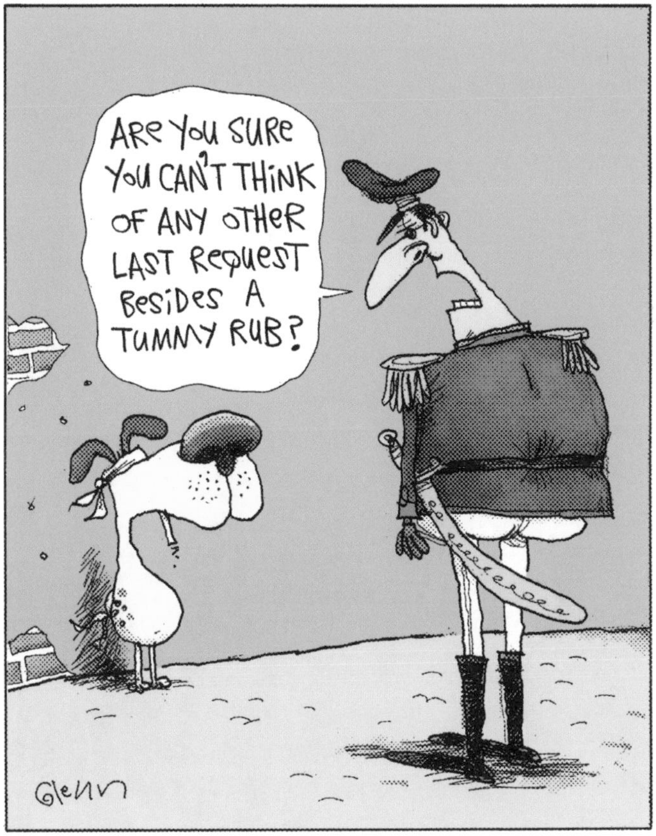
ARE YOU SURE YOU CAN'T THINK OF ANY OTHER LAST REQUEST BESIDES A TUMMY RUB?

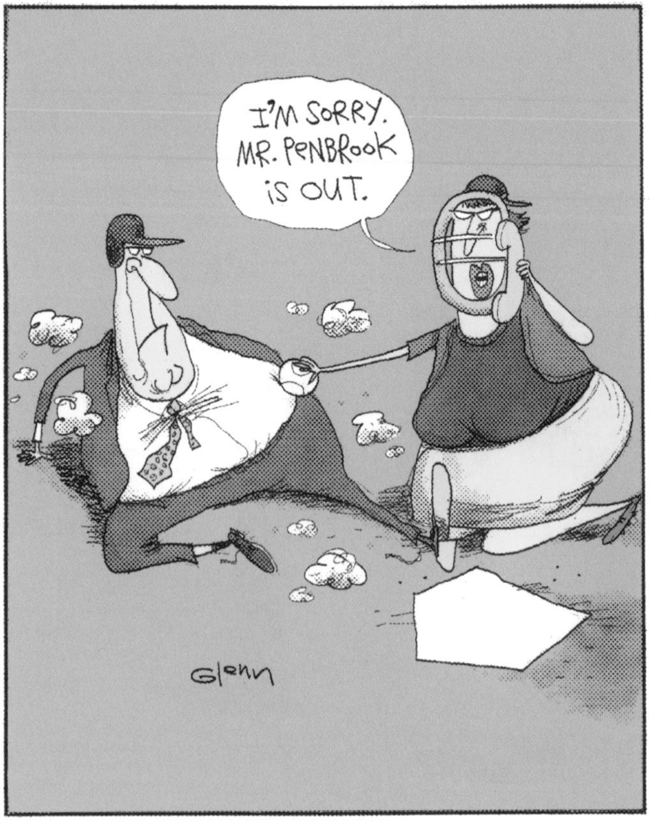
I'M SORRY. MR. PENBROOK IS OUT.
Glenn

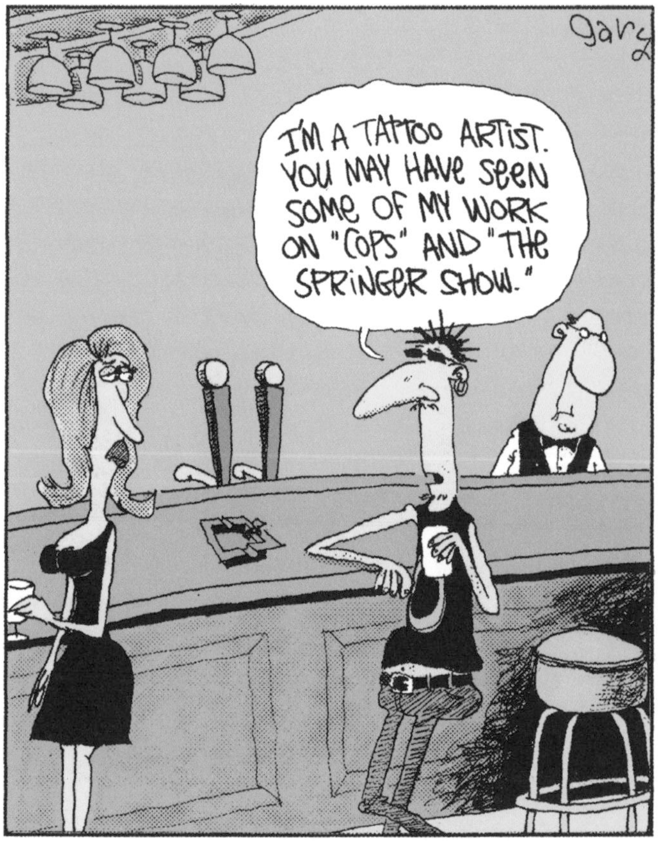
gary
I'M A TATTOO ARTIST. YOU MAY HAVE SEEN SOME OF MY WORK ON "COPS" AND "THE SPRINGER SHOW."

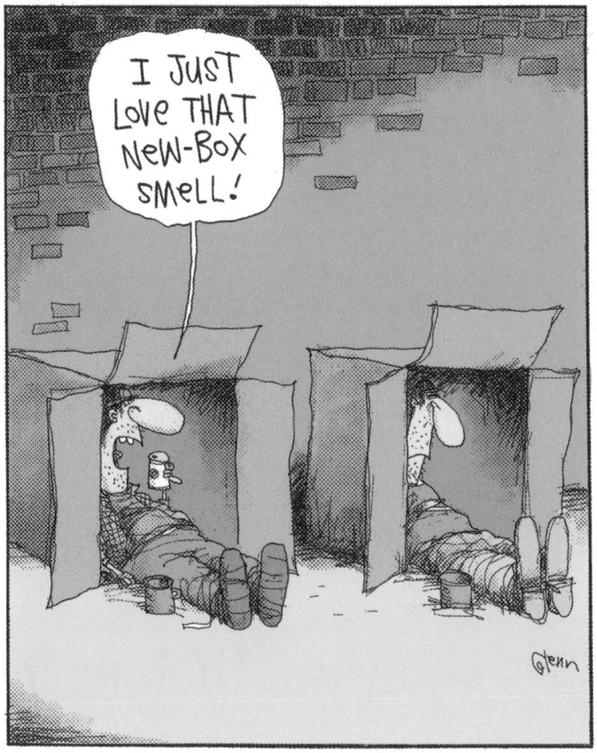
I JUST LOVE THAT NEW-BOX SMELL!
Glenn

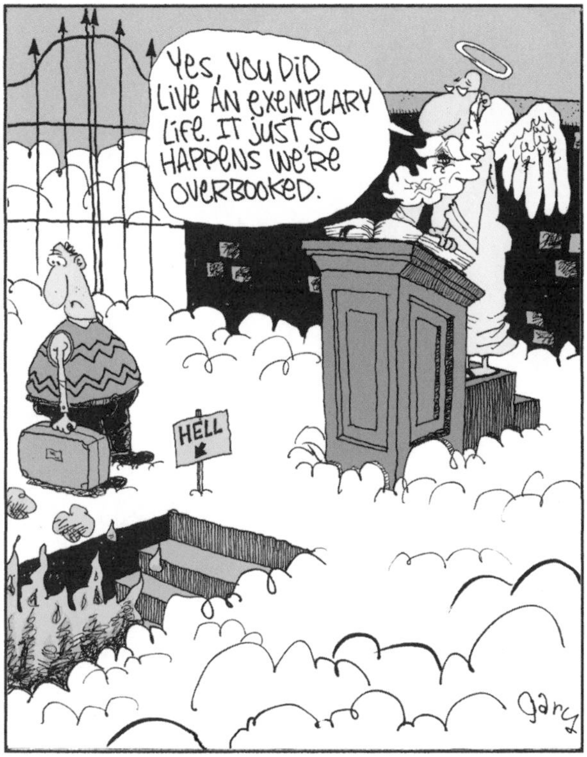
YES, YOU DID LIVE AN EXEMPLARY LIFE. IT JUST SO HAPPENS WE'RE OVERBOOKED.
HELL
gary

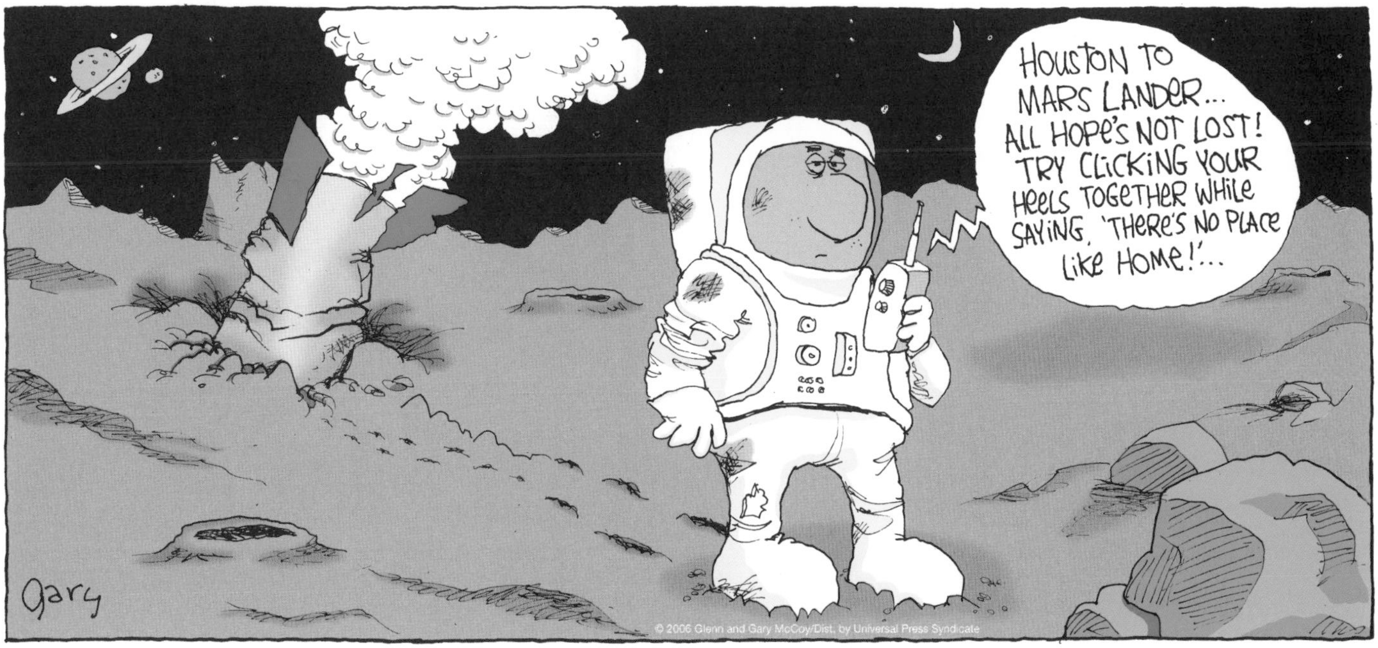
HOUSTON TO MARS LANDER... ALL HOPE'S NOT LOST! TRY CLICKING YOUR HEELS TOGETHER WHILE SAYING, 'THERE'S NO PLACE LIKE HOME!'...
gary
© 2006 Glenn and Gary McCoy/Dist. by Universal Press Syndicate

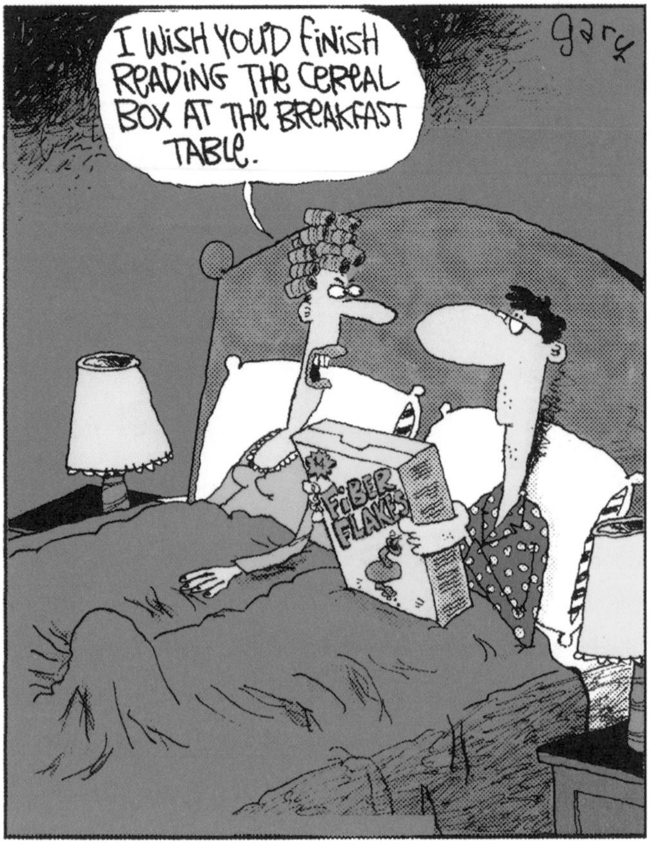
I WISH YOU'D FINISH READING THE CEREAL BOX AT THE BREAKFAST TABLE.
FIBER FLAKES
gary

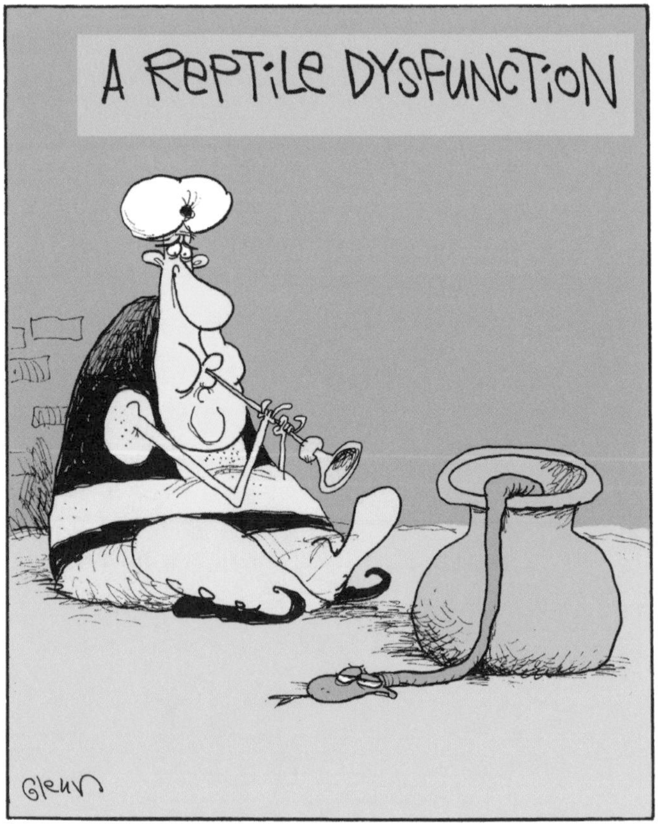
A REPTILE DYSFUNCTION
Glenn

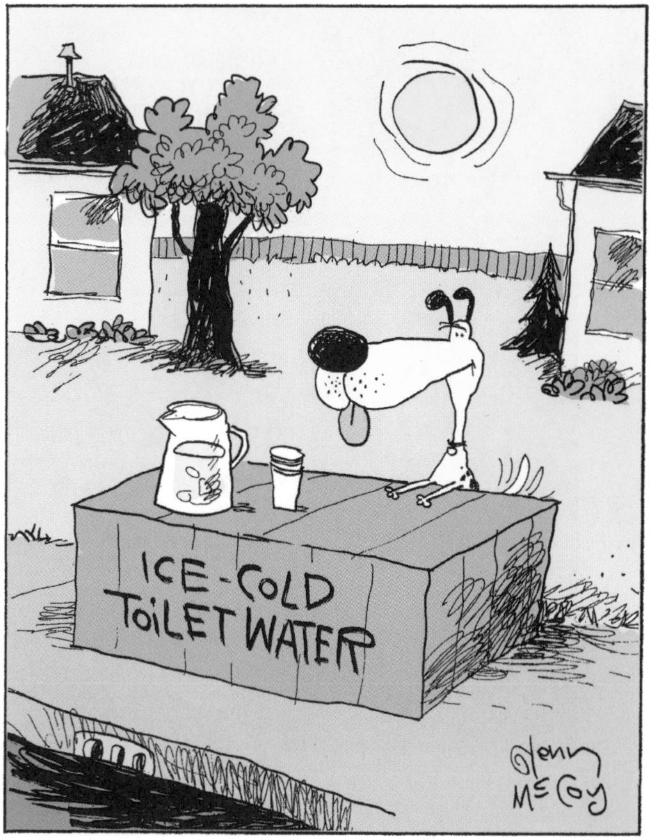
ICE-COLD
TOILET WATER
Glenn McCoy

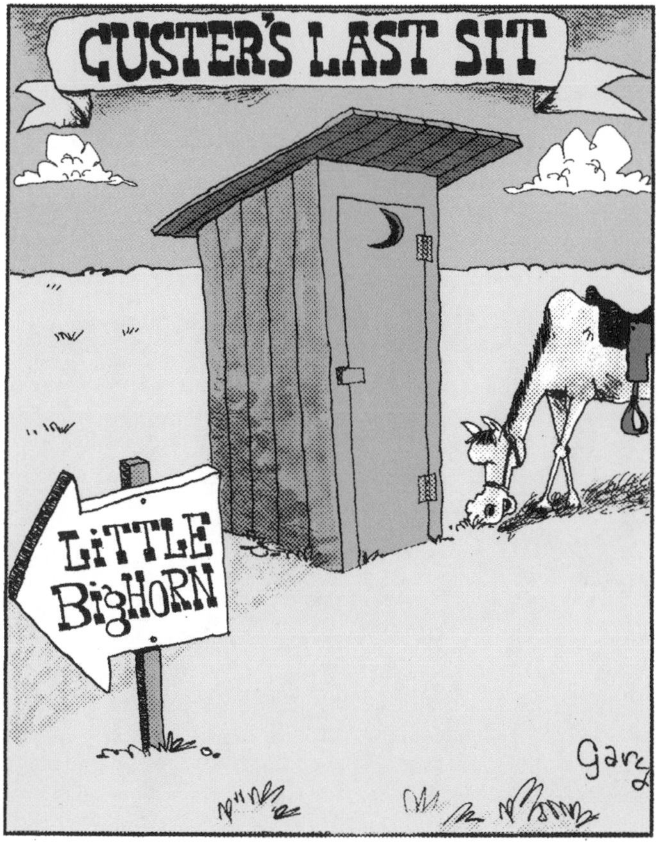
CUSTER'S LAST SIT
LITTLE BIGHORN
Gary

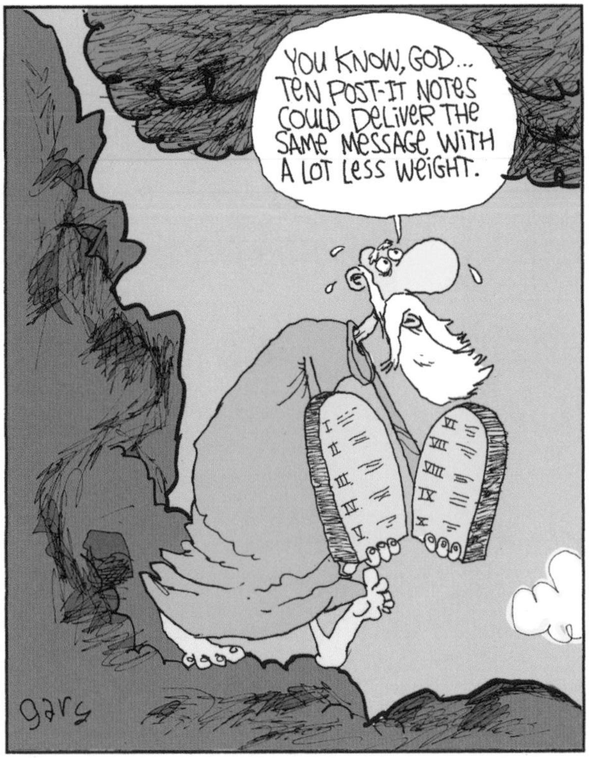
YOU KNOW, GOD... TEN POST-IT NOTES COULD DELIVER THE SAME MESSAGE WITH A LOT LESS WEIGHT.
gary

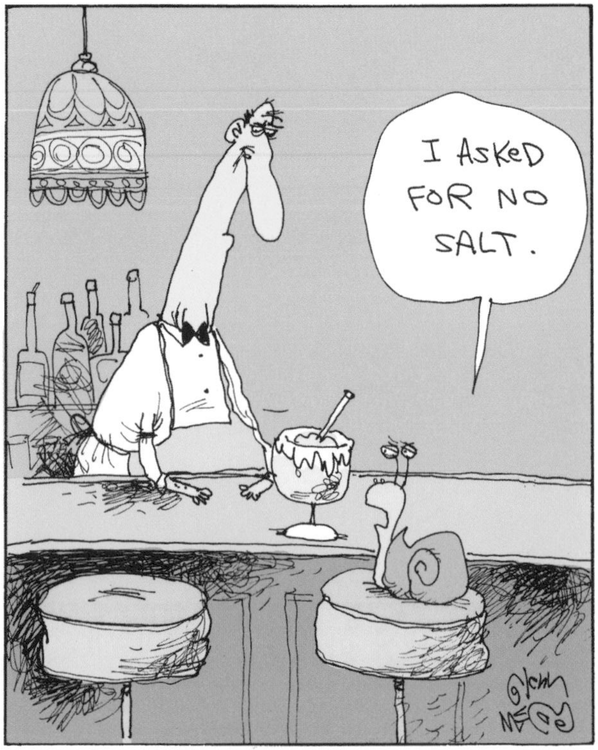
I ASKED FOR NO SALT.

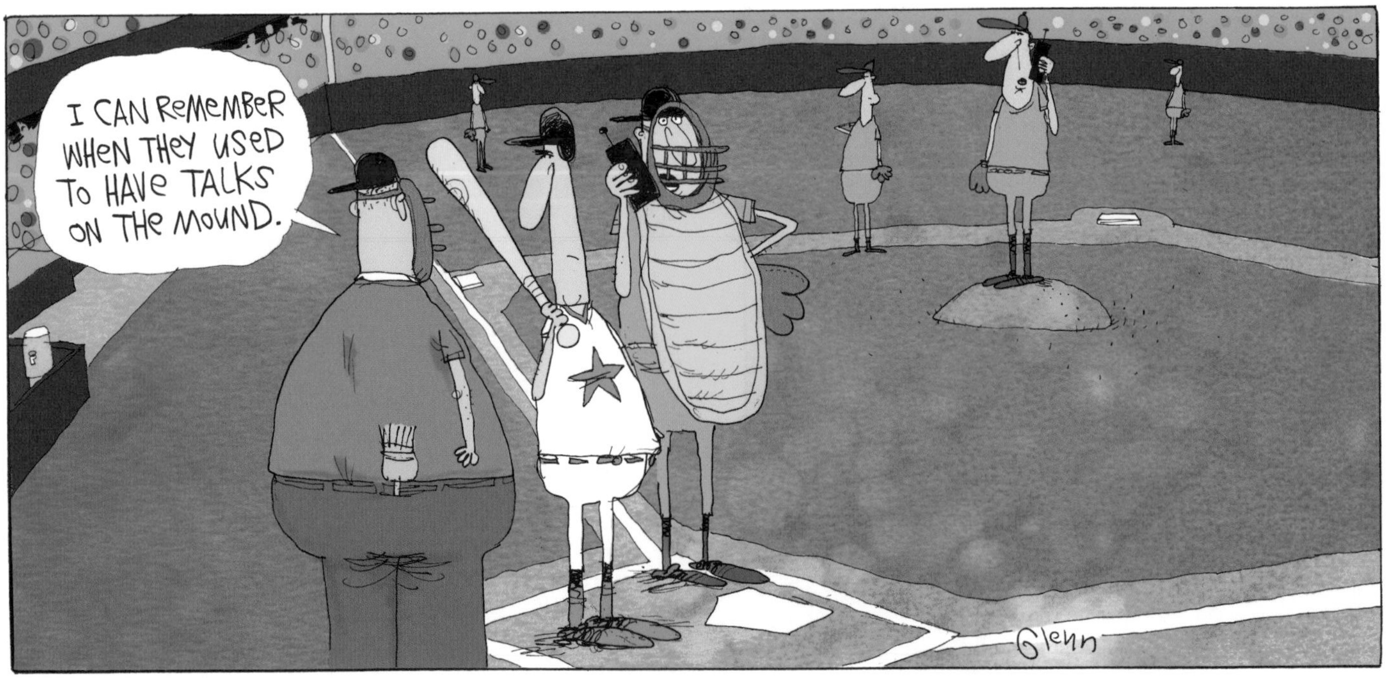
I CAN REMEMBER WHEN THEY USED TO HAVE TALKS ON THE MOUND.
Glenn

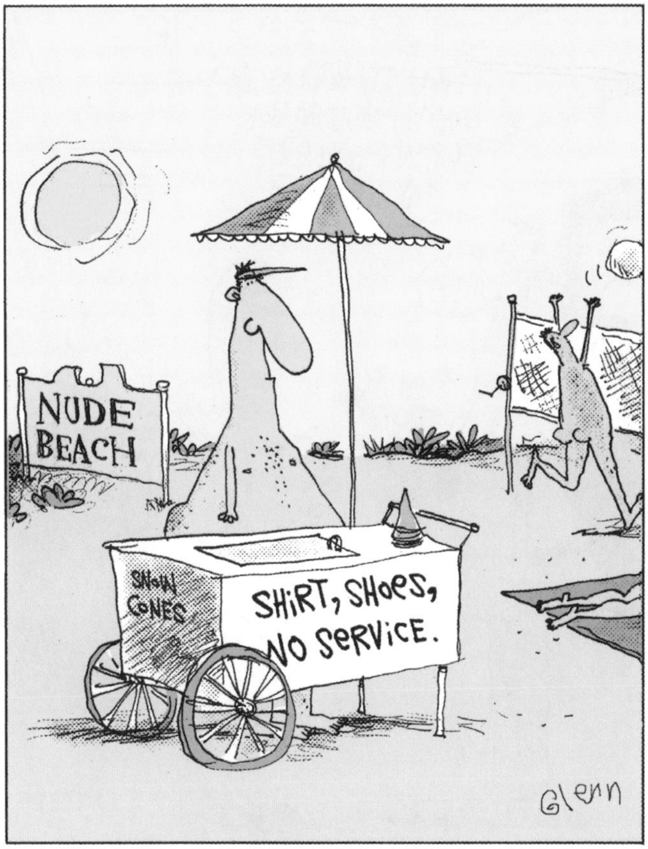
NUDE BEACH
SNOW CONES
SHIRT, SHOES, NO SERVICE.
Glenn

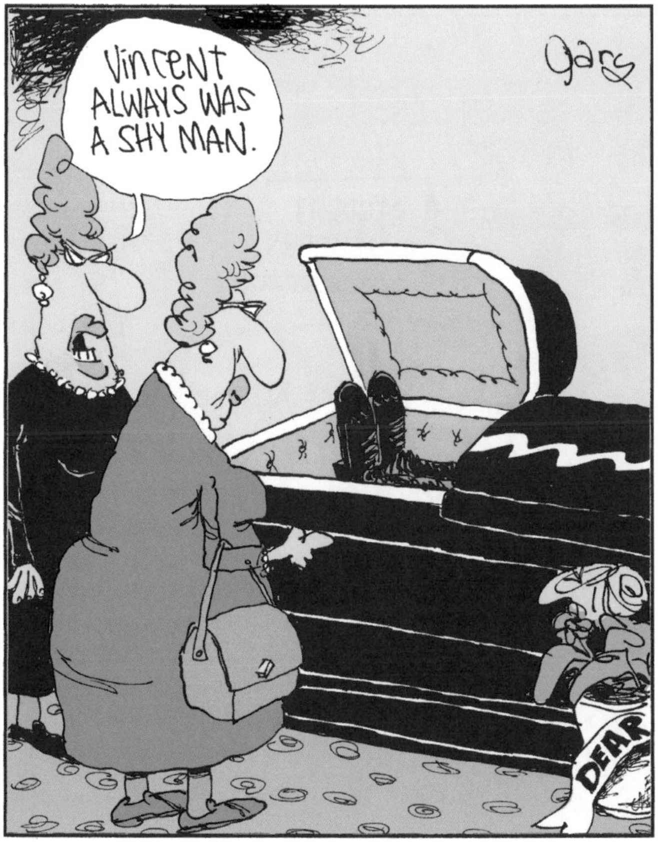
Gary
VINCENT ALWAYS WAS A SHY MAN.
DEAR

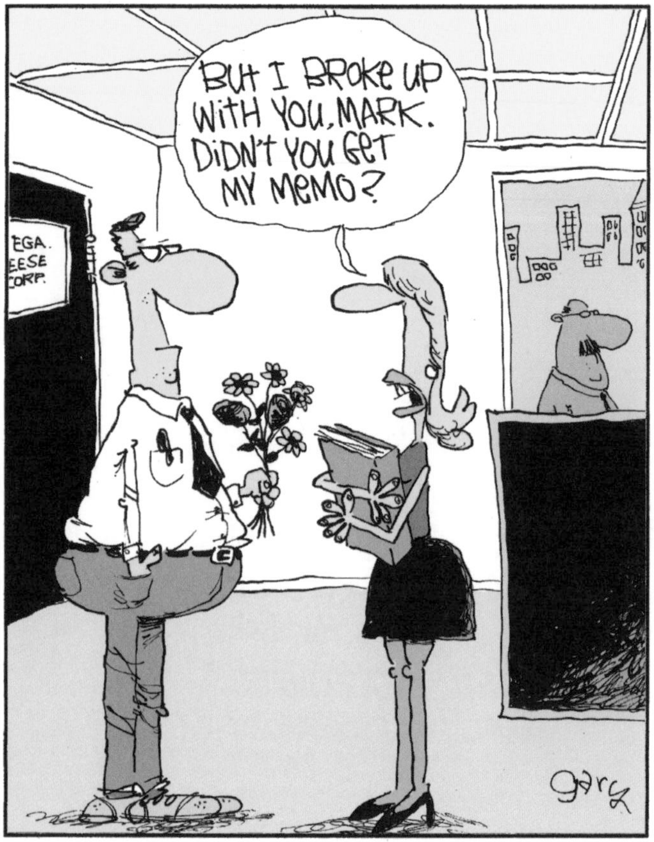
BUT I BROKE UP WITH YOU, MARK. DIDN'T YOU GET MY MEMO?
EGA.
EESE
CORP.
gary

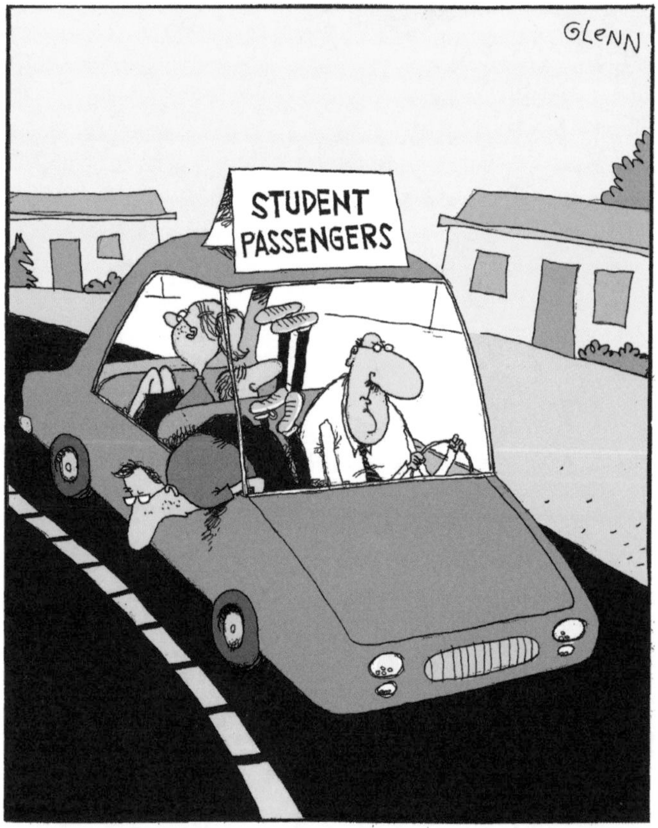
GLENN
STUDENT PASSENGERS

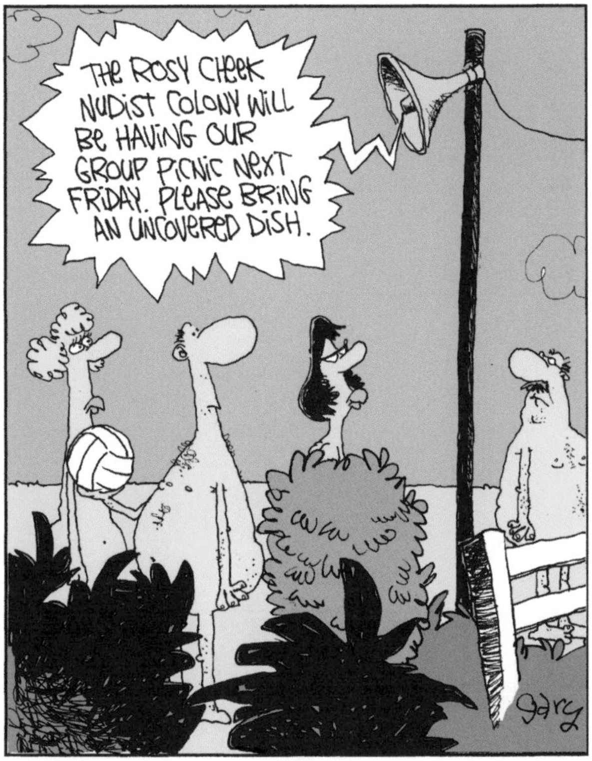
THE ROSY CHEEK NUDIST COLONY WILL BE HAVING OUR GROUP PICNIC NEXT FRIDAY. PLEASE BRING AN UNCOVERED DISH.
Gary

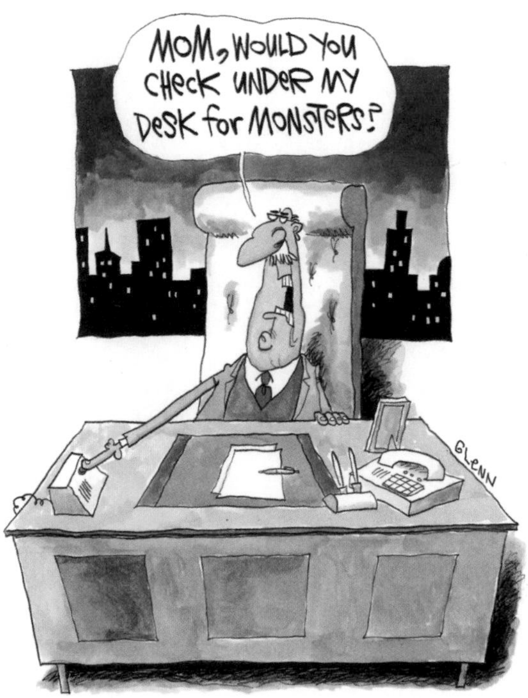
MOM, WOULD YOU CHECK UNDER MY DESK FOR MONSTERS?
GLENN

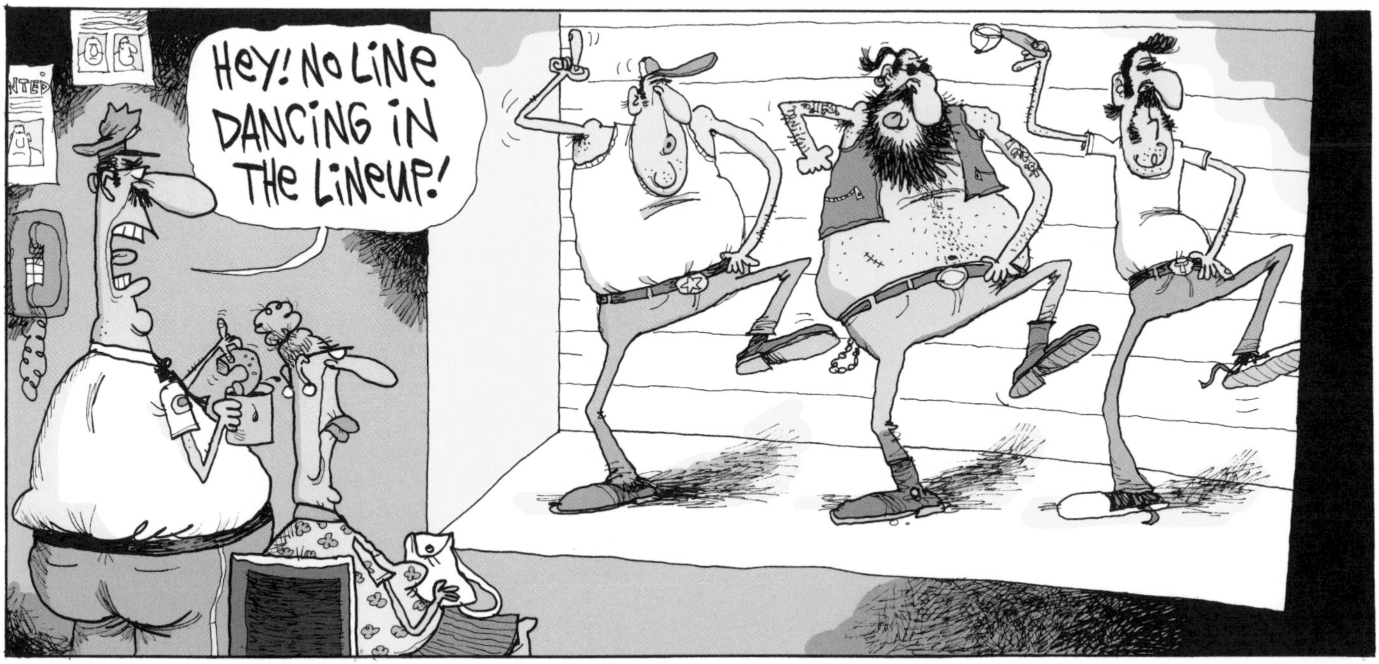
HEY! NO LINE DANCING IN THE LINEUP!

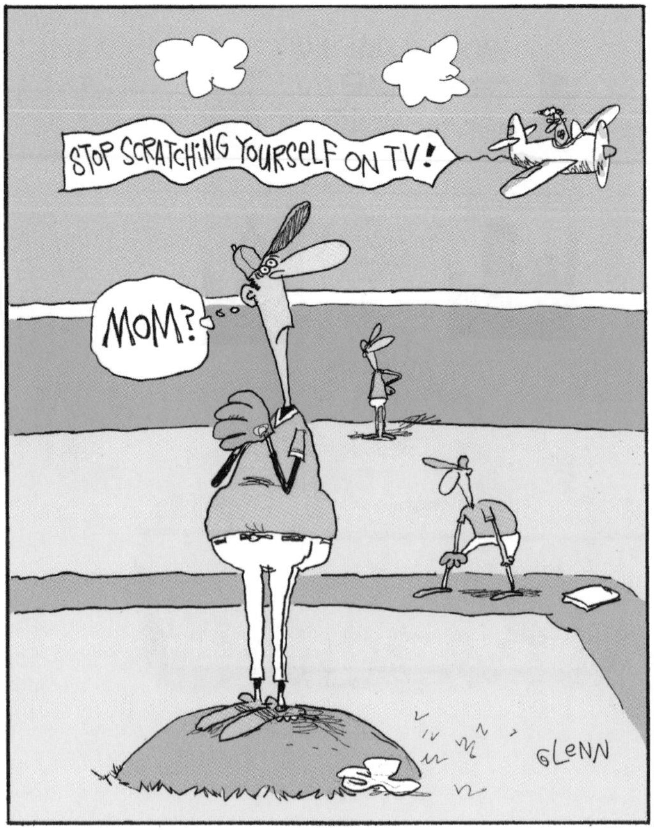
STOP SCRATCHING YOURSELF ON TV!
MOM?
GLENN

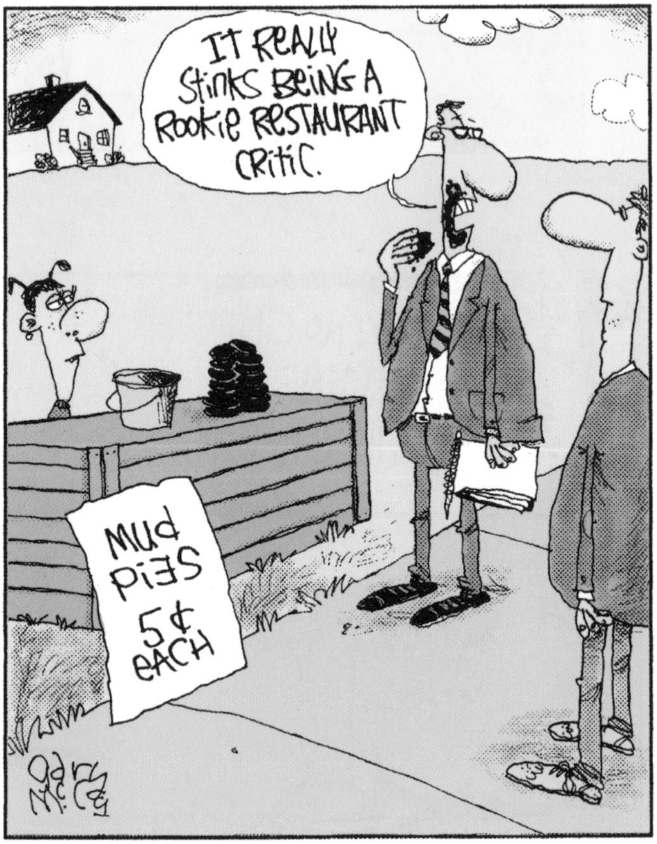
IT REALLY STINKS BEING A ROOKIE RESTAURANT CRITIC.
MUD PIES 5¢ EACH

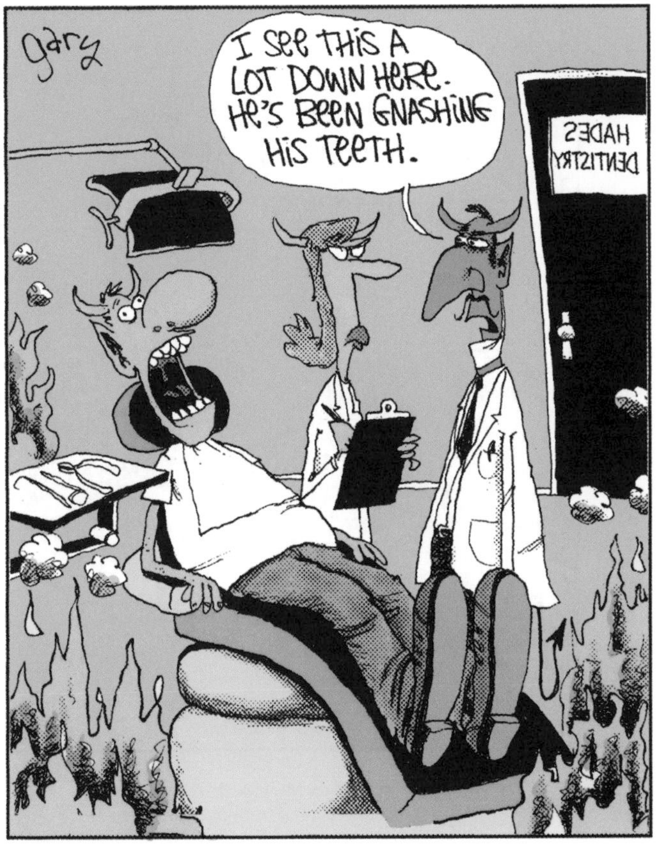
gary
I SEE THIS A LOT DOWN HERE. HE'S BEEN GNASHING HIS TEETH.
HADES DENTISTRY

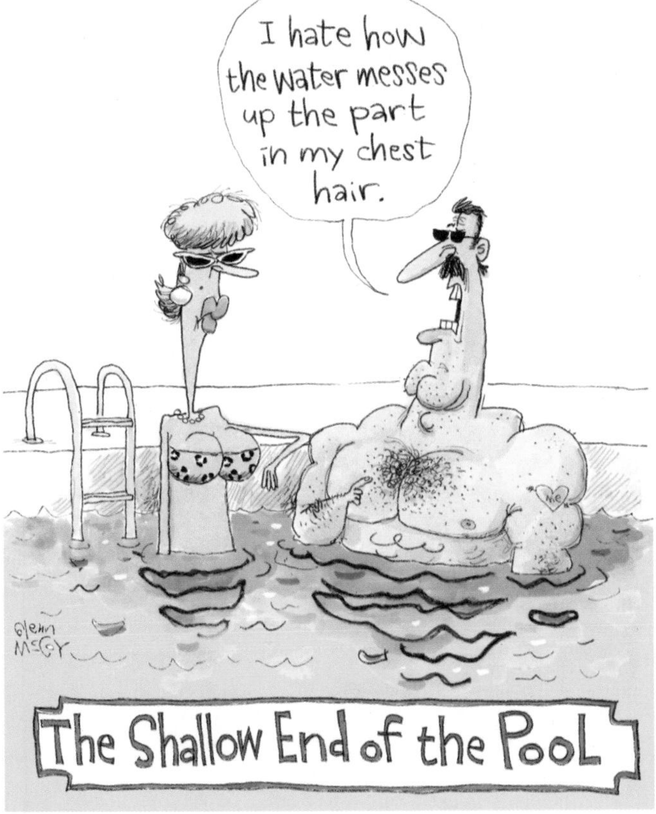
I hate how the water messes up the part in my chest hair.
Glenn McCoy

The Shallow End of the PooL

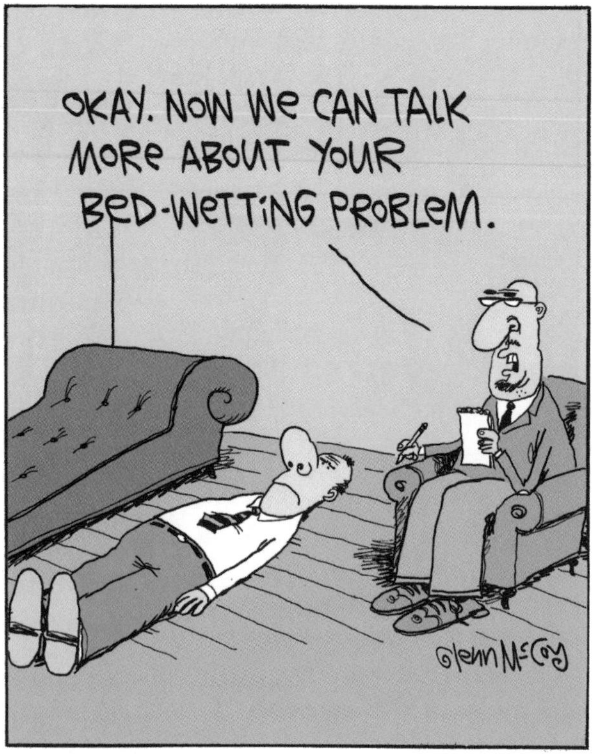
OKAY. NOW WE CAN TALK MORE ABOUT YOUR BED-WETTING PROBLEM.
Glenn McCoy

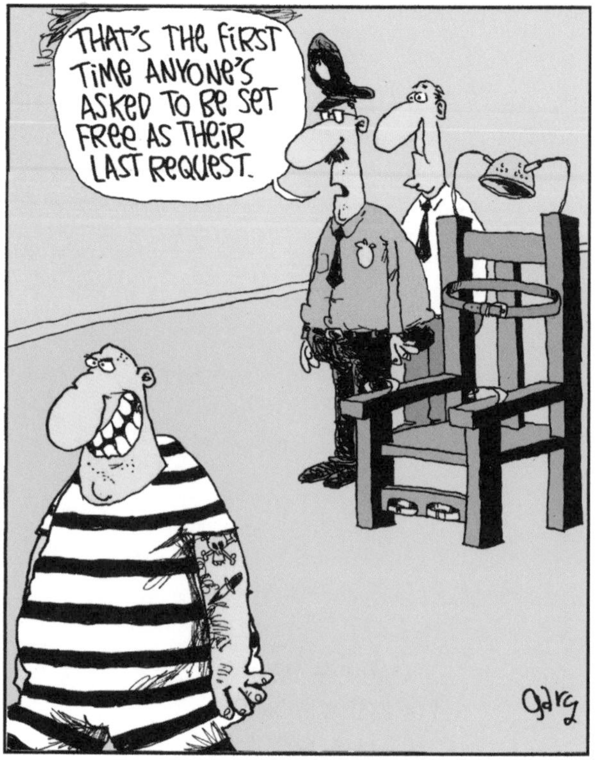
THAT'S THE FIRST TIME ANYONE'S ASKED TO BE SET FREE AS THEIR LAST REQUEST.
Gary

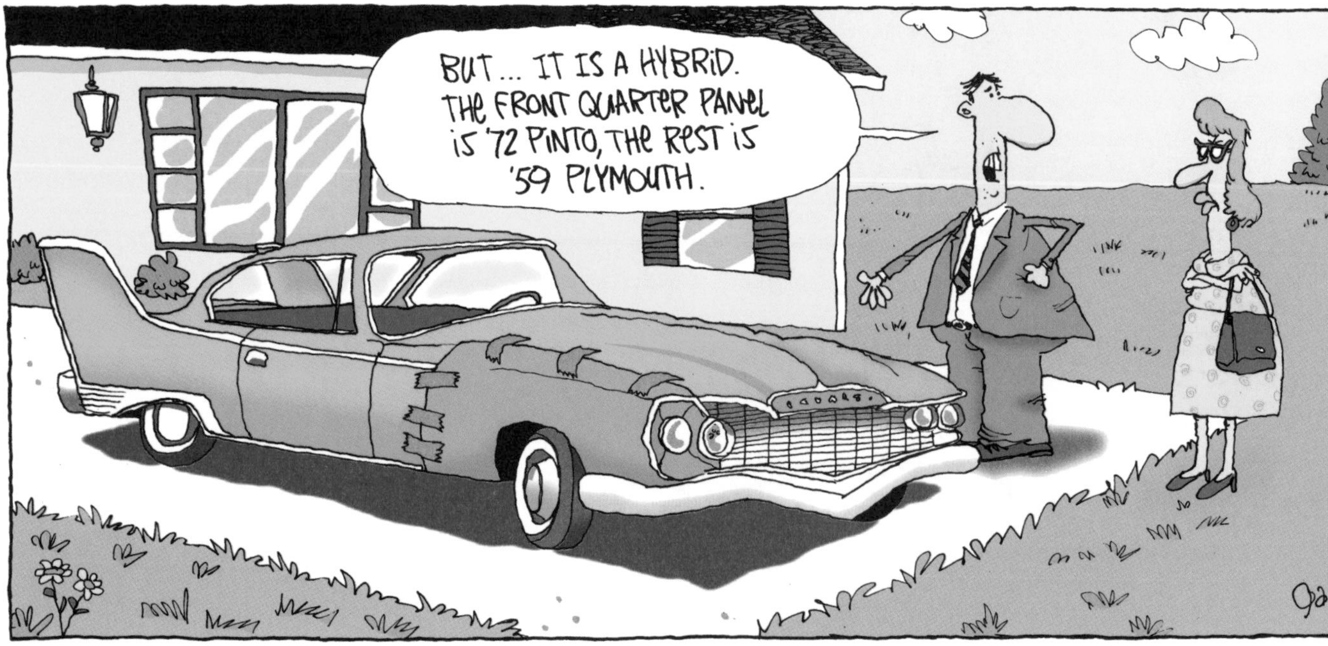
BUT... IT IS A HYBRID. THE FRONT QUARTER PANEL IS '72 PINTO, THE REST IS '59 PLYMOUTH.
Gary

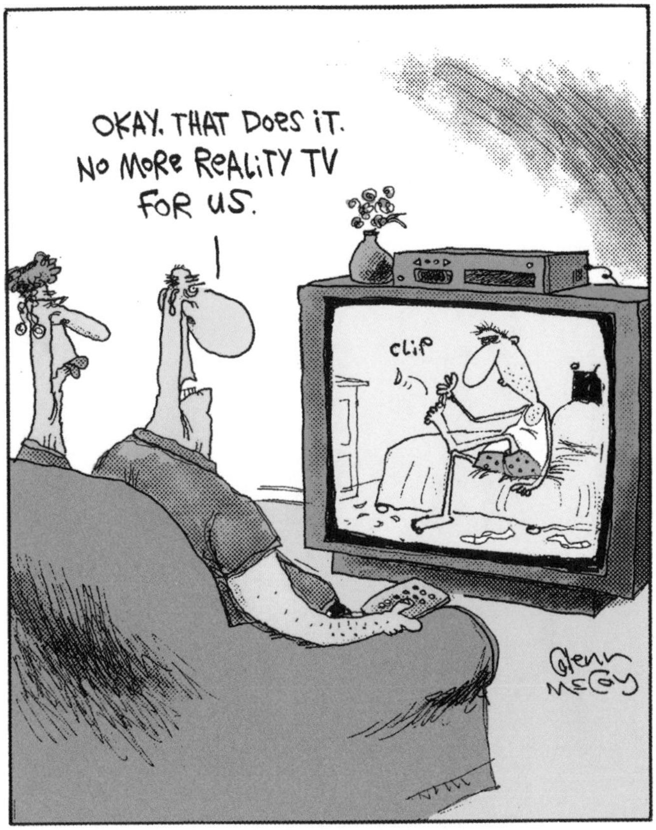
OKAY. THAT DOES IT. NO MORE REALITY TV FOR US.
CLIP
Glenn McCoy

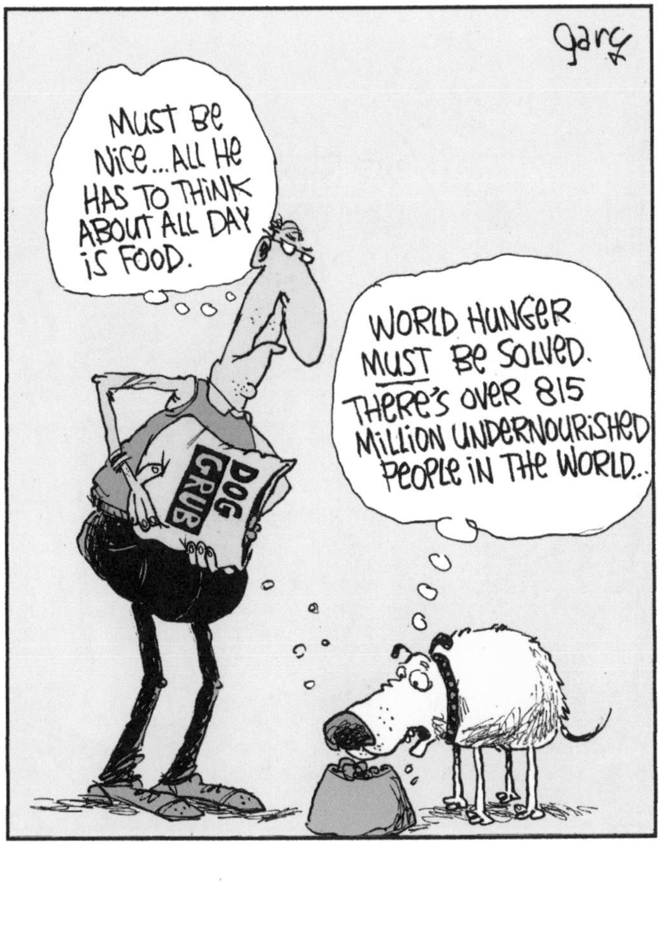
gary
MUST BE NICE... ALL HE HAS TO THINK ABOUT ALL DAY IS FOOD.
WORLD HUNGER MUST BE SOLVED. THERE'S OVER 815 MILLION UNDERNOURISHED PEOPLE IN THE WORLD...
DOG GRUB

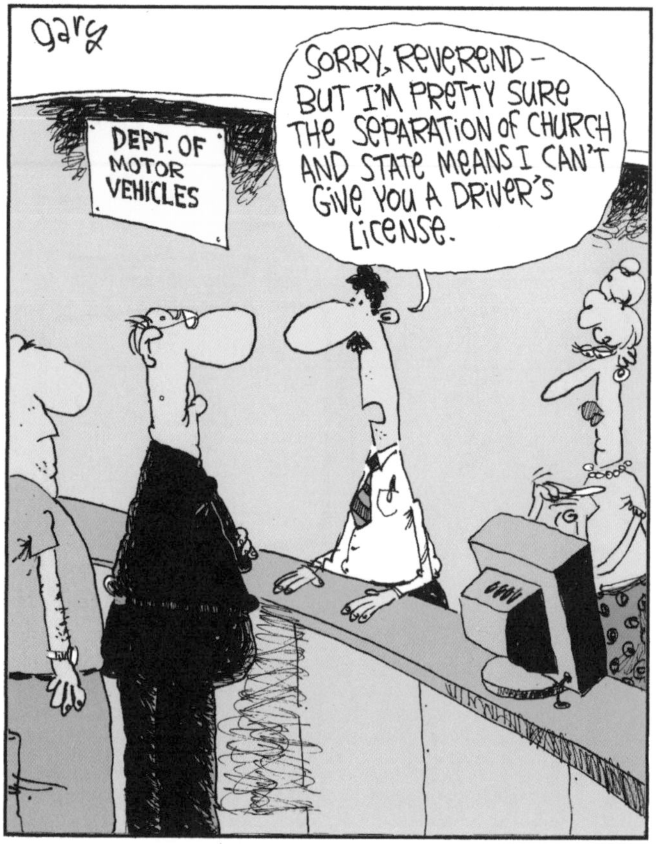
gary
DEPT. OF MOTOR VEHICLES
SORRY, REVEREND – BUT I'M PRETTY SURE THE SEPARATION OF CHURCH AND STATE MEANS I CAN'T GIVE YOU A DRIVER'S LICENSE.

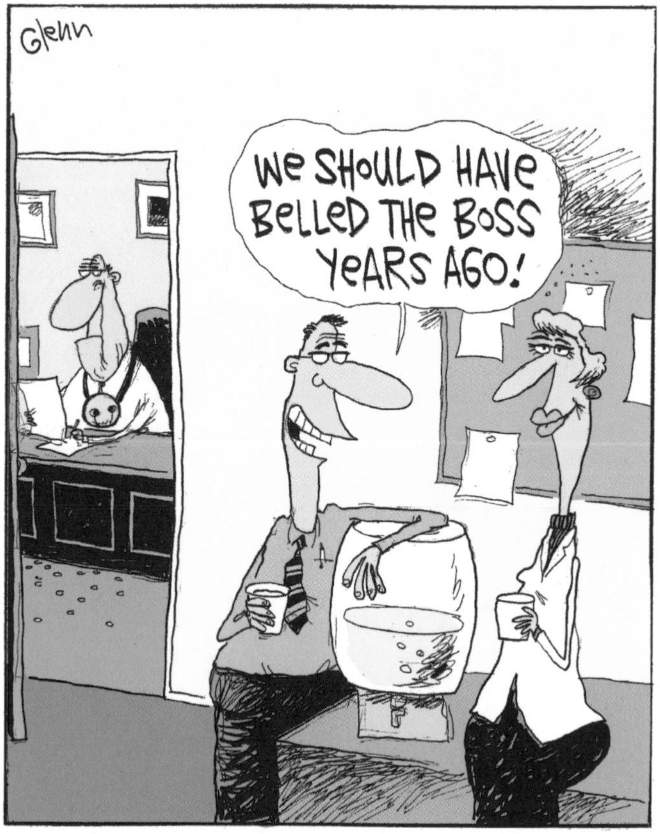
Glenn
WE SHOULD HAVE BELLED THE BOSS YEARS AGO!

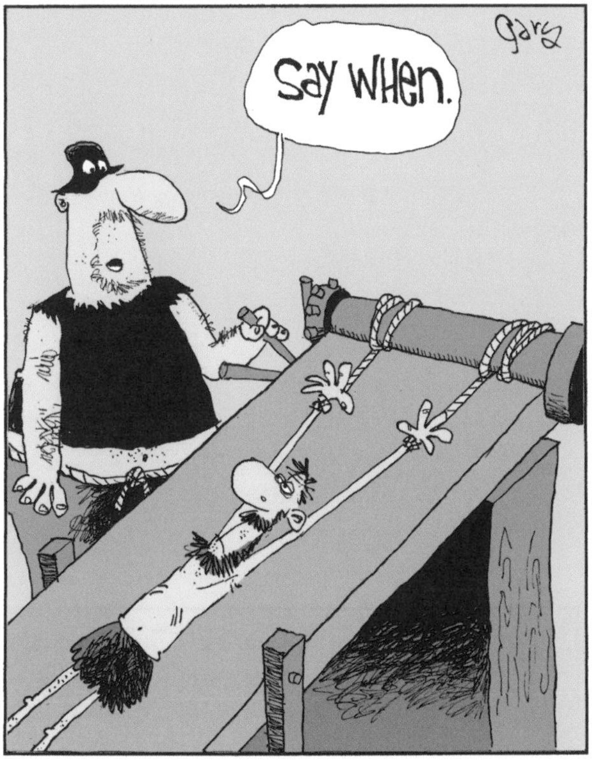
Say WHEN.
gary

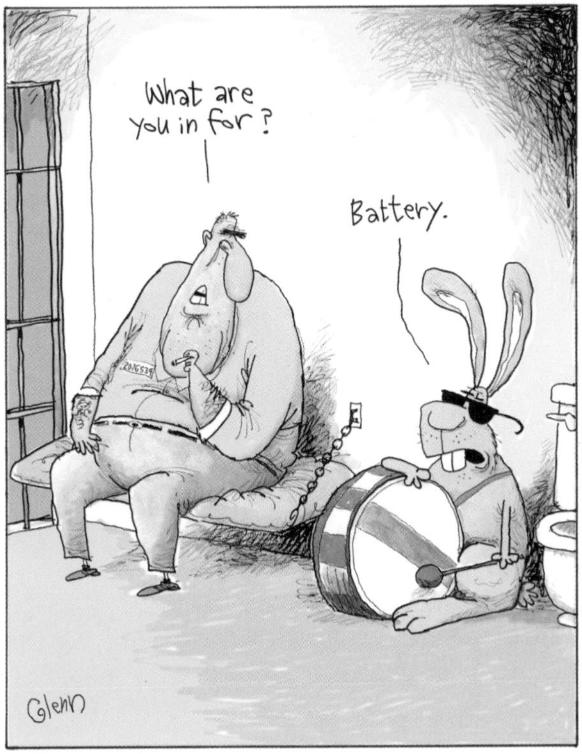
What are you in for?
Battery.
Glenn

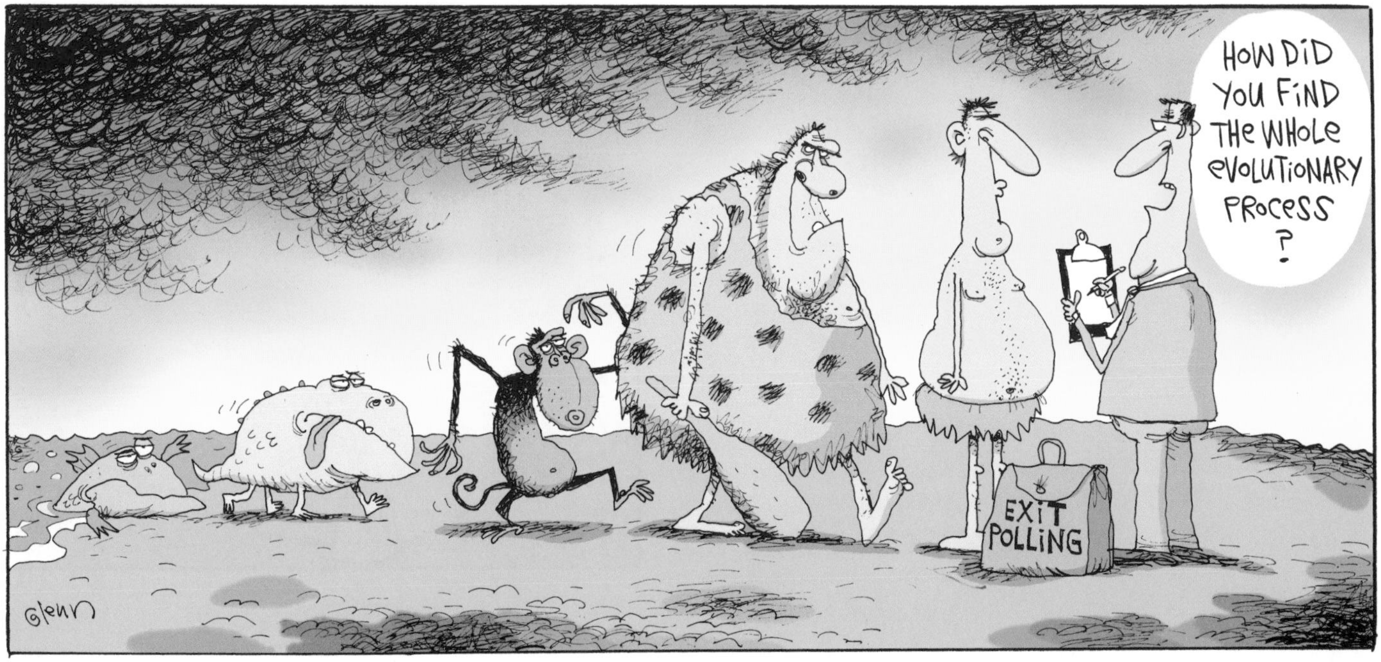
HOW DID YOU FIND THE WHOLE EVOLUTIONARY PROCESS ?
EXIT POLLING
Glenn

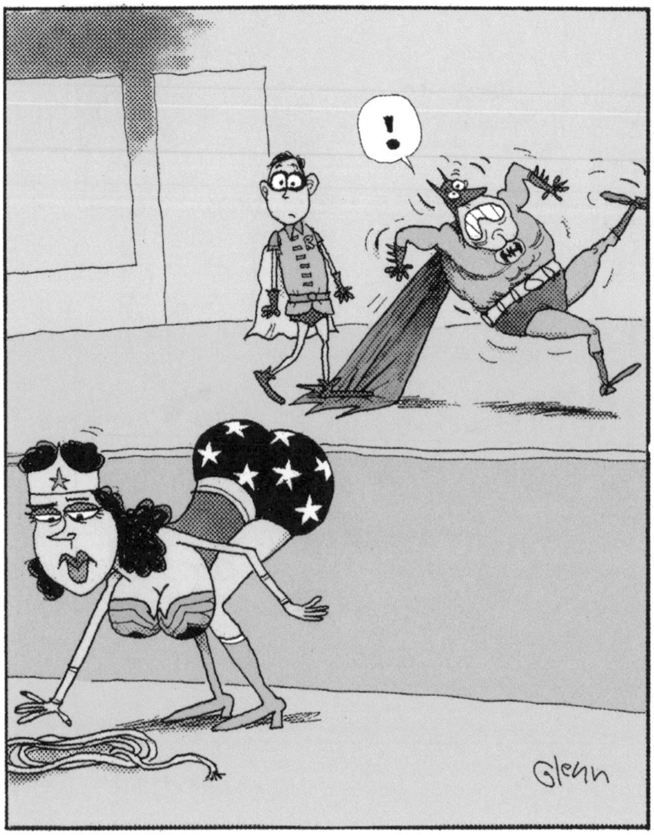
!
Glenn

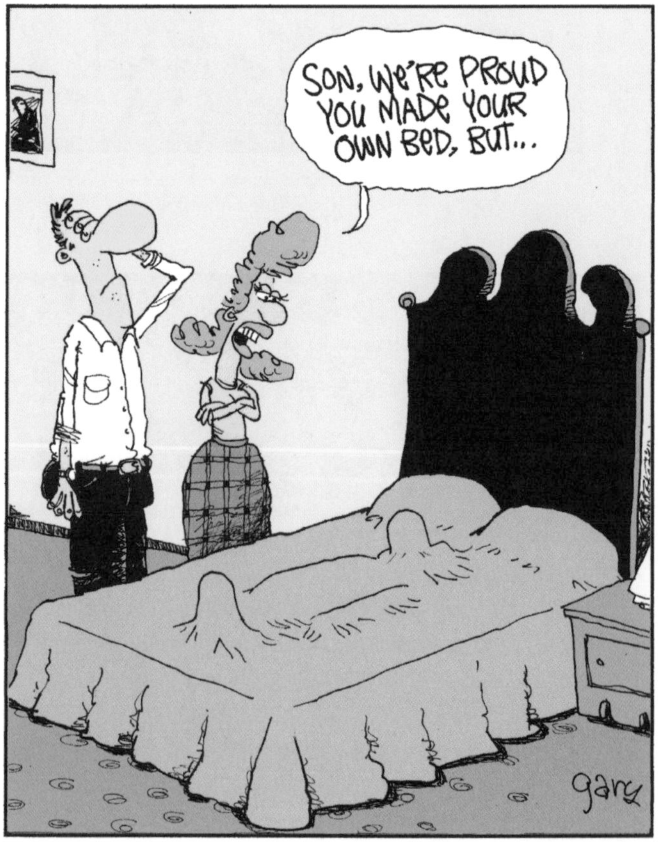
SON, WE'RE PROUD YOU MADE YOUR OWN BED, BUT...
gary

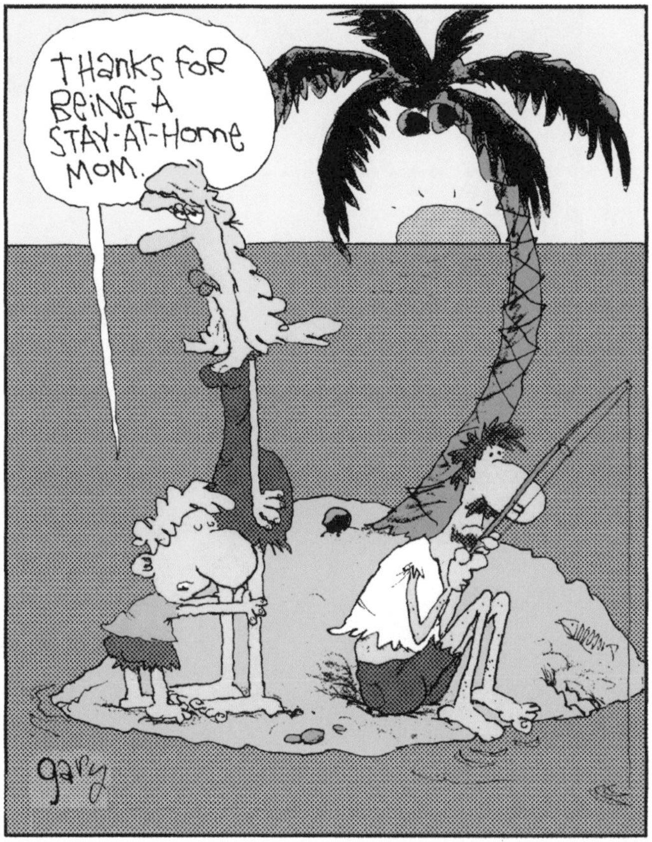
THANKS FOR BEING A STAY-AT-HOME MOM.
gary

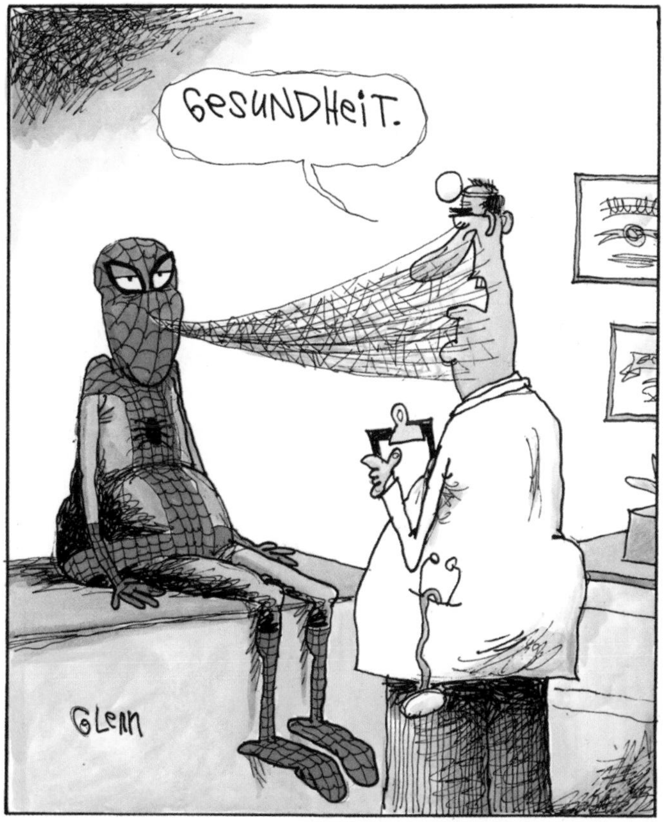
GESUNDHEIT.
GLENN

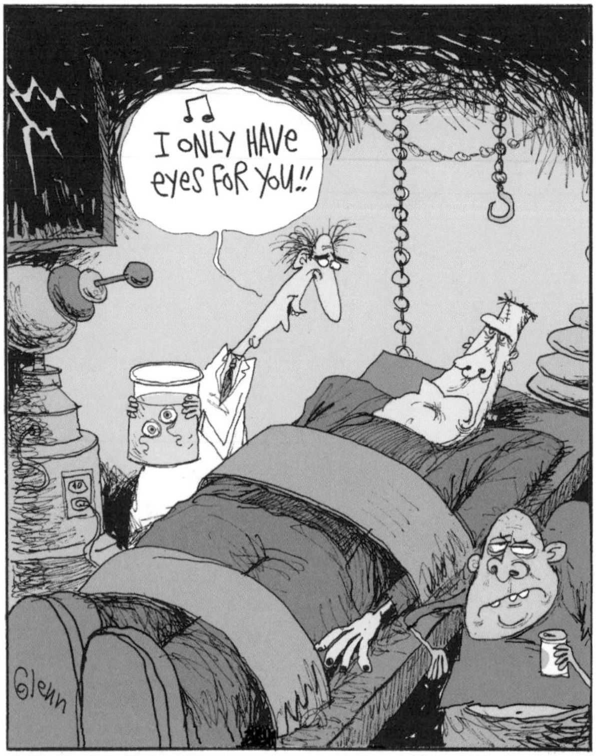
I ONLY HAVE eyes FOR YOU!!
Glenn

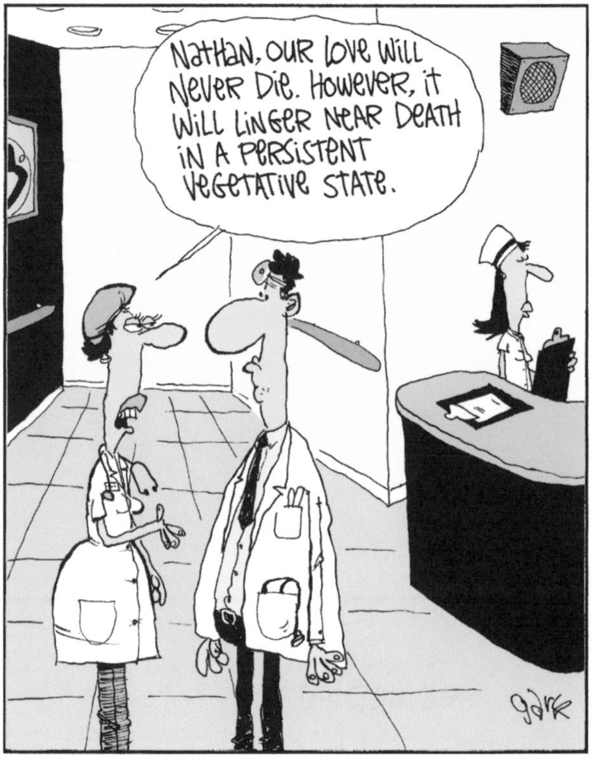
NatHan, OUR Love Will Never Die. However, it Will Linger Near Death in A Persistent Vegetative State.
Garg

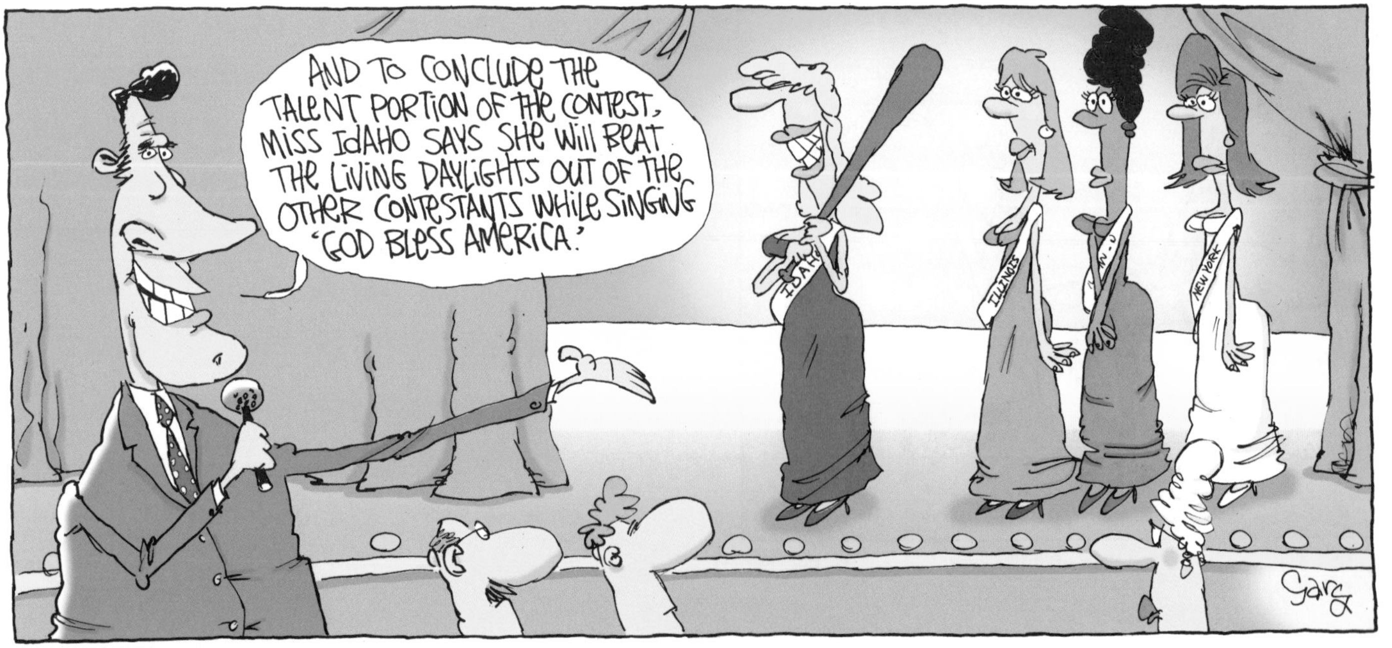
AND TO CONCLUDE THE TALENT PORTION OF THE CONTEST, MISS IDAHO SAYS SHE WILL BEAT THE LIVING DAYLIGHTS OUT OF THE OTHER CONTESTANTS WHILE SINGING 'GOD BLESS AMERICA.'
IDAHO
ILLINOIS
N.J.
NEW YORK
Garg

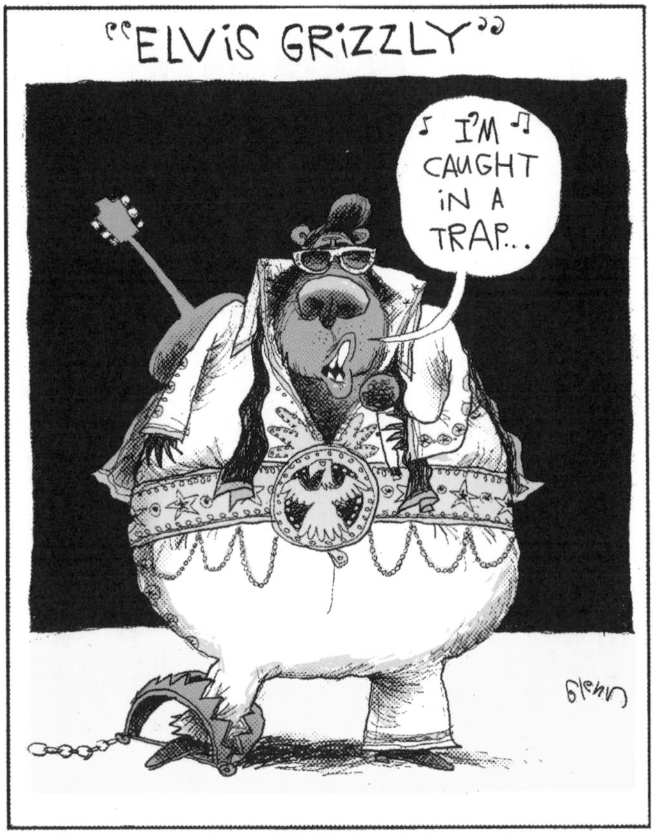
"ELVIS GRIZZLY"
♪ I'M ♫ CAUGHT IN A TRAP...
Glenn

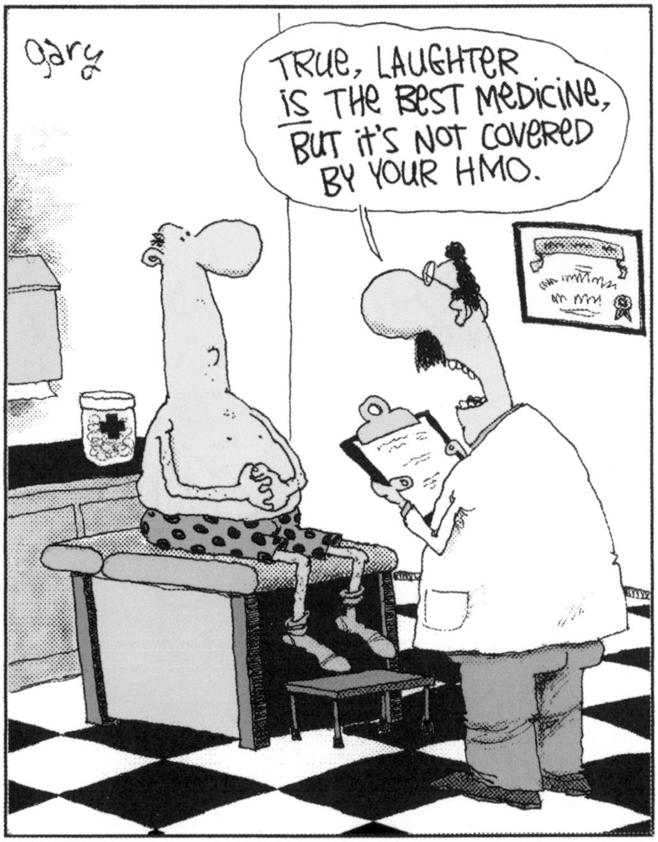
gary
TRUE, LAUGHTER IS THE BEST MEDICINE, BUT IT'S NOT COVERED BY YOUR HMO.

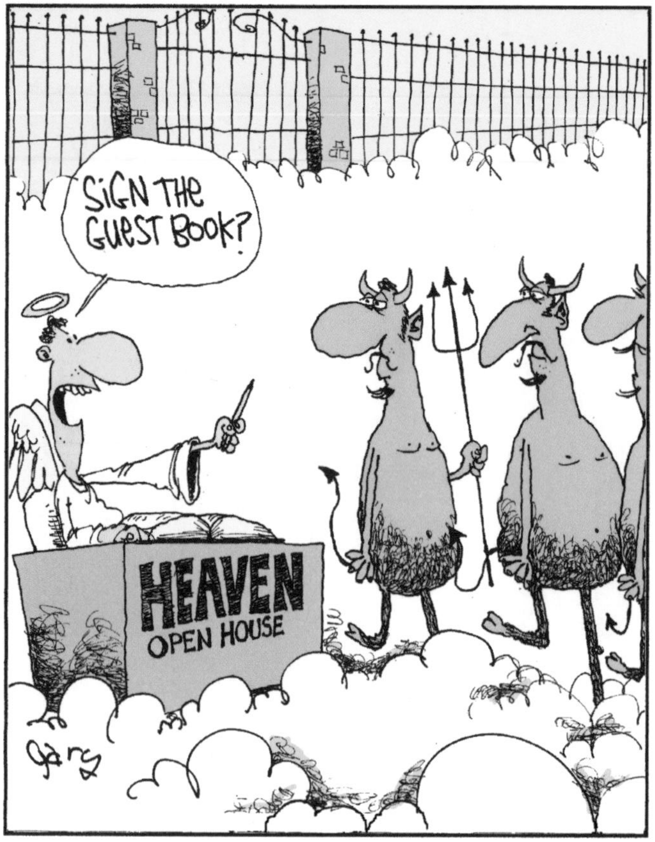
SIGN THE GUEST BOOK?
HEAVEN
OPEN HOUSE
Gary

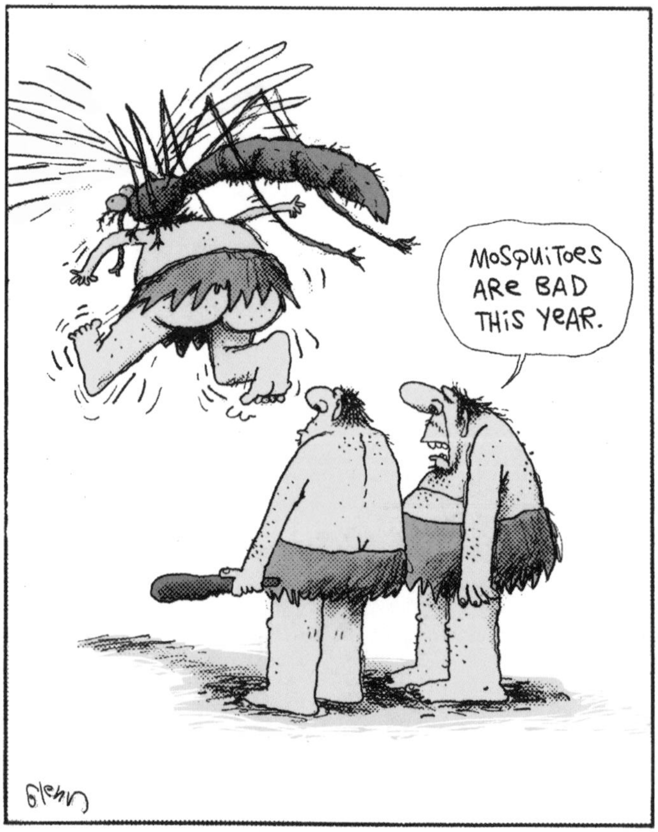
MOSQUITOES ARE BAD THIS YEAR.
Glenn

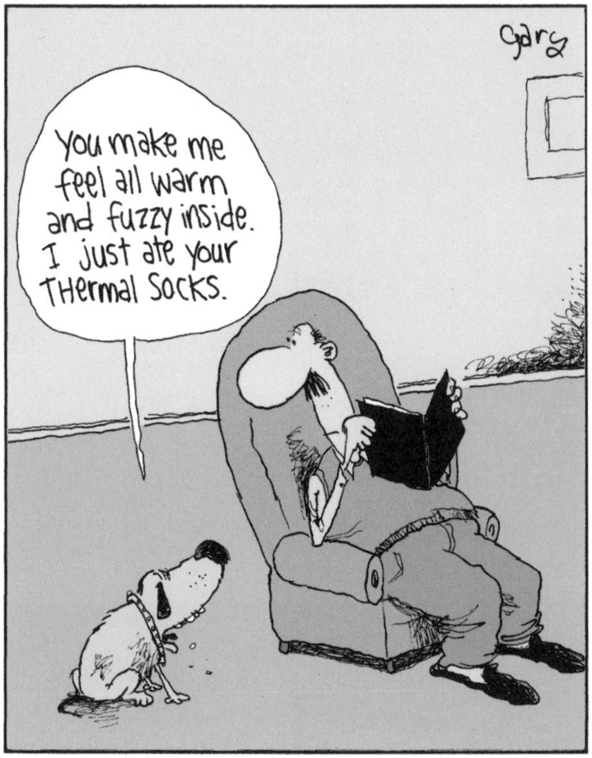
Gary
You make me feel all warm and fuzzy inside. I just ate your THermal SocKs.

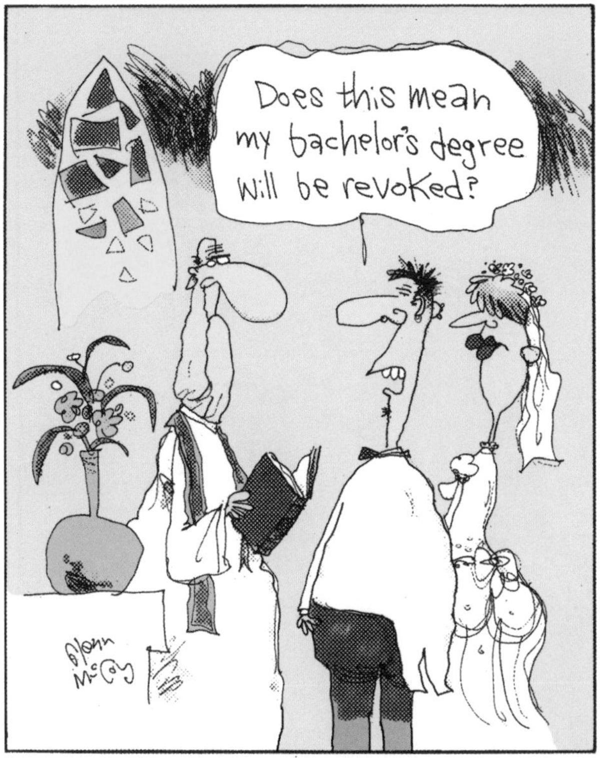
Does this mean my bachelor's degree will be revoked?
Glenn McCoy

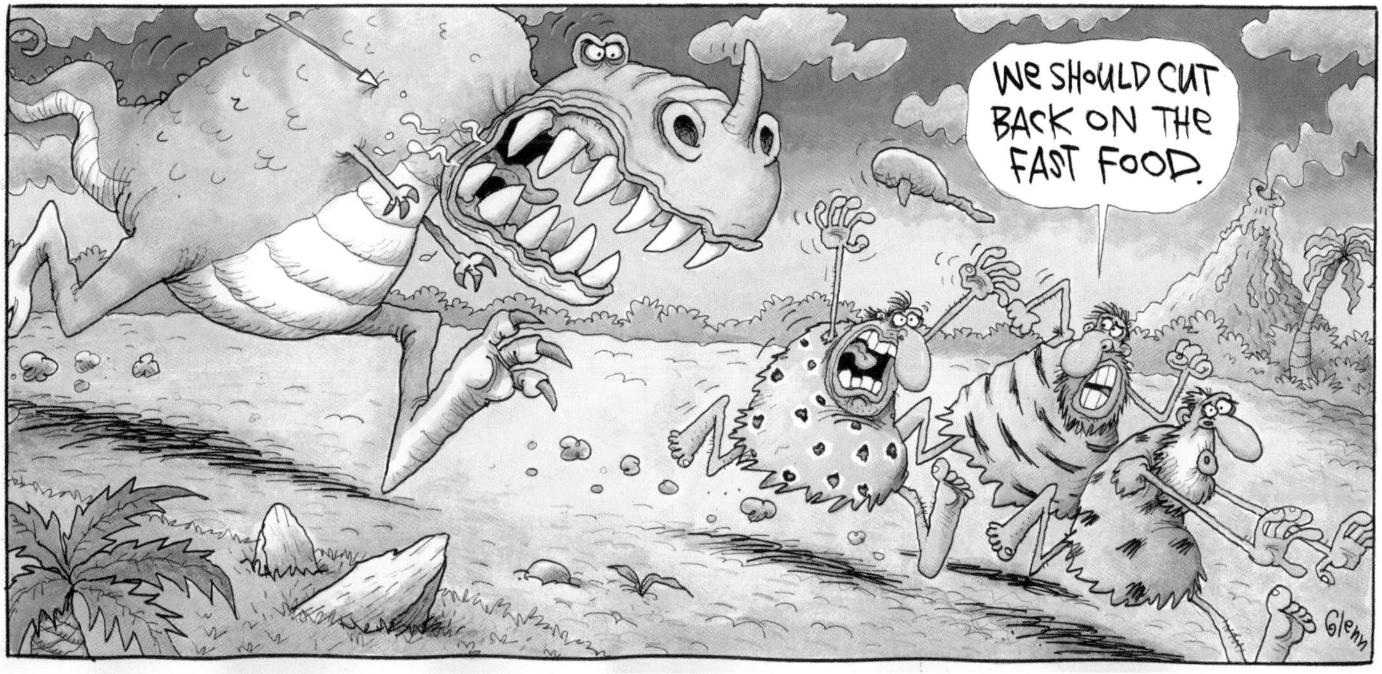
WE SHOULD CUT BACK ON THE FAST FOOD.
Glenn

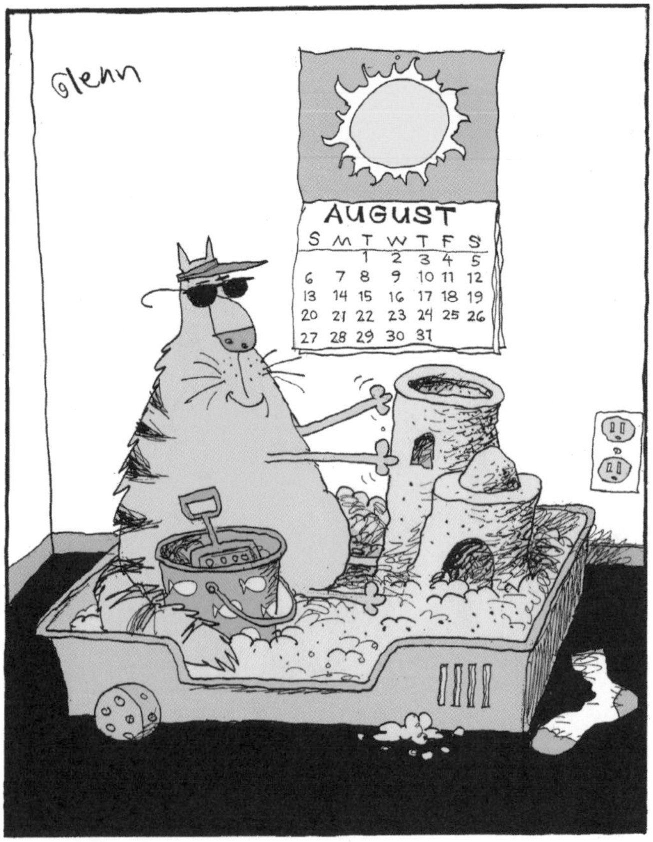
Glenn
AUGUST
S M T W T F S
1 2 3 4 5
6 7 8 9 10 11 12
13 14 15 16 17 18 19
20 21 22 23 24 25 26
27 28 29 30 31

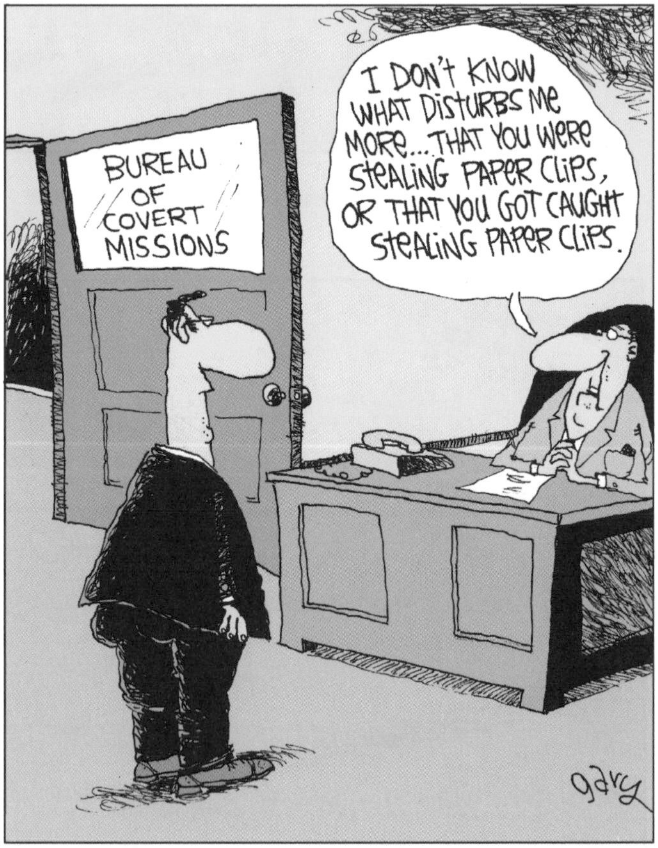
BUREAU OF COVERT MISSIONS
I DON'T KNOW WHAT DISTURBS ME MORE... THAT YOU WERE STEALING PAPER CLIPS, OR THAT YOU GOT CAUGHT STEALING PAPER CLIPS.
gary

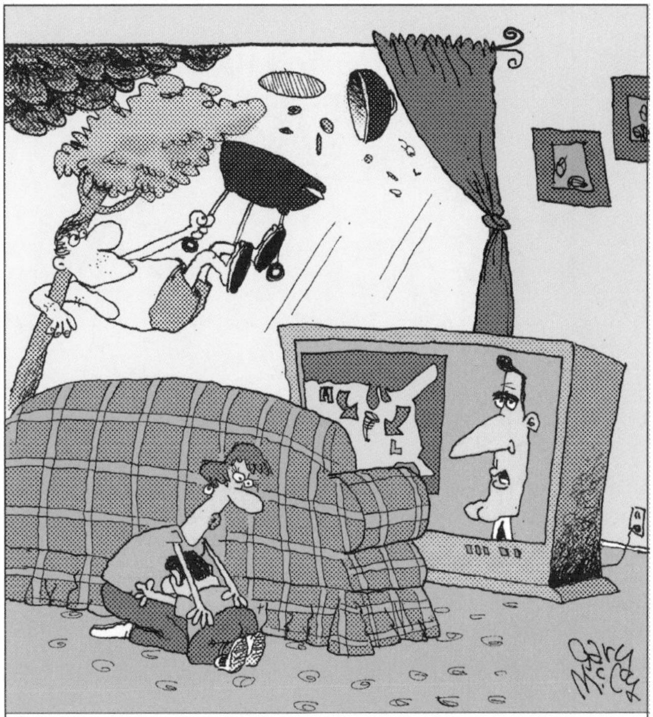
Gary McCoy

"THESE STORMS WILL PRODUCE LIGHTNING, HAIL, AND TORNADOS. WOMEN AND CHILDREN SEEK SHELTER. AND MEN MAY WANT TO CONSIDER CANCELING THEIR BARBECUES."

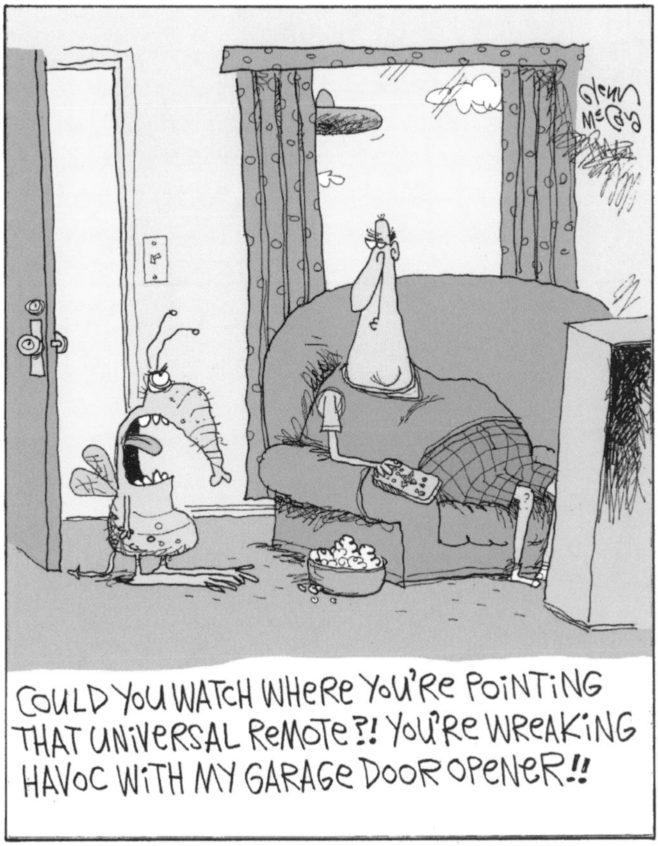
Glenn McCoy

COULD YOU WATCH WHERE YOU'RE POINTING THAT UNIVERSAL REMOTE?! YOU'RE WREAKING HAVOC WITH MY GARAGE DOOR OPENER!!

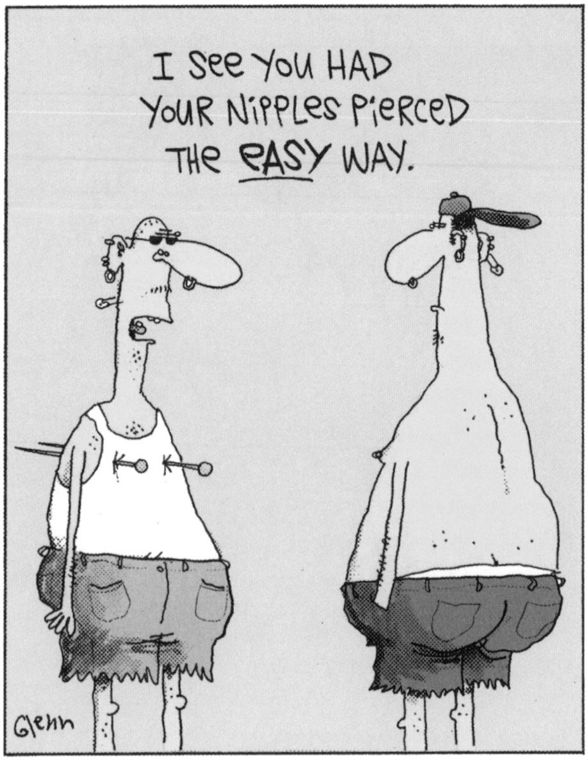
I SEE YOU HAD YOUR NIPPLES PIERCED THE EASY WAY.
Glenn

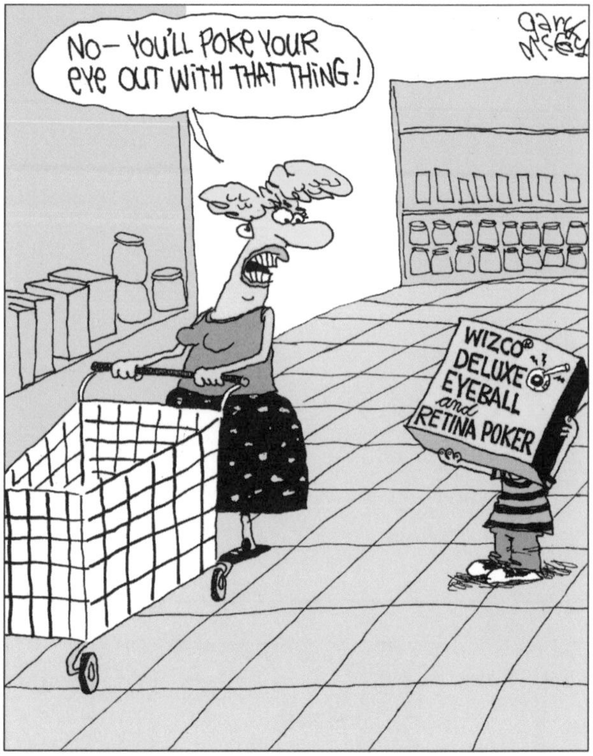
NO– YOU'LL POKE YOUR EYE OUT WITH THAT THING!
WIZCO® DELUXE EYEBALL and RETINA POKER

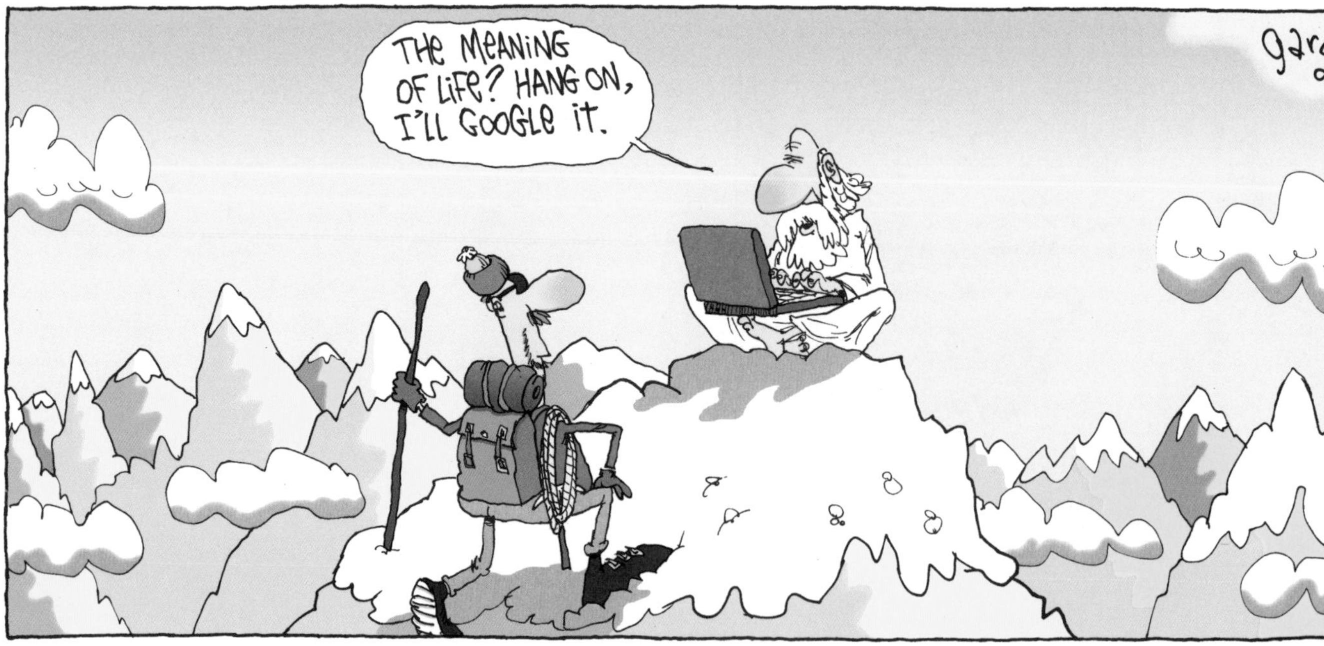
THE MEANING OF LIFE? HANG ON, I'LL GOOGLE IT.
gary

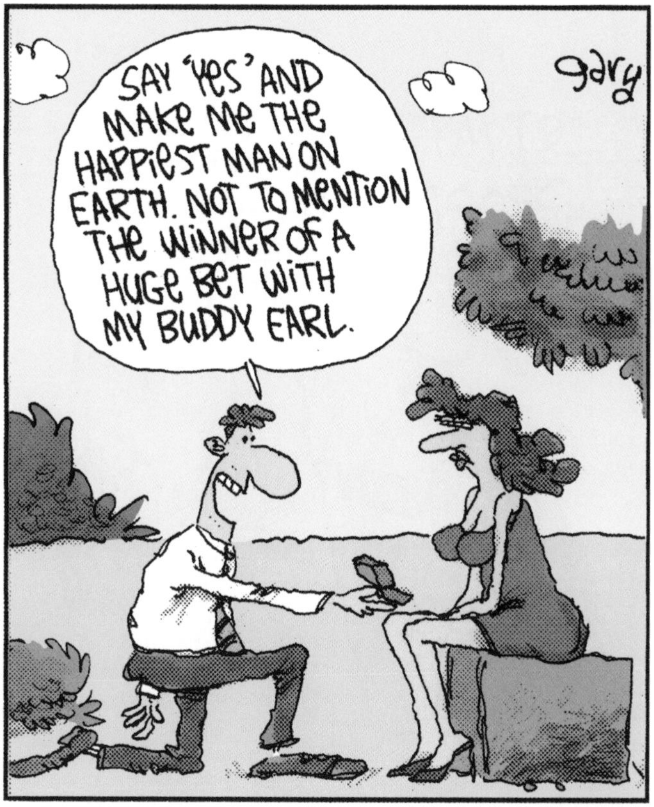
SAY 'YES' AND MAKE ME THE HAPPIEST MAN ON EARTH. NOT TO MENTION THE WINNER OF A HUGE BET WITH MY BUDDY EARL.
gary

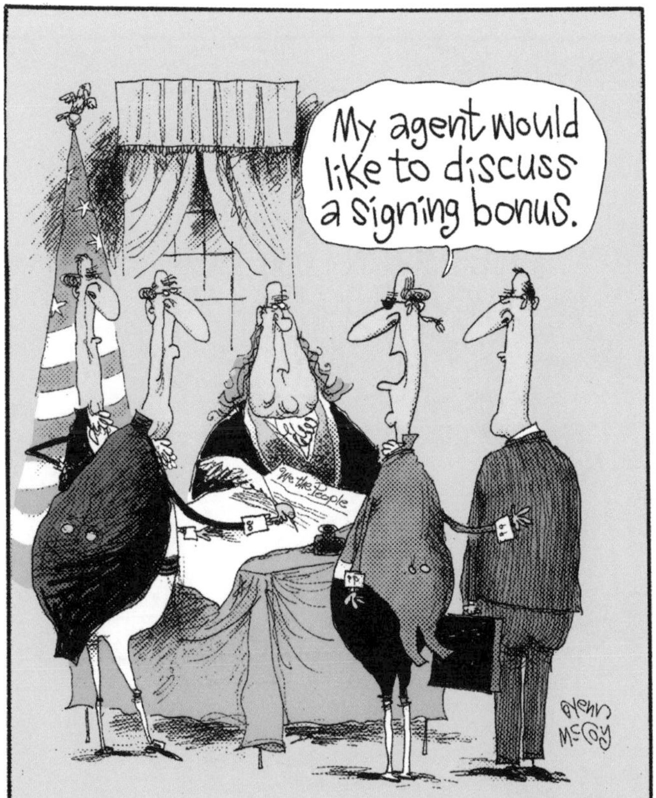
My agent would like to discuss a signing bonus.
We the People
Glenn McCoy

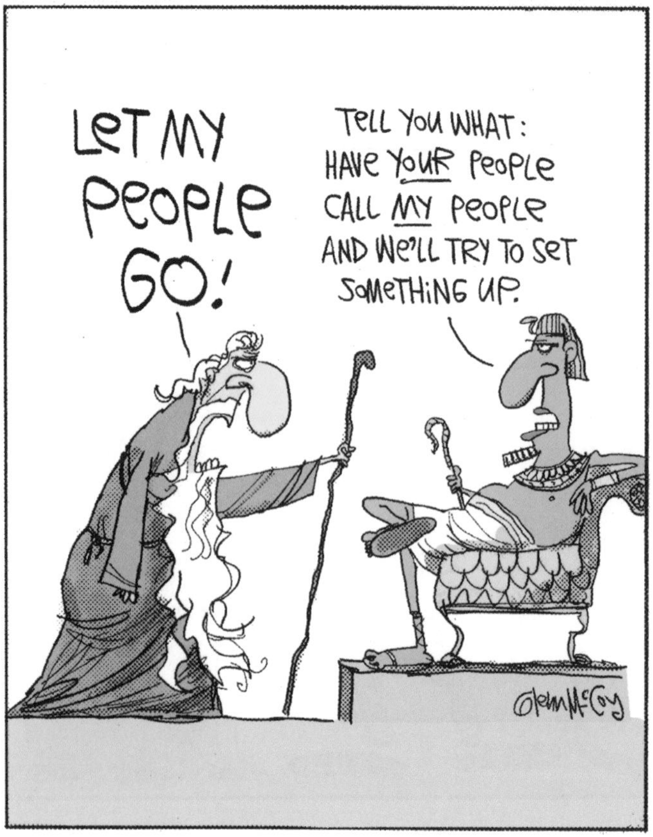
LET MY PEOPLE GO!
TELL YOU WHAT: HAVE YOUR PEOPLE CALL MY PEOPLE AND WE'LL TRY TO SET SOMETHING UP.
Glenn McCoy

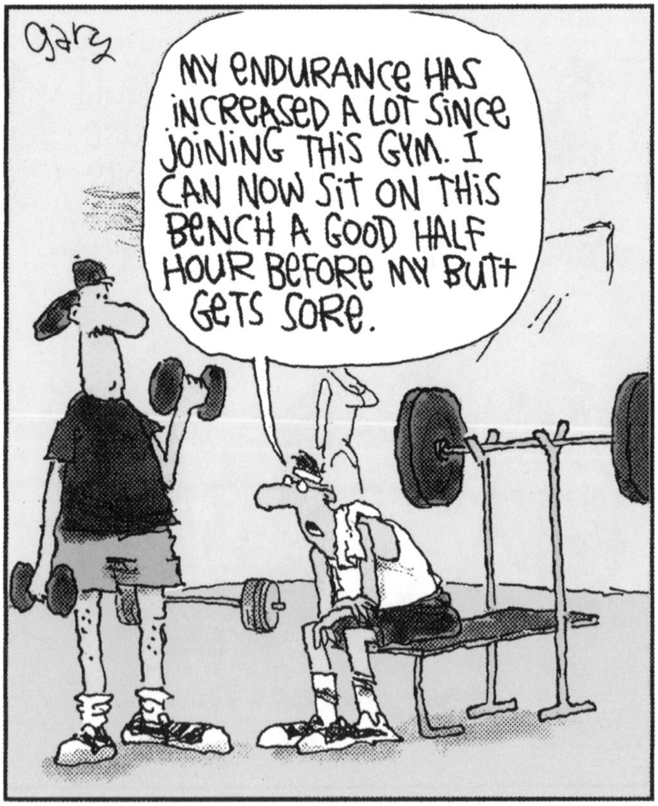
Gary
MY ENDURANCE HAS INCREASED A LOT SINCE JOINING THIS GYM. I CAN NOW SIT ON THIS BENCH A GOOD HALF HOUR BEFORE MY BUTT GETS SORE.

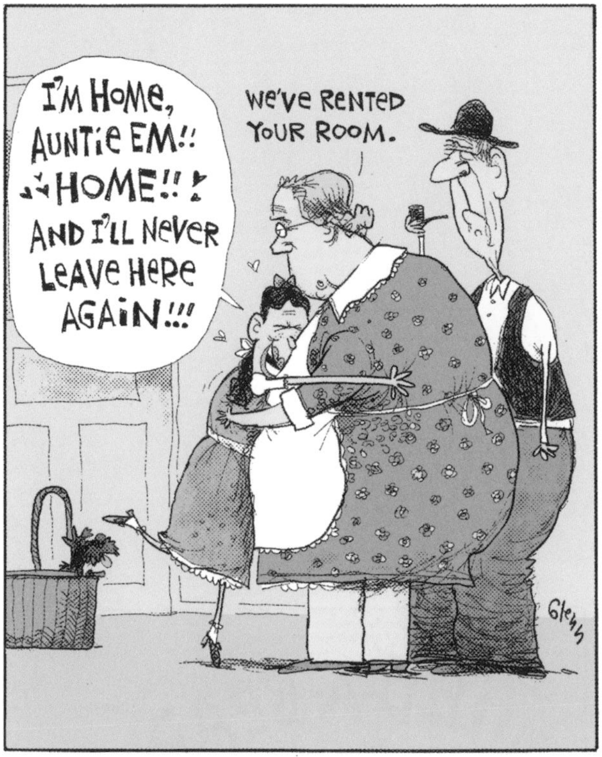
I'M HOME, AUNTIE EM!! HOME!! AND I'LL NEVER LEAVE HERE AGAIN!!!
WE'VE RENTED YOUR ROOM.
Glenn

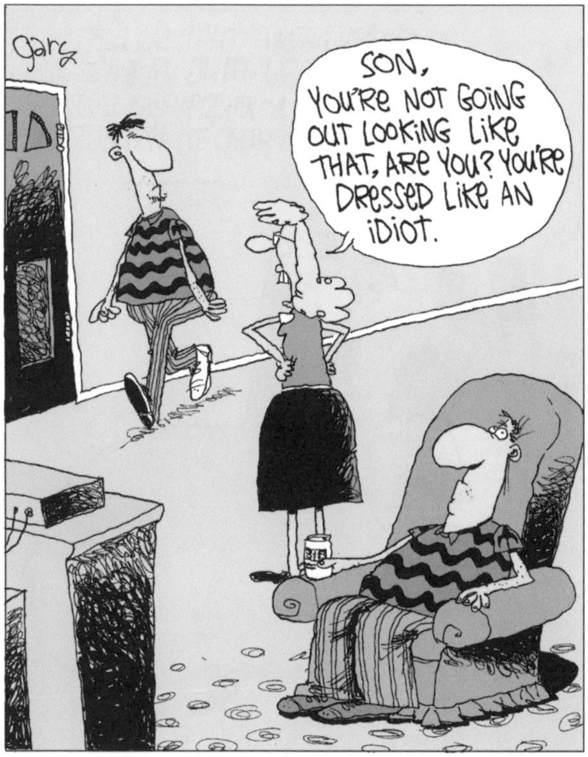
Gary
SON, YOU'RE NOT GOING OUT LOOKING LIKE THAT, ARE YOU? YOU'RE DRESSED LIKE AN IDIOT.

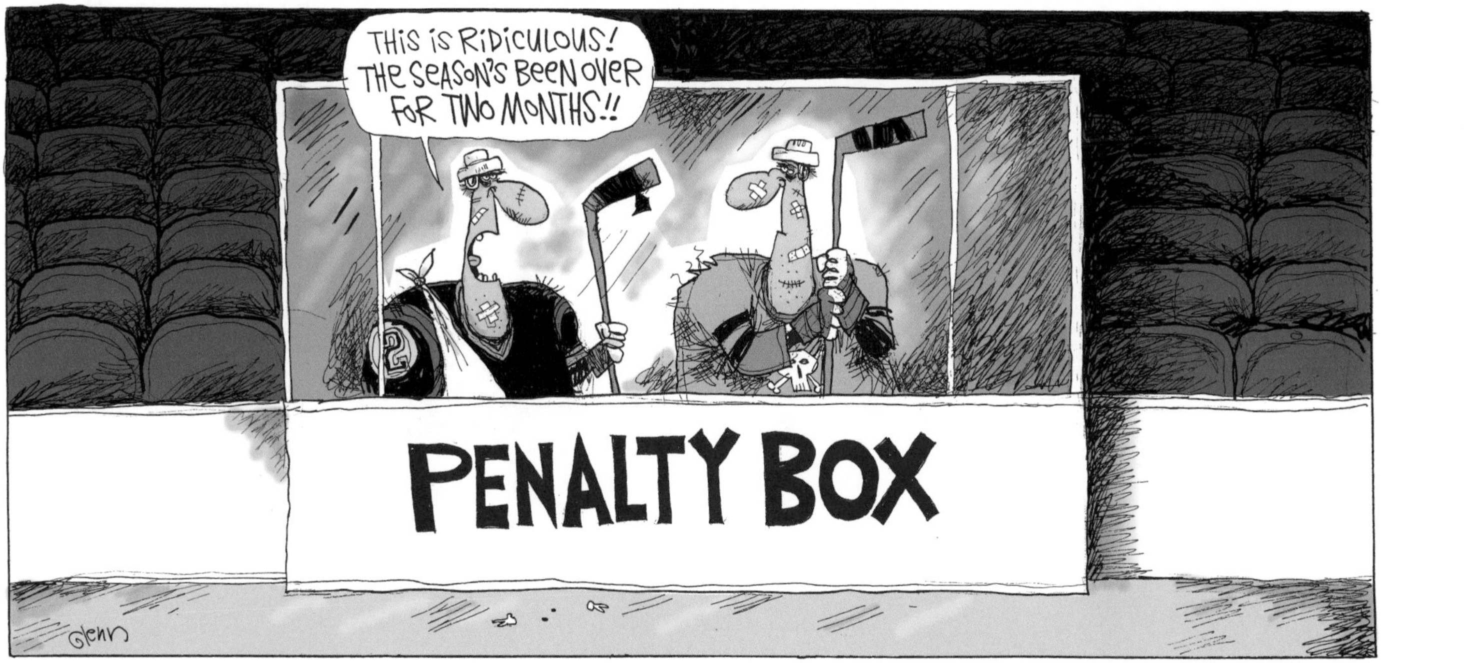
THIS IS RIDICULOUS! THE SEASON'S BEEN OVER FOR TWO MONTHS!!
PENALTY BOX
Glenn

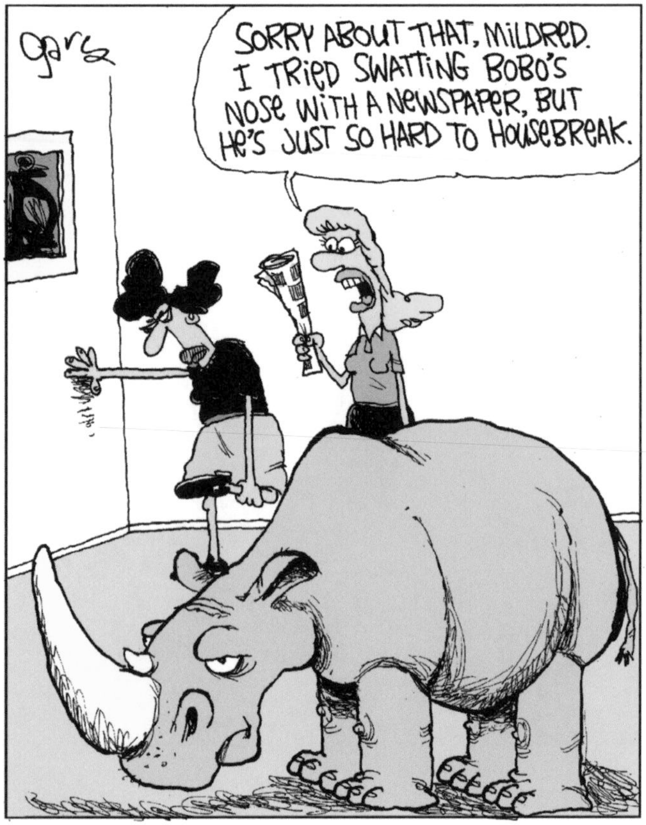
SORRY ABOUT THAT, MILDRED. I TRIED SWATTING BOBO'S NOSE WITH A NEWSPAPER, BUT HE'S JUST SO HARD TO HOUSEBREAK.

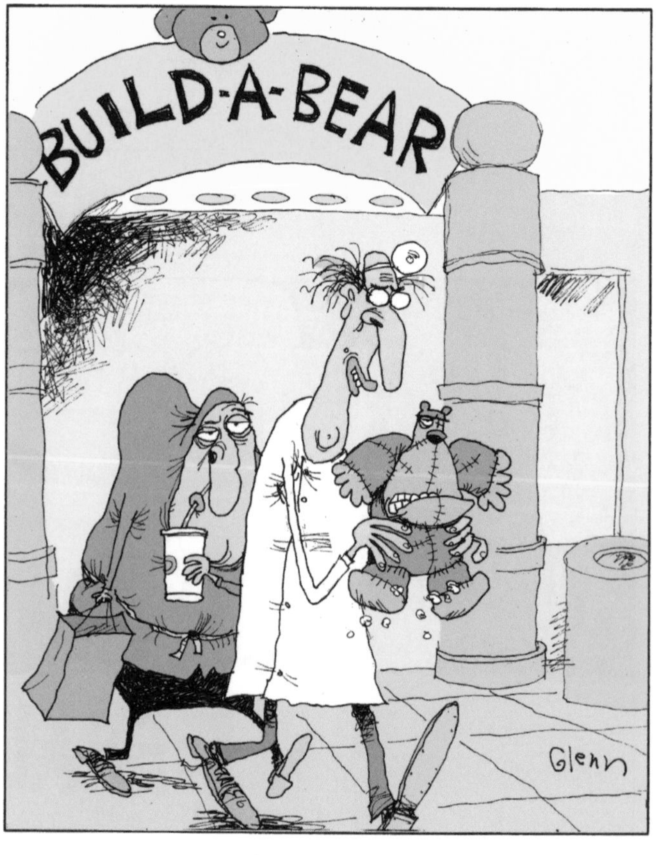
BUILD-A-BEAR
Glenn

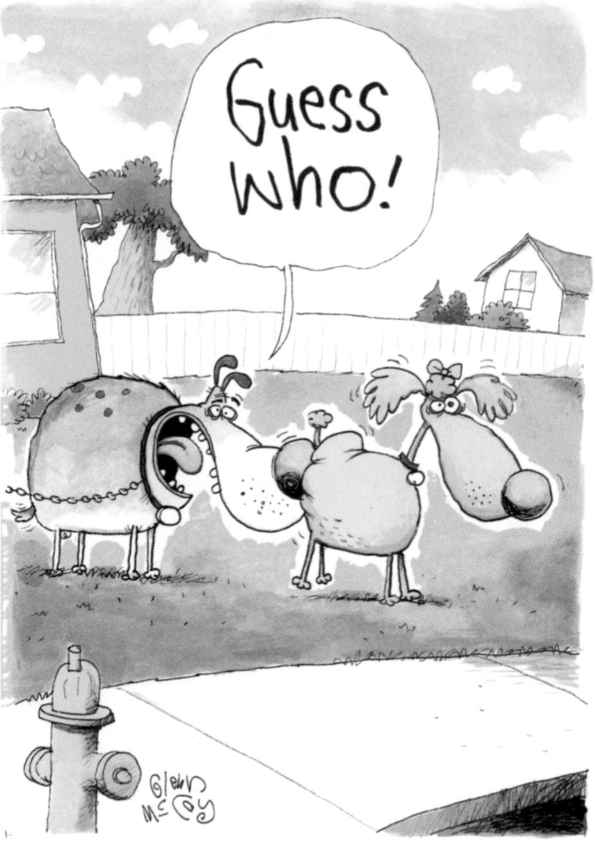
Guess who!
Glenn McCoy

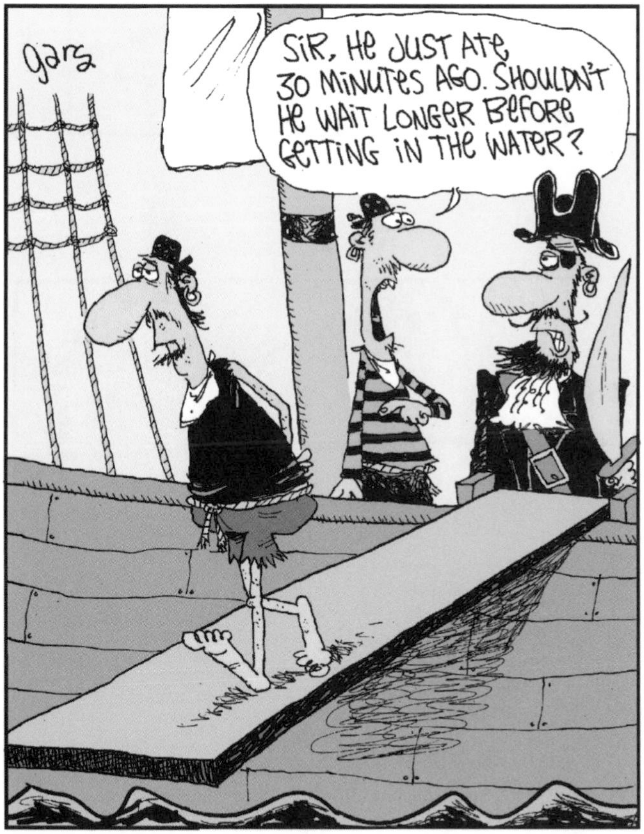
gary
SIR, HE JUST ATE 30 MINUTES AGO. SHOULDN'T HE WAIT LONGER BEFORE GETTING IN THE WATER?

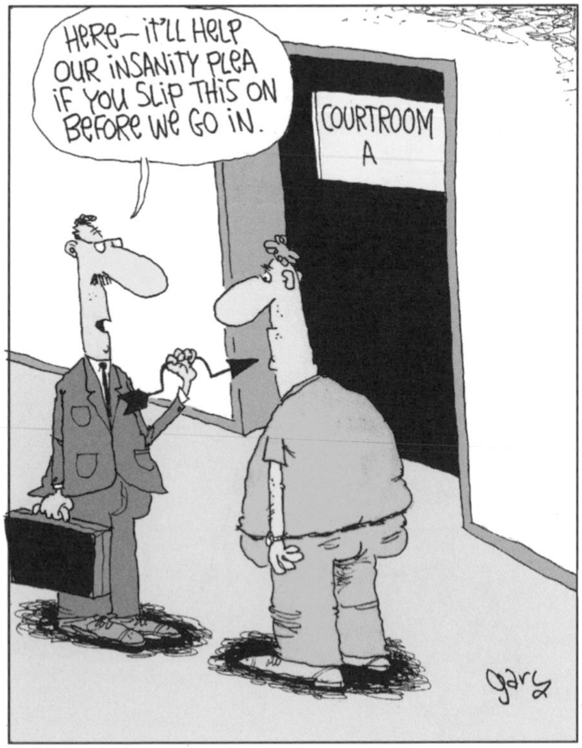
HERE—IT'LL HELP OUR INSANITY PLEA IF YOU SLIP THIS ON BEFORE WE GO IN.
COURTROOM A
gary

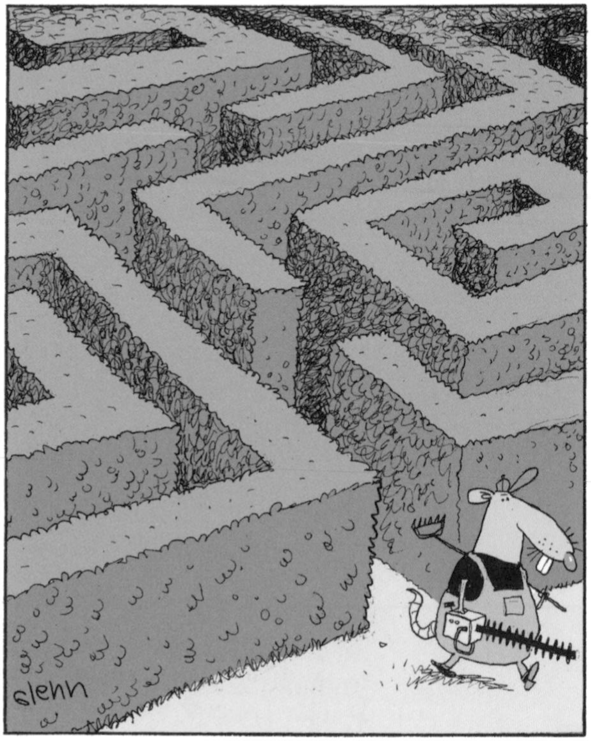
glenn

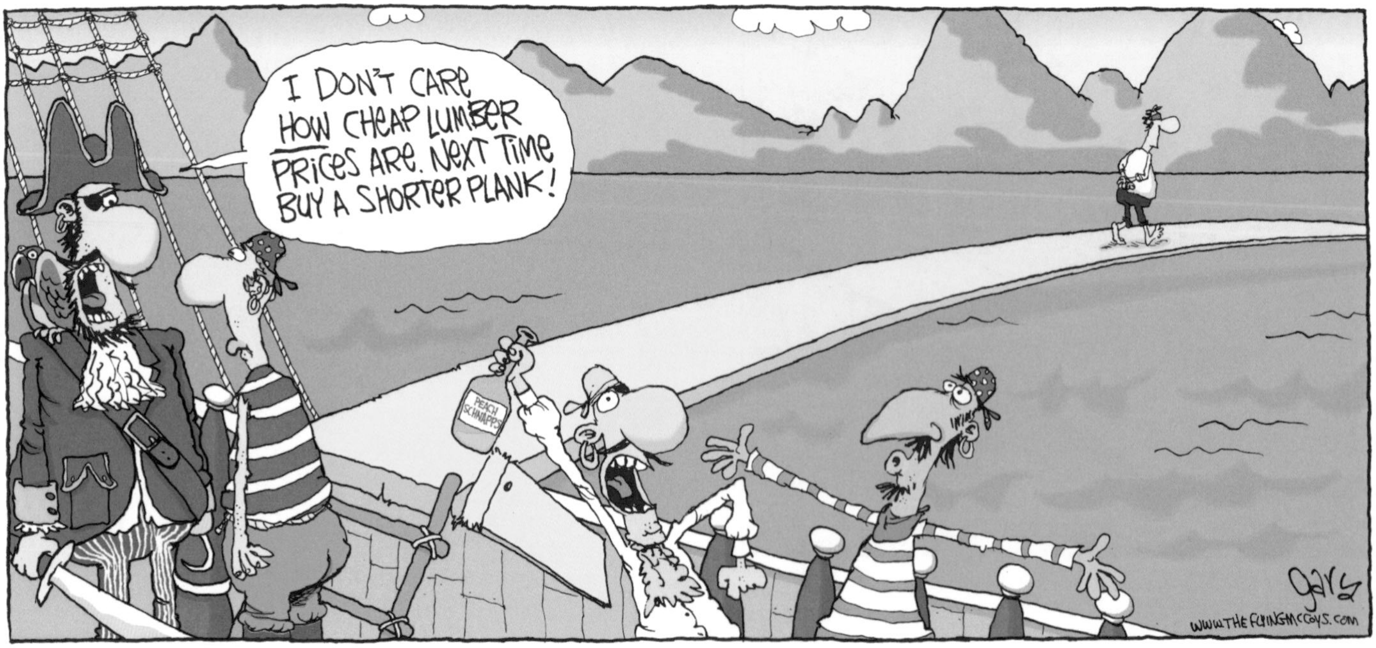
I DON'T CARE HOW CHEAP LUMBER PRICES ARE. NEXT TIME BUY A SHORTER PLANK!
PEACH SCHNAPPS
gary
WWW.THEFLYINGMCCOYS.COM

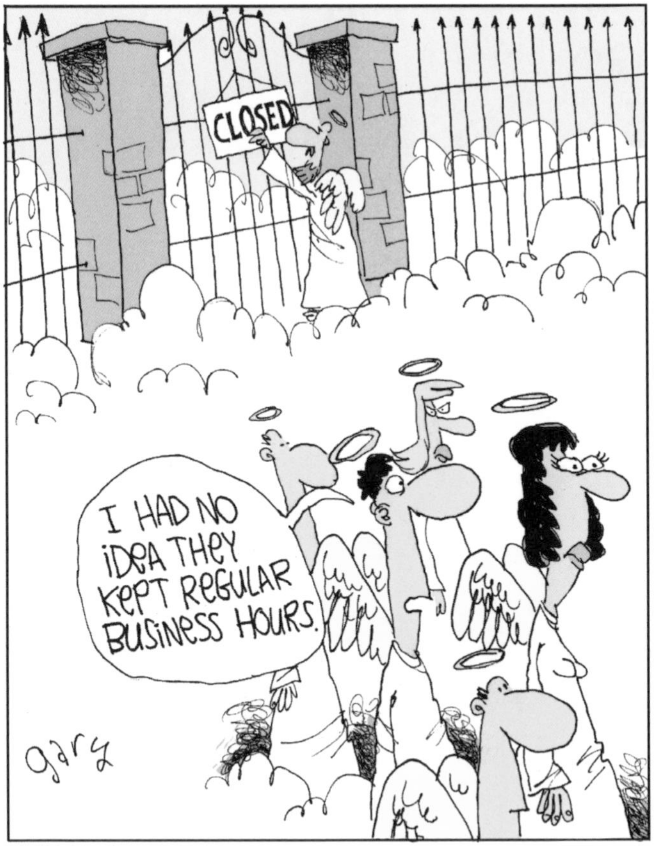
CLOSED
I HAD NO iDEA THEY KEPT REGULAR BUSINESS HOURS.
gary

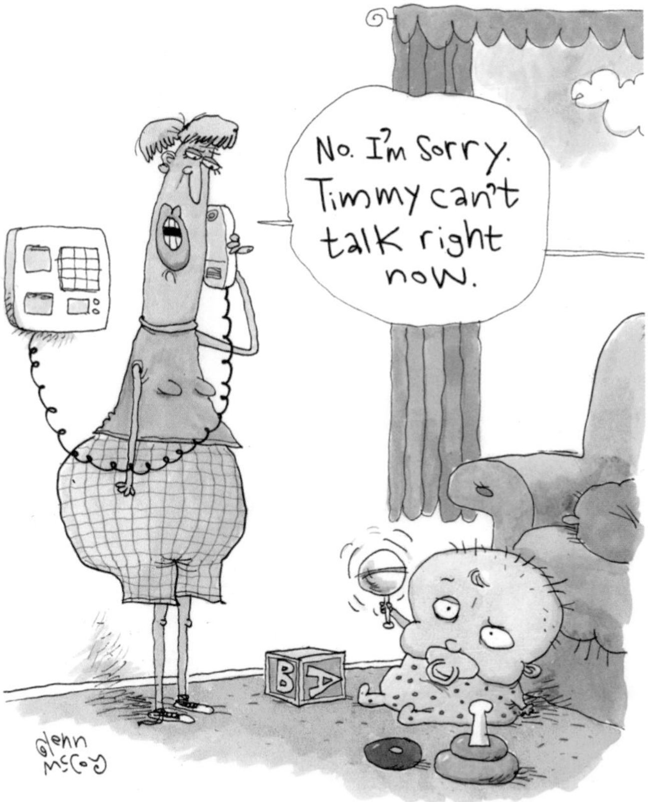
No. I'm Sorry. Timmy can't talk right now.
B A
glenn McCoy

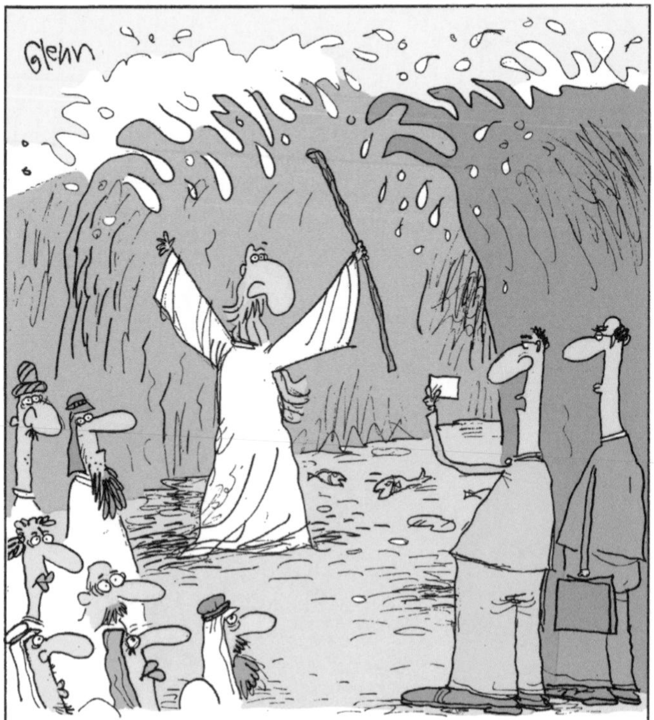
Glenn

WE'RE FROM THE E.P.A.—ARE YOU AWARE THAT THIS IS A FEDERALLY PROTECTED WETLAND?

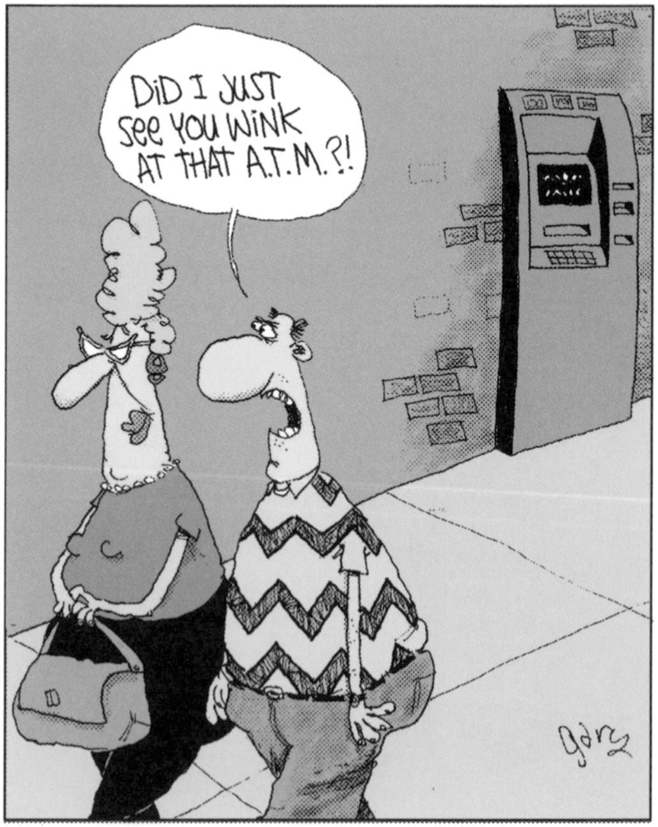
DID I JUST SEE YOU WINK AT THAT A.T.M.?!
Gary

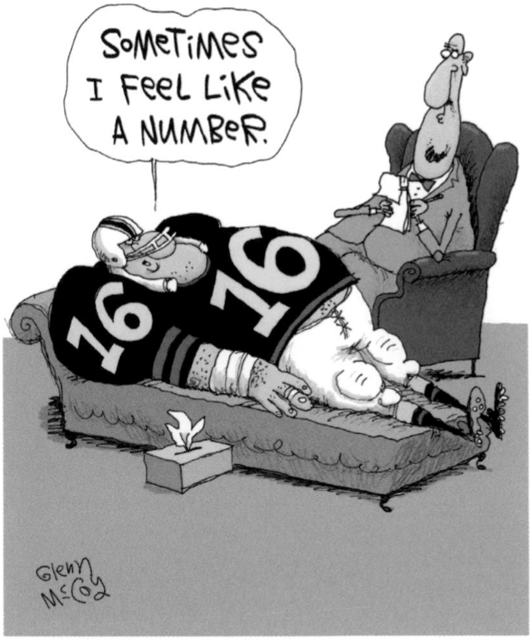
SOMETIMES I FEEL LIKE A NUMBER.
16
16
Glenn McCoy

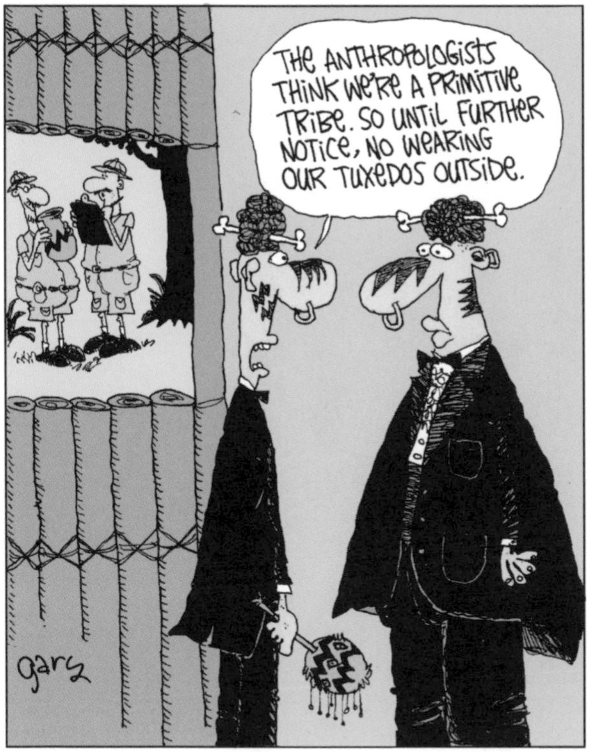
THE ANTHROPOLOGISTS THINK WE'RE A PRIMITIVE TRIBE. SO UNTIL FURTHER NOTICE, NO WEARING OUR TUXEDOS OUTSIDE.
gary

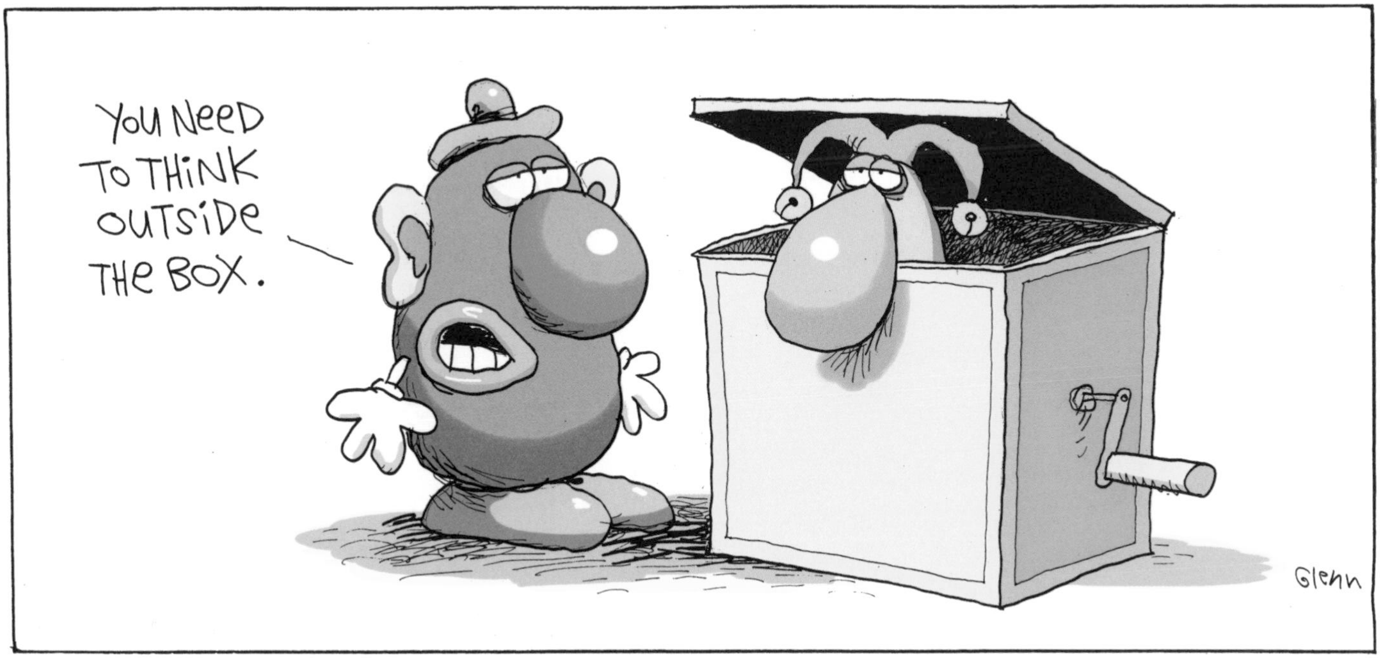
YOU NEED TO THINK OUTSIDE THE BOX.
Glenn

gary

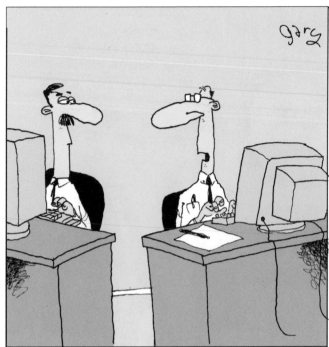

"AFTER THIRTY YEARS AS A RESPECTED AND RESPONSIBLE PRESIDENTIAL SPEECHWRITER, WHY DO I SUDDENLY HAVE THE URGE TO WORK 'FUNKILICIOUS' INTO THE STATE OF THE UNION ADDRESS?"

YOUR DELUSIONS SEEM TO BE GETTING WORSE. I WANT YOU TO START TAKING ONE OF THESE PILLS TWICE A DAY.
glenn

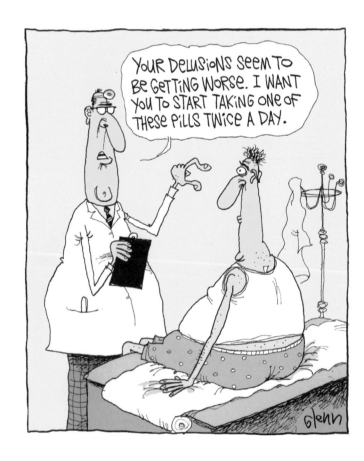

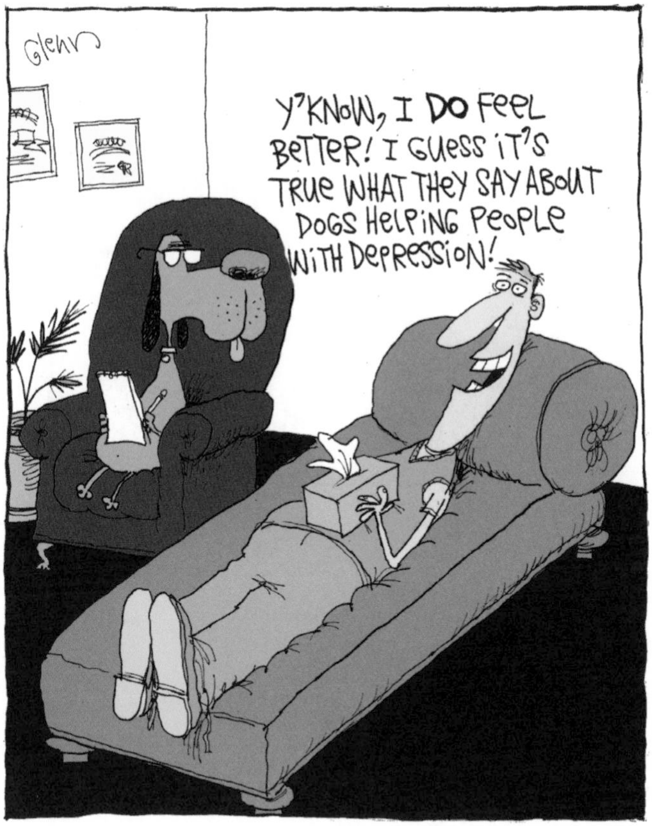
Glenn
Y'KNOW, I DO FEEL BETTER! I GUESS IT'S TRUE WHAT THEY SAY ABOUT DOGS HELPING PEOPLE WITH DEPRESSION!

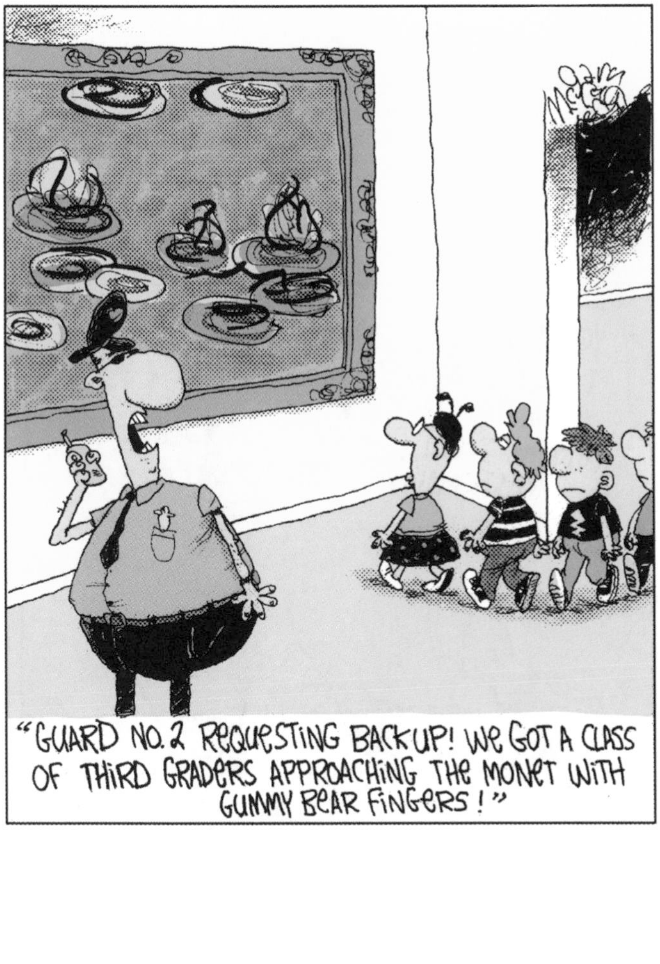
"GUARD NO. 2 REQUESTING BACKUP! WE GOT A CLASS OF THIRD GRADERS APPROACHING THE MONET WITH GUMMY BEAR FINGERS!"

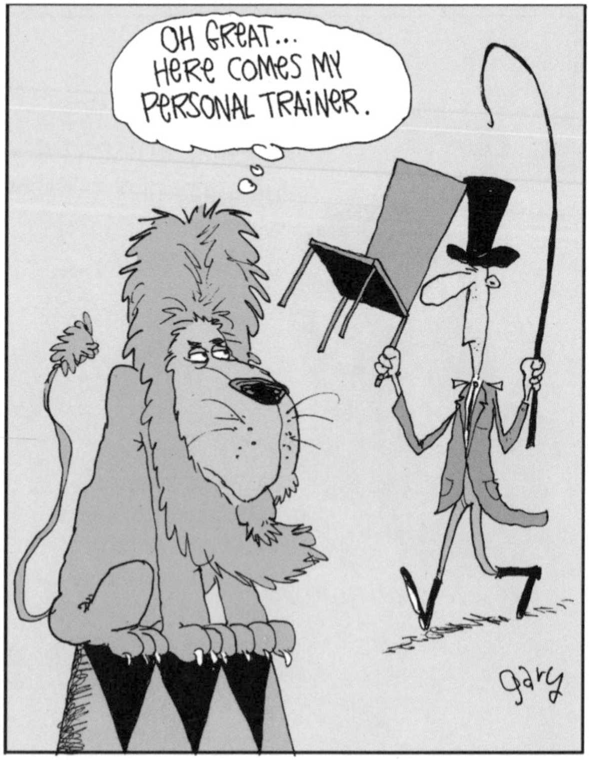
OH GREAT...
HERE COMES MY
PERSONAL TRAINER.

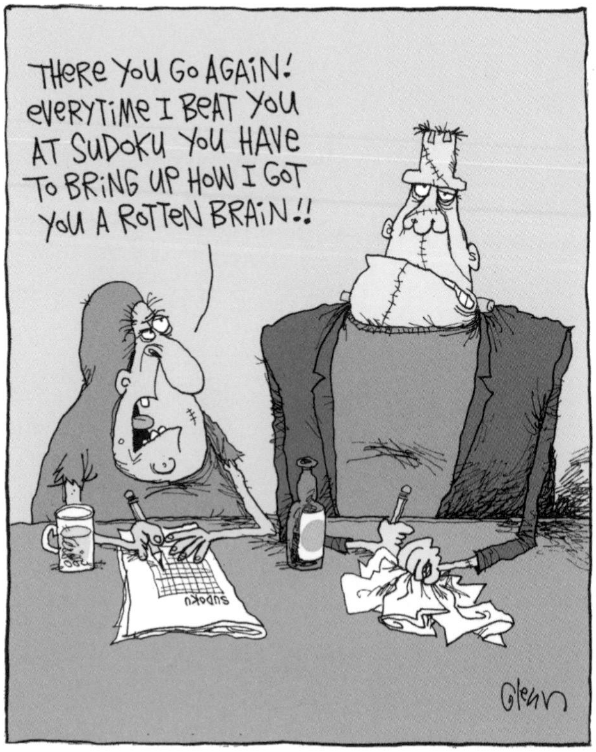
THERE YOU GO AGAIN!
EVERYTIME I BEAT YOU
AT SUDOKU YOU HAVE
TO BRING UP HOW I GOT
YOU A ROTTEN BRAIN!!
SUDOKU

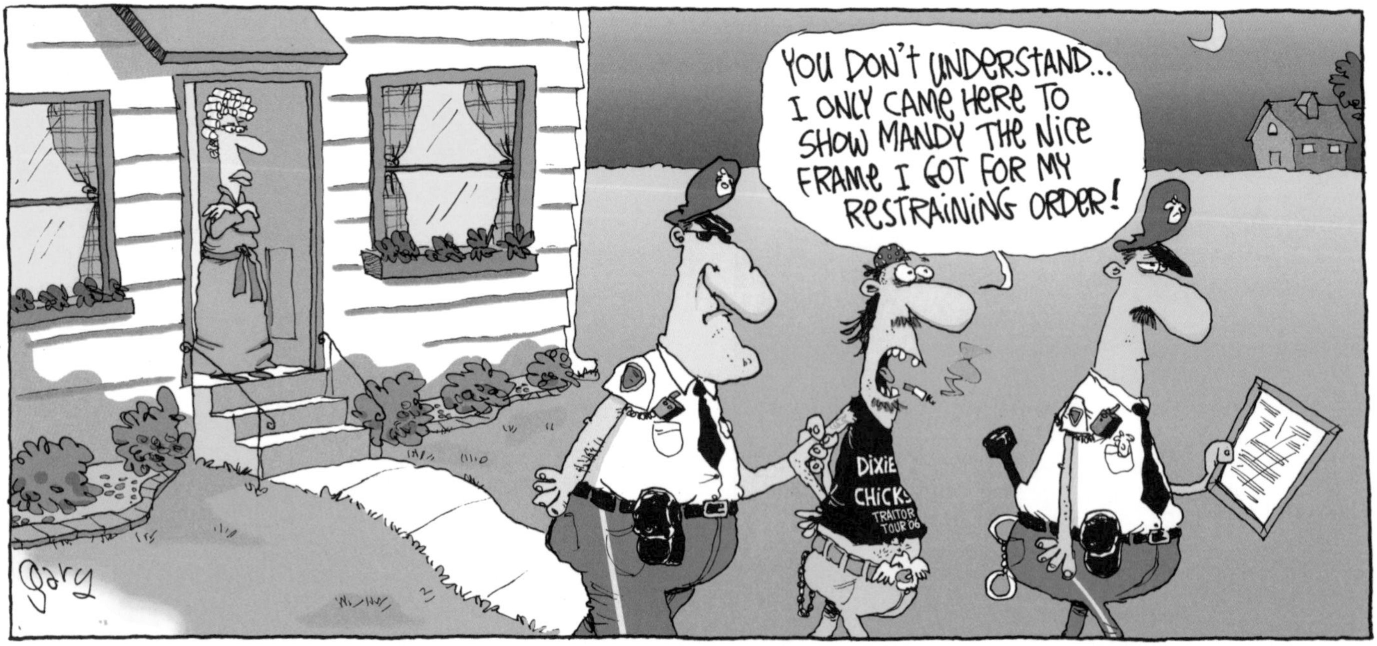
YOU DON'T UNDERSTAND...
I ONLY CAME HERE TO
SHOW MANDY THE NICE
FRAME I GOT FOR MY
RESTRAINING ORDER!
DIXIE
CHICKS
TRAITOR
TOUR 06

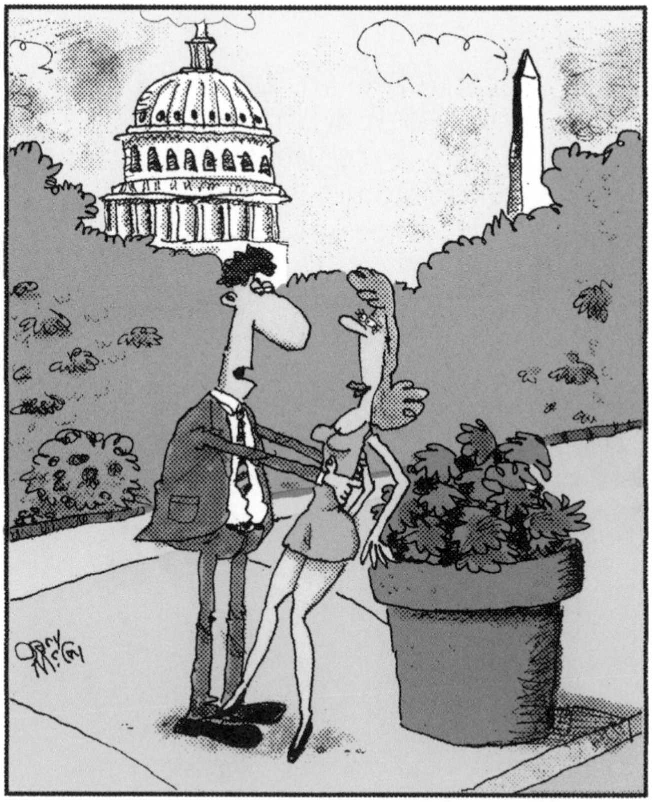

"Francine, I think I love you-with a margin of error of plus or minus five percentage points."

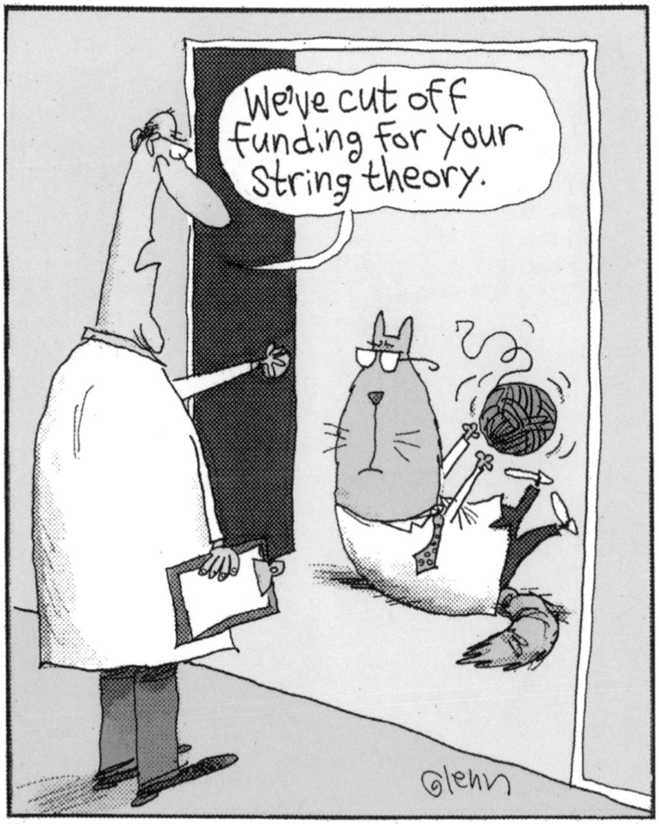

We've cut off funding for your string theory.
Glenn

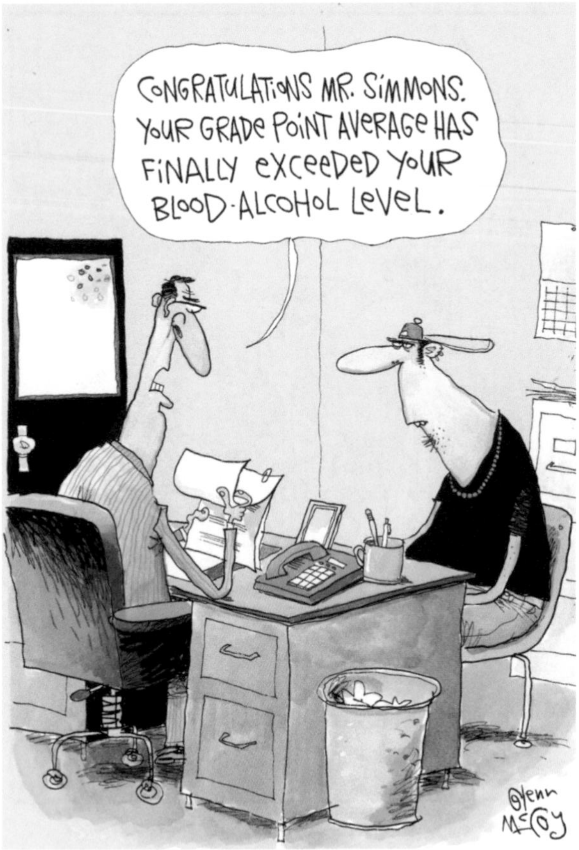
CONGRATULATIONS MR. SIMMONS. YOUR GRADE POINT AVERAGE HAS FINALLY EXCEEDED YOUR BLOOD-ALCOHOL LEVEL.
Glenn McCoy

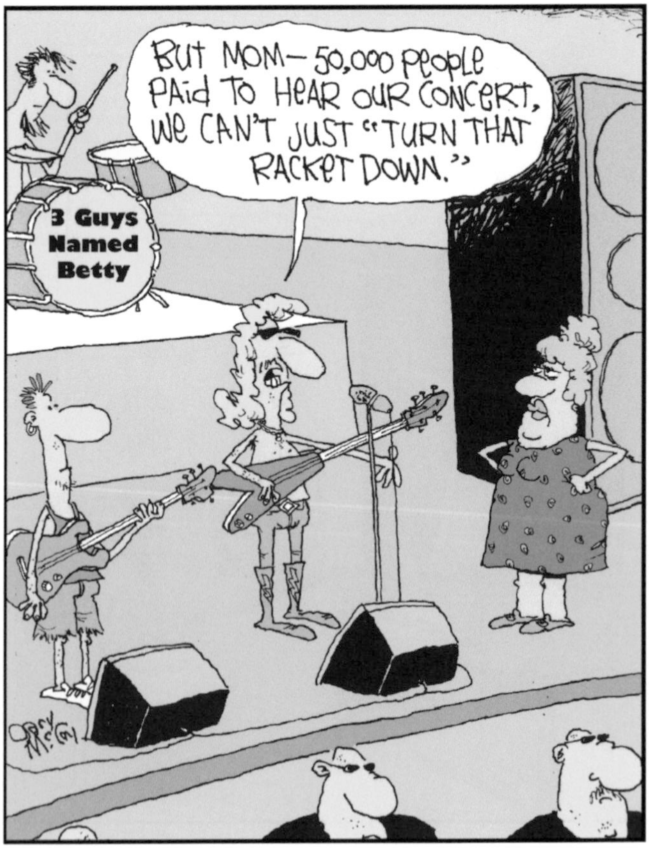
BUT MOM—50,000 PEOPLE PAID TO HEAR OUR CONCERT, WE CAN'T JUST "TURN THAT RACKET DOWN."
3 Guys Named Betty
Gary McCoy

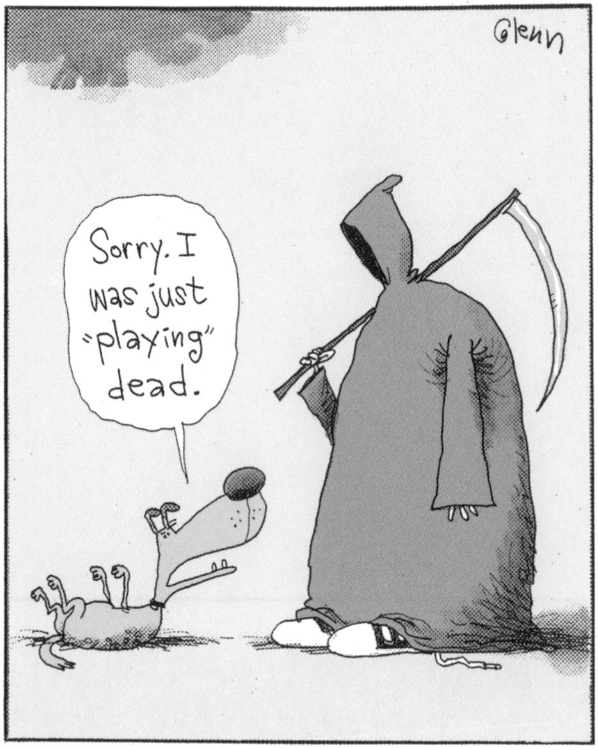
Glenn
Sorry. I was just "playing" dead.

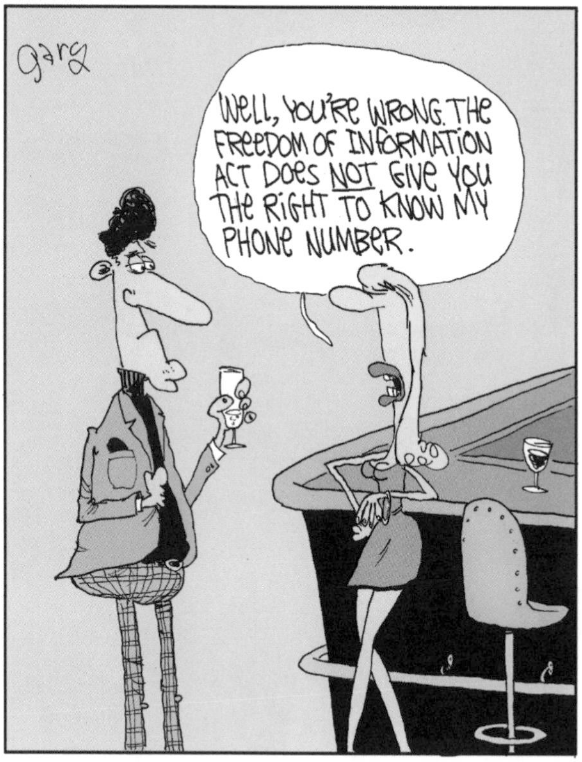
gary
WELL, YOU'RE WRONG. THE FREEDOM OF INFORMATION ACT DOES NOT GIVE YOU THE RIGHT TO KNOW MY PHONE NUMBER.

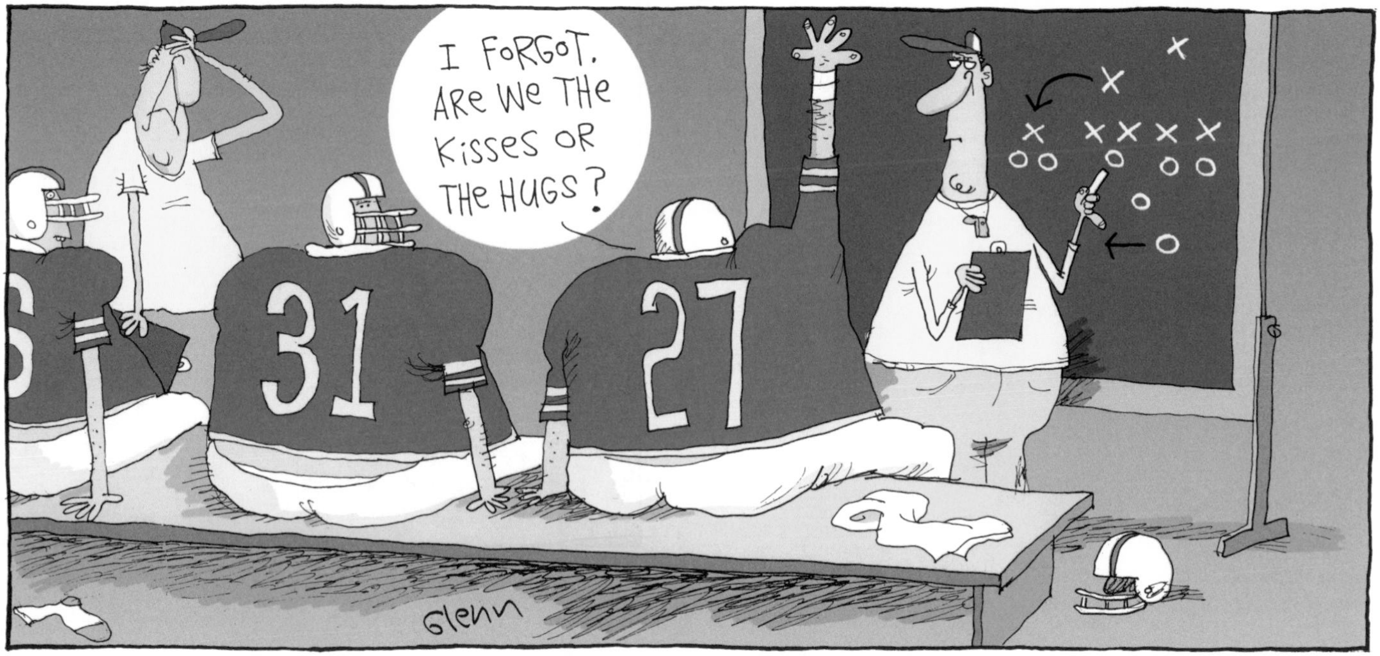
I FORGOT. ARE WE THE KISSES OR THE HUGS?
31
27
Glenn

I DON'T GET IT... WE CAN PUT A MAN ON THE MOON. BUT WE CAN'T GET HIM TO MOONWALK.
Gary

CUTTING CORNERS AT THE CHURCH CARNIVAL
BAPTISMAL DUNKING BOOTH
Glenn McCoy

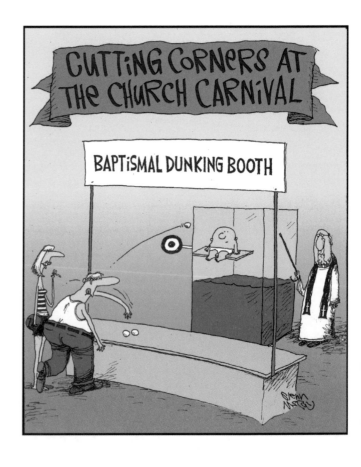

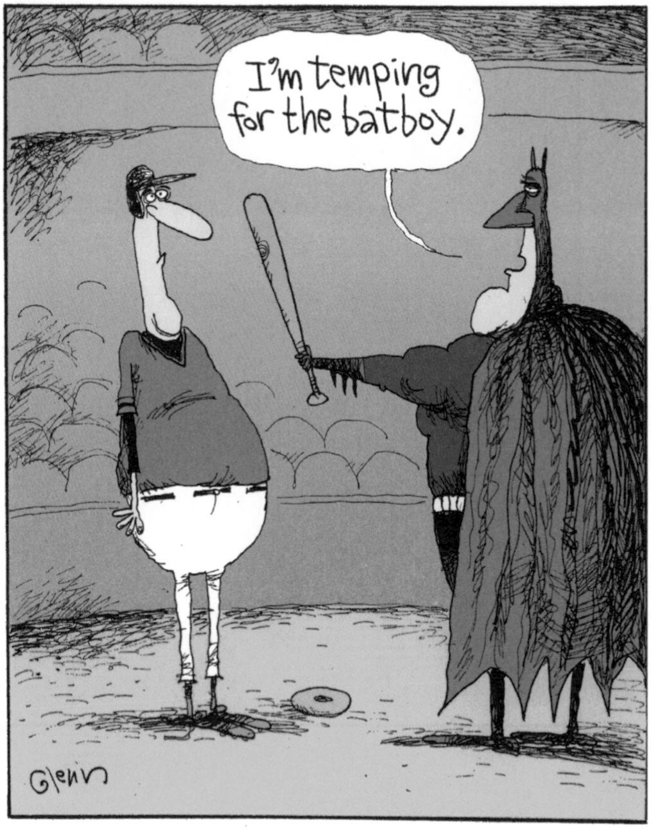
I'm temping for the batboy.
Glenn

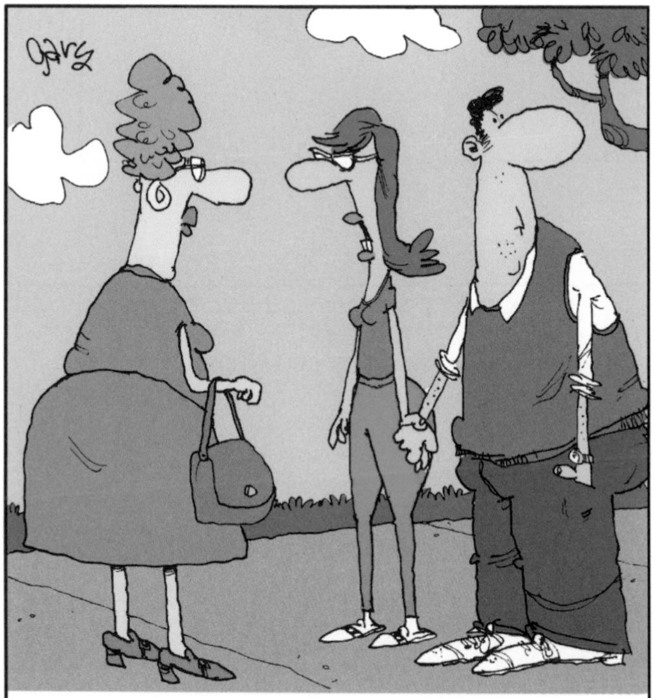
Gary

"I'm a Jay Leno fan, but Jerry prefers David Letterman. We still haven't decided how we're going to raise our kids."

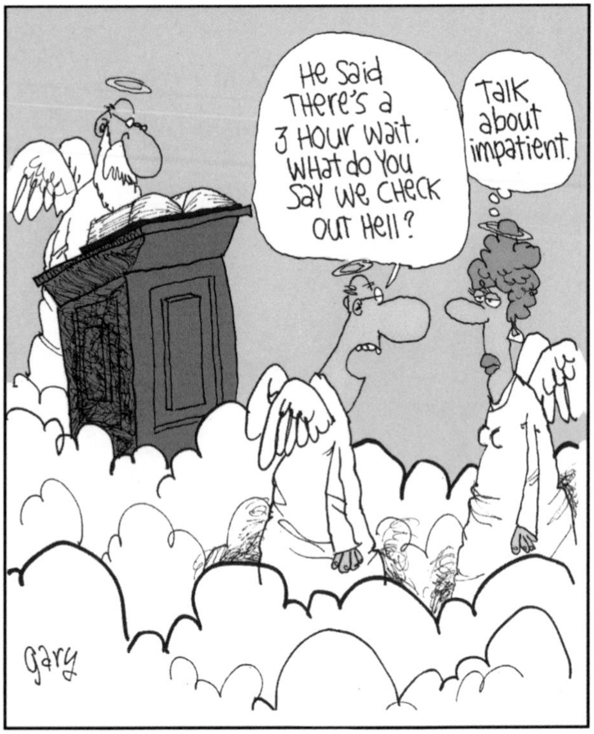
He said There's a 3 Hour wait. What do You Say we Check out Hell?
Talk about impatient.
gary

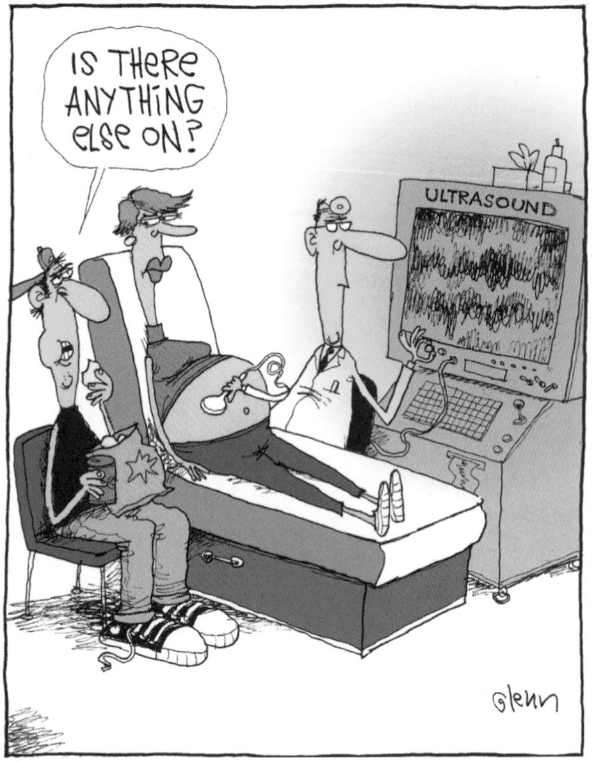
IS THERE ANYTHING ELSE ON?
ULTRASOUND
glenn

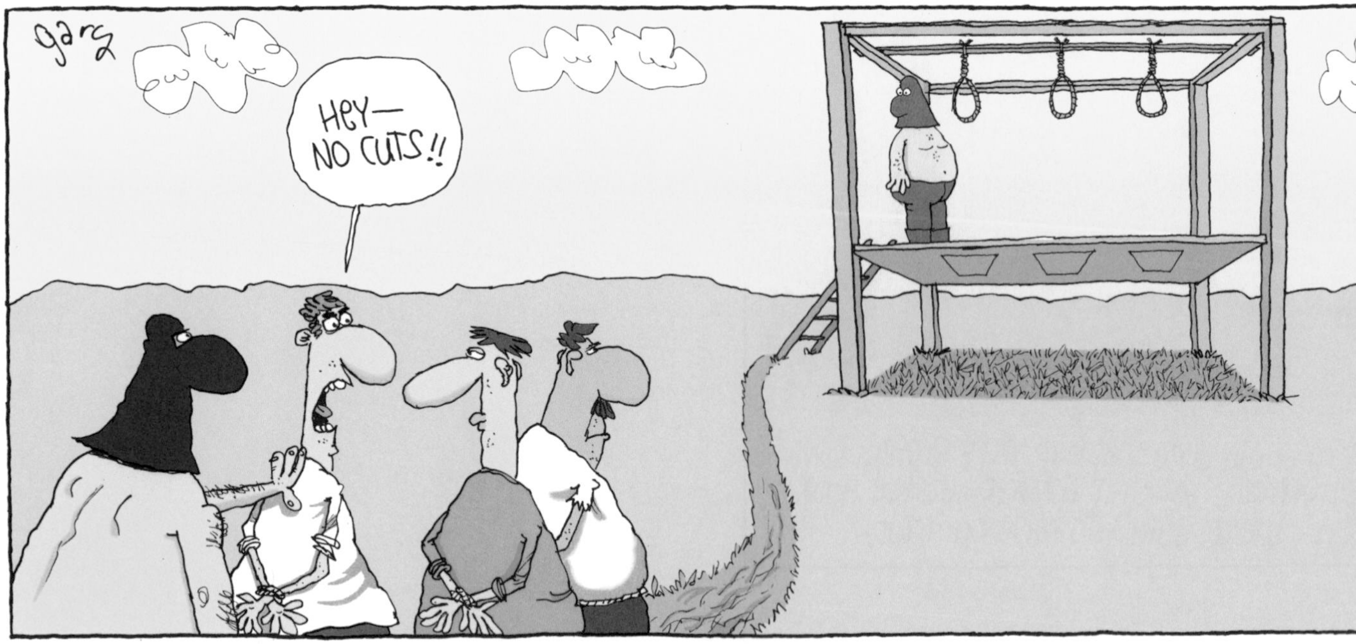
gary
HEY— NO CUTS!!

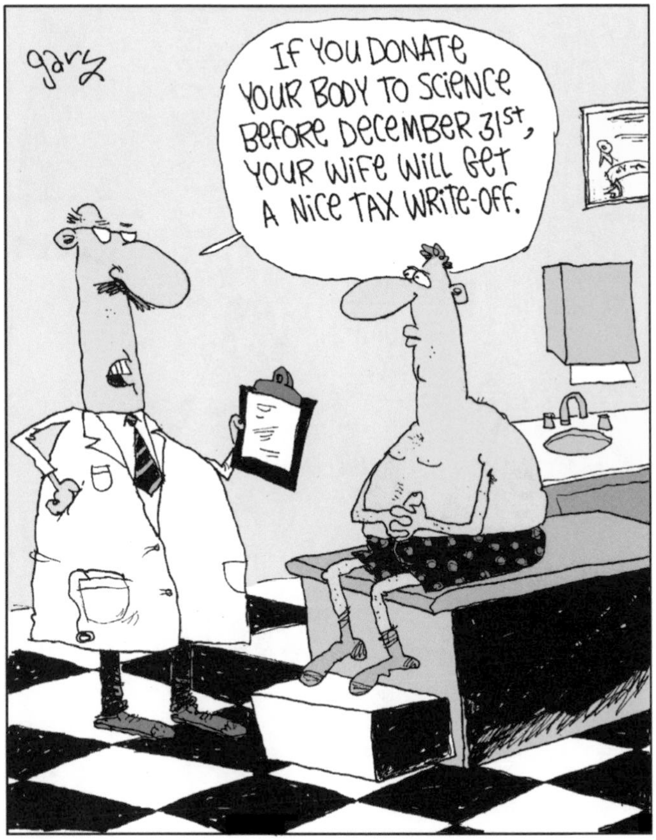
gary
IF YOU DONATE YOUR BODY TO SCIENCE BEFORE DECEMBER 31st, YOUR WIFE WILL GET A NICE TAX WRITE-OFF.

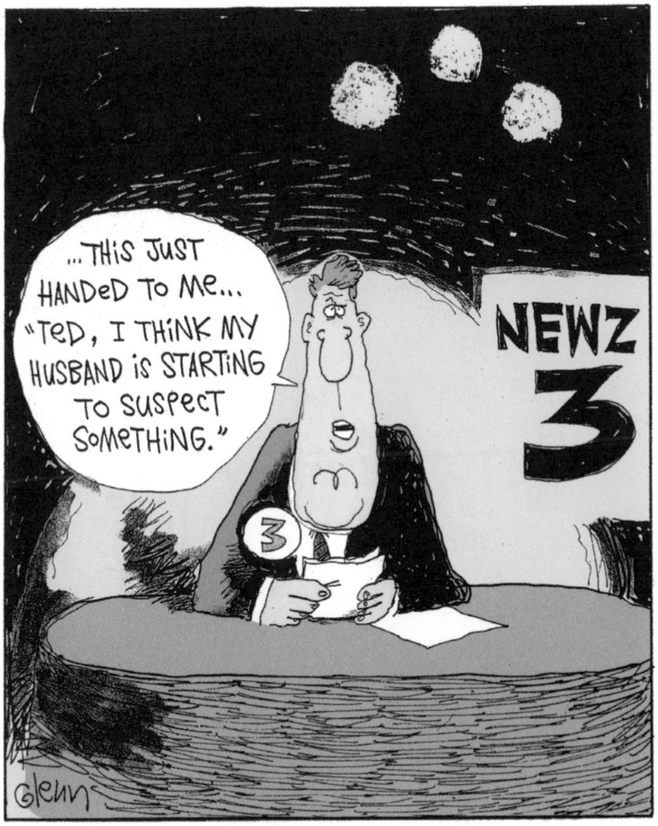
...THIS JUST HANDED TO ME... "TED, I THINK MY HUSBAND IS STARTING TO SUSPECT SOMETHING."
NEWZ
3
3
glenn

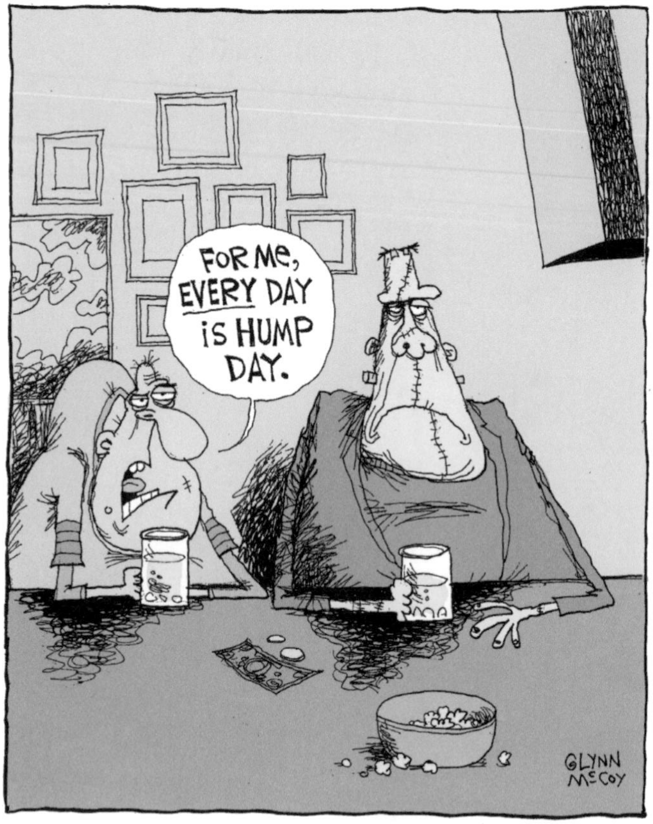
FOR ME, EVERY DAY is HUMP DAY.
GLYNN McCOY

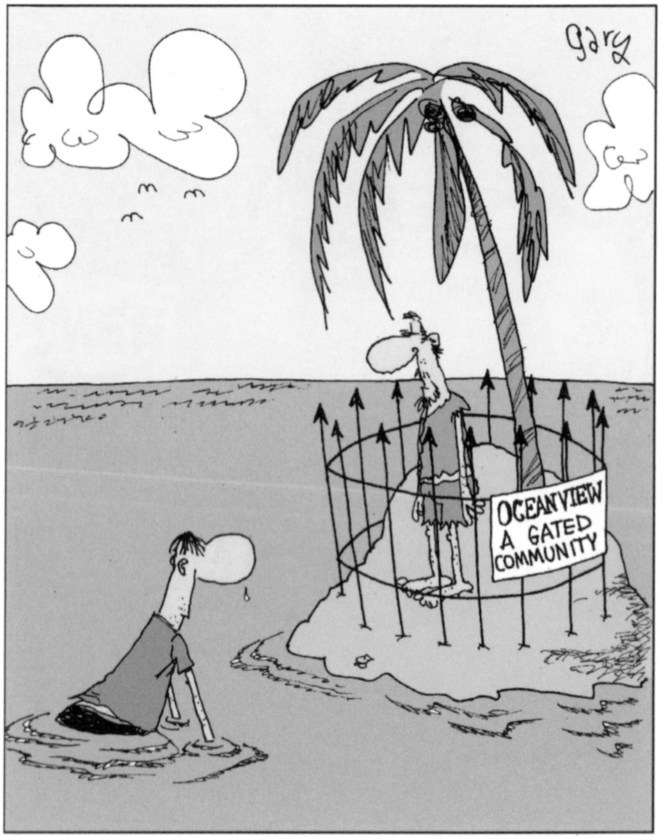
gary
OCEANVIEW
A GATED COMMUNITY

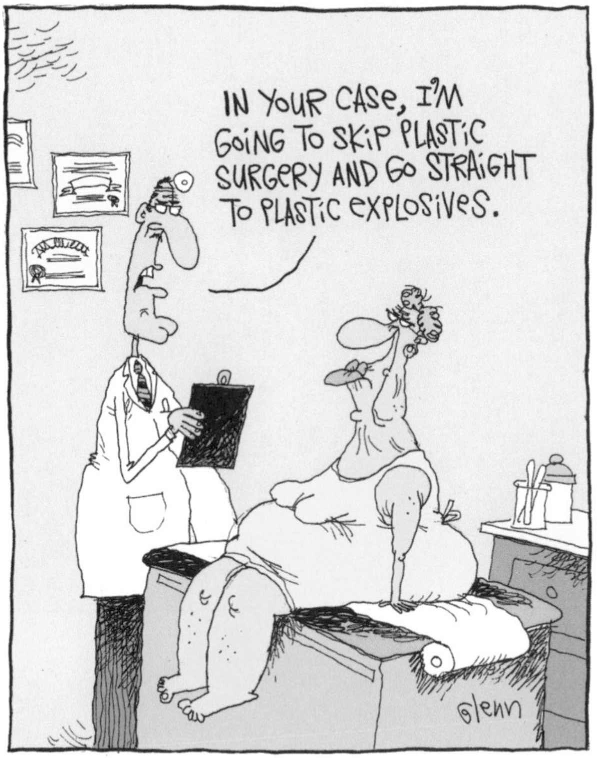
IN YOUR CASE, I'M GOING TO SKIP PLASTIC SURGERY AND GO STRAIGHT TO PLASTIC EXPLOSIVES.
glenn

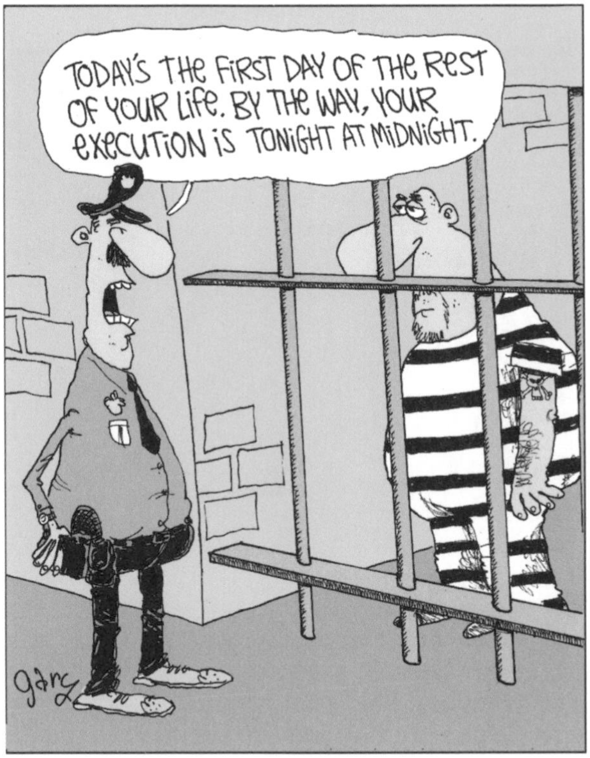
TODAY'S THE FIRST DAY OF THE REST OF YOUR LIFE. BY THE WAY, YOUR EXECUTION IS TONIGHT AT MIDNIGHT.
gary

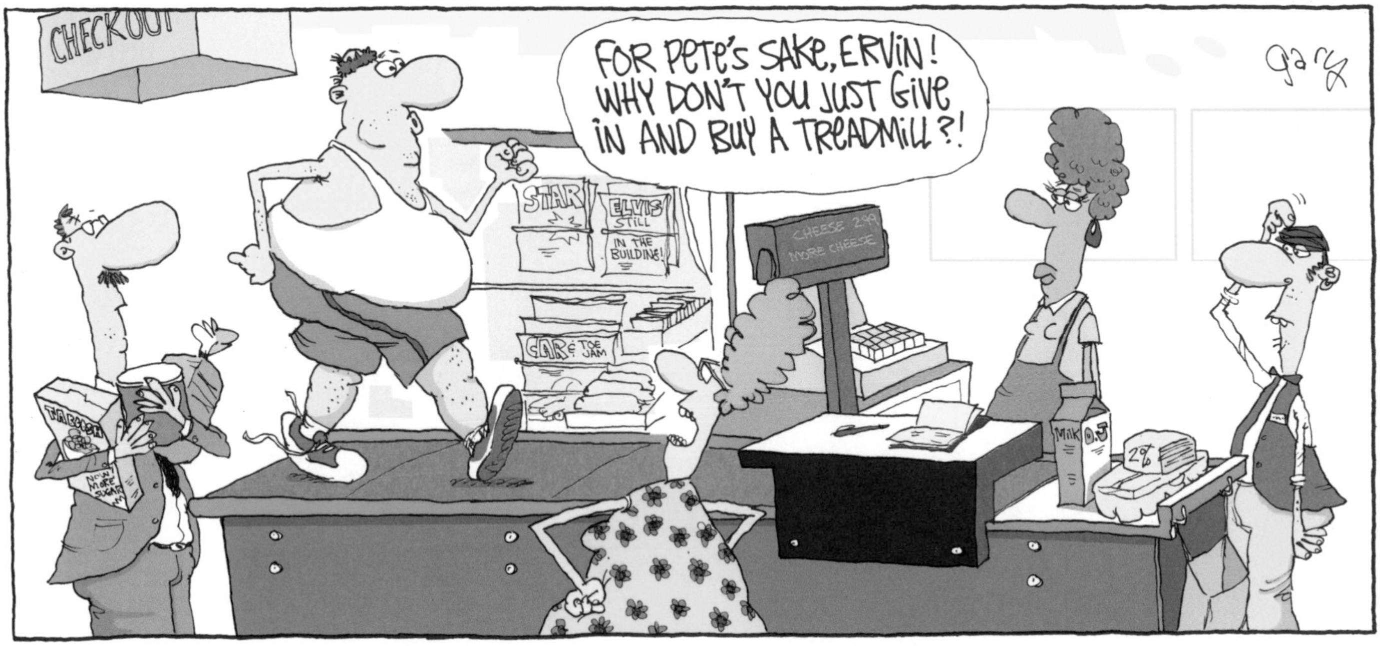
CHECKOUT
FOR PETE'S SAKE, ERVIN! WHY DON'T YOU JUST GIVE IN AND BUY A TREADMILL?!
gary
STAR
ELVIS STILL IN THE BUILDING!
CAR & TOE JAM
MILK
O.J
2%

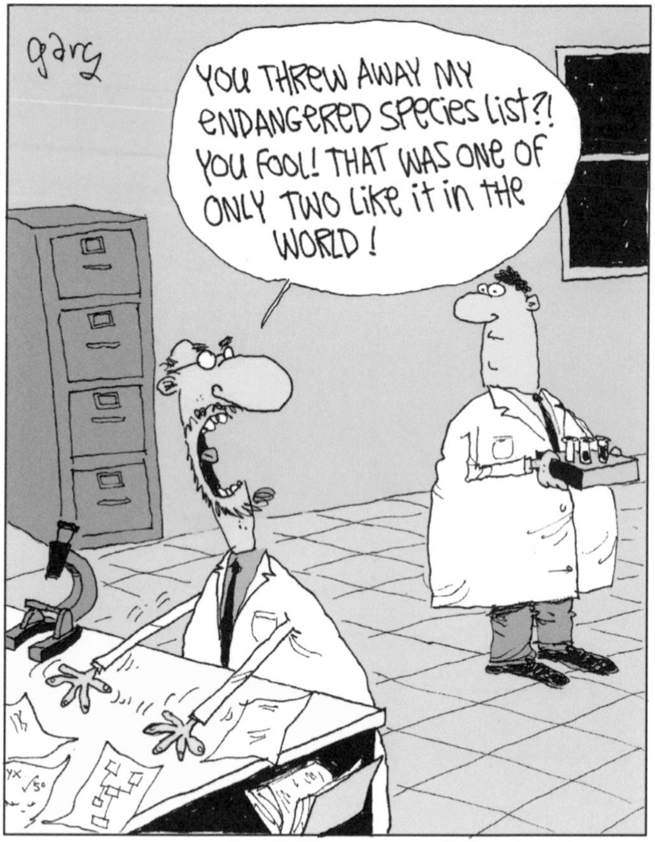
gary
YOU THREW AWAY MY ENDANGERED SPECIES LIST?! YOU FOOL! THAT WAS ONE OF ONLY TWO LIKE IT IN THE WORLD!

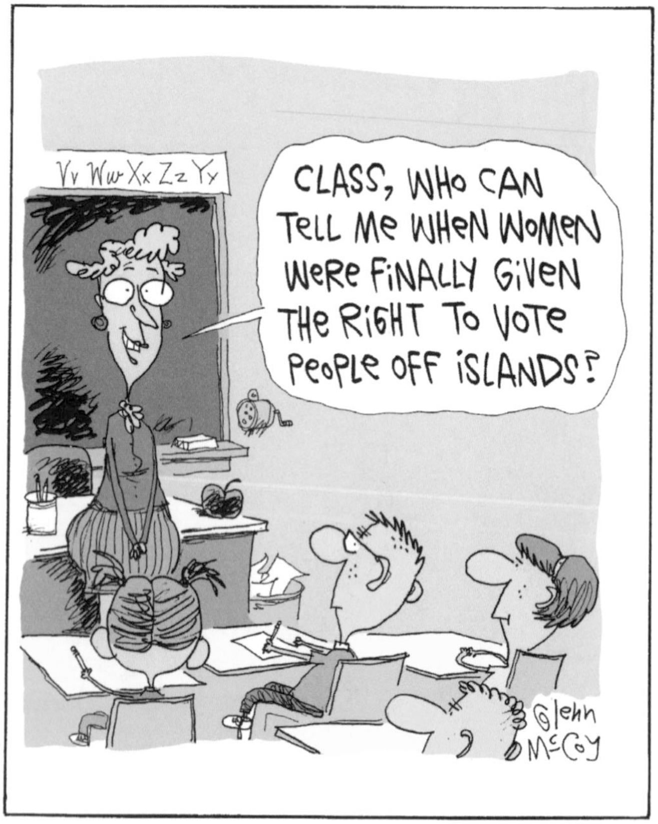
Vv Ww Xx Zz Yy
CLASS, WHO CAN TELL ME WHEN WOMEN WERE FINALLY GIVEN THE RIGHT TO VOTE PEOPLE OFF ISLANDS?
Glenn McCoy

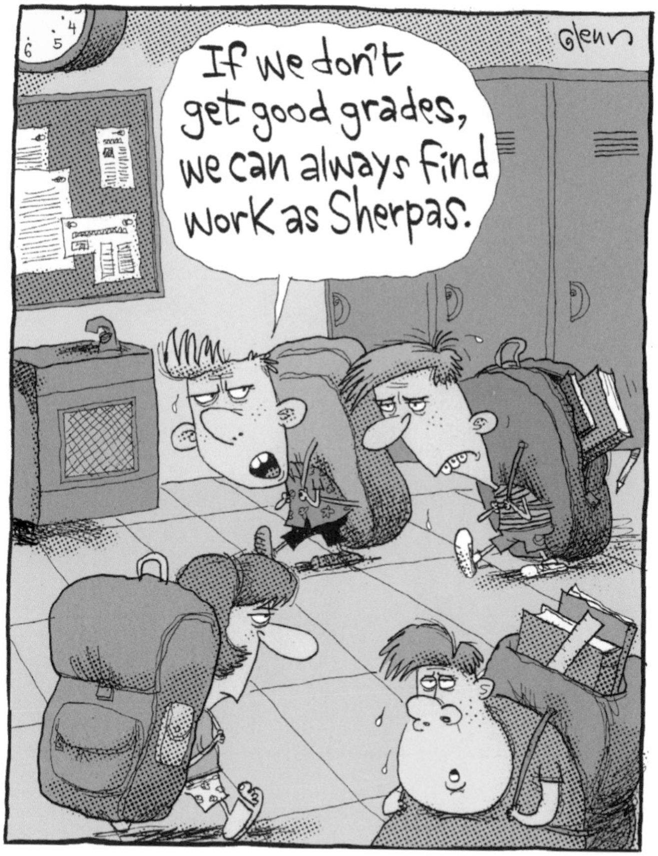
glenn
If we don't get good grades, we can always find work as Sherpas.

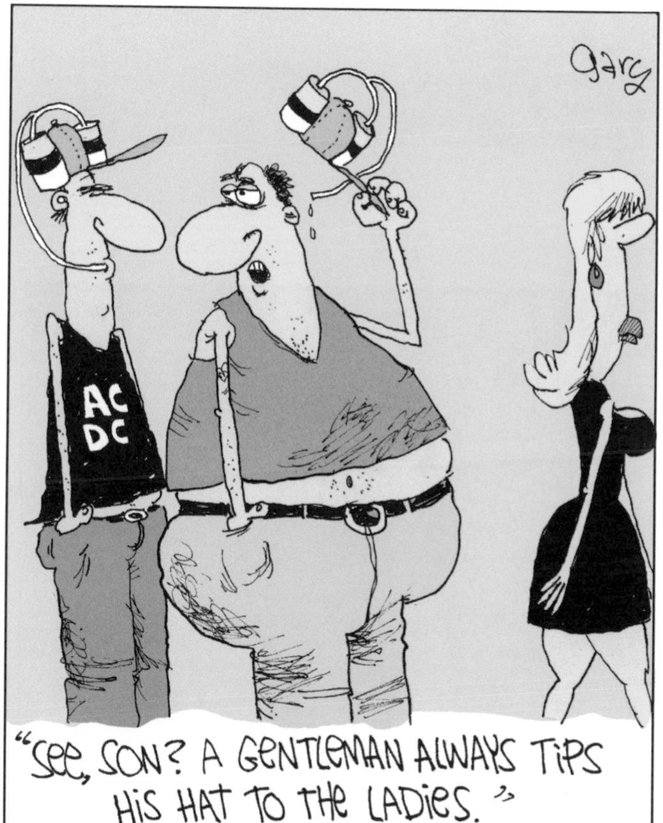
gary
AC
DC

"SEE, SON? A GENTLEMAN ALWAYS TIPS HIS HAT TO THE LADIES."

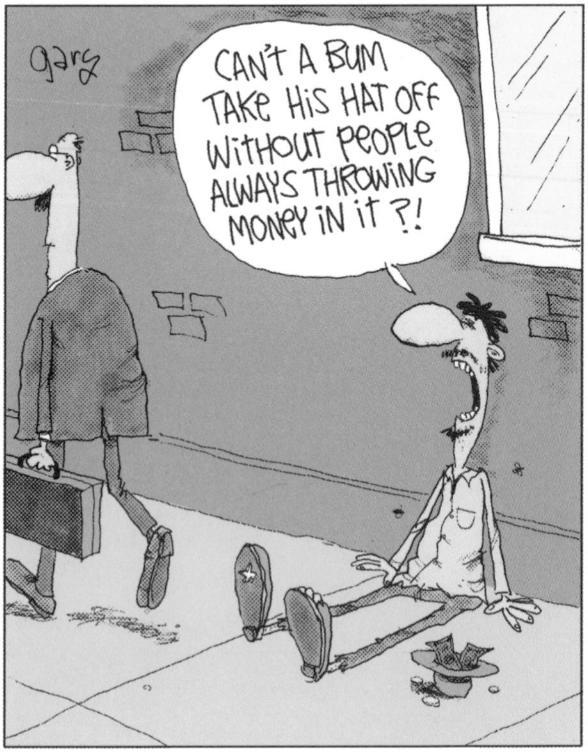
gary
CAN'T A BUM TAKE HIS HAT OFF WITHOUT PEOPLE ALWAYS THROWING MONEY IN IT ?!

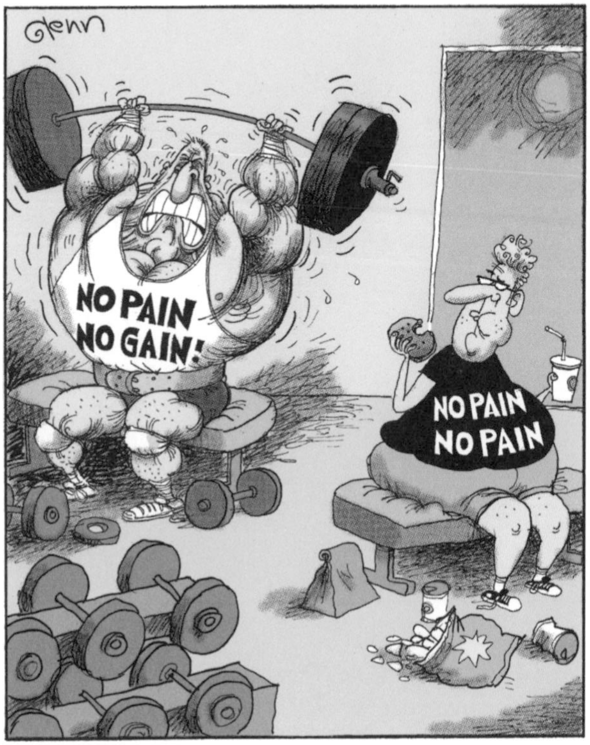
Glenn
NO PAIN NO GAIN!
NO PAIN NO PAIN

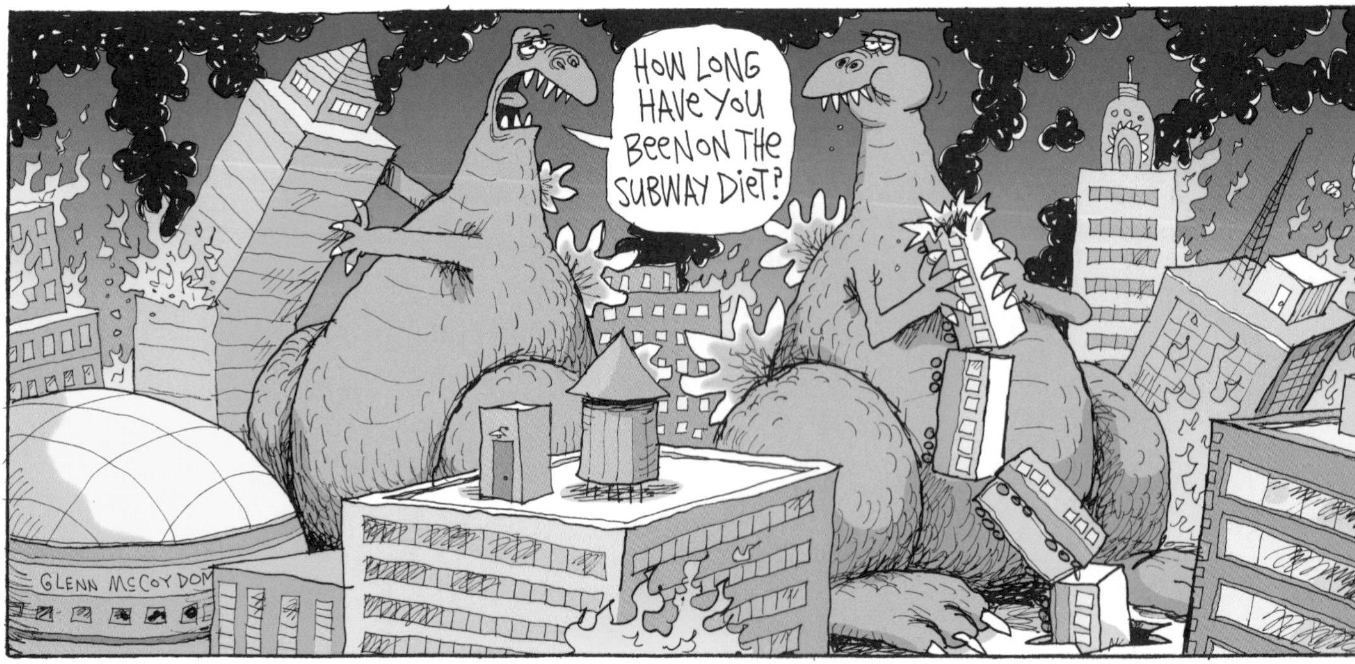
HOW LONG HAVE YOU BEEN ON THE SUBWAY DIET?
GLENN McCOY DOM

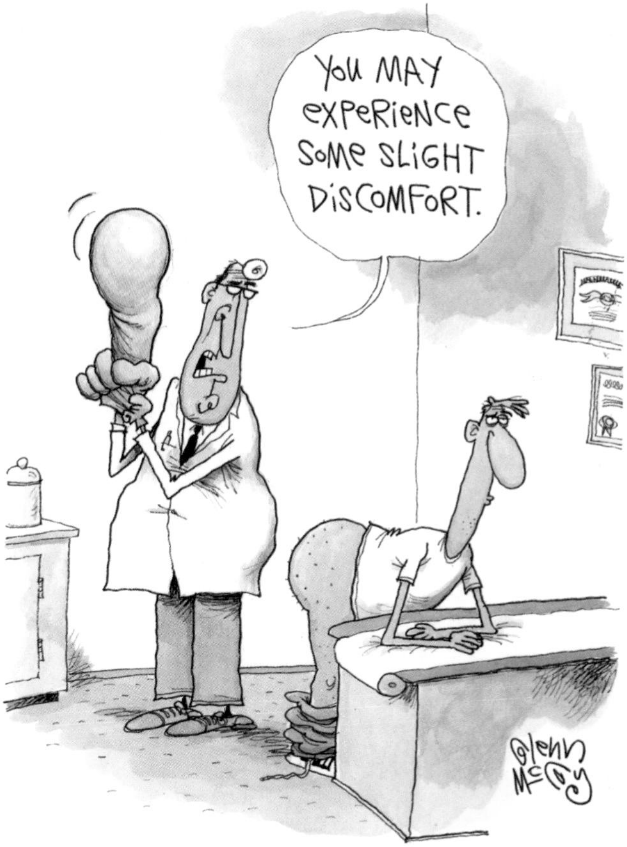
YOU MAY EXPERIENCE SOME SLIGHT DISCOMFORT.
Glenn McCoy

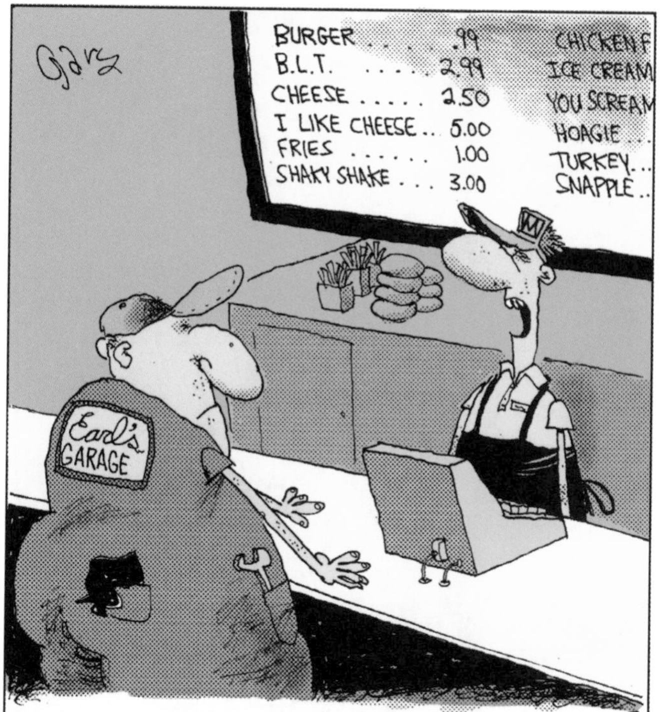
Gary
BURGER 99
B.L.T. 2.99
CHEESE 2.50
I LIKE CHEESE . . 5.00
FRIES 1.00
SHAKY SHAKE . . . 3.00
CHICKEN F
ICE CREAM
YOU SCREAM
HOAGIE . .
TURKEY. . .
SNAPPLE . .
Earl's GARAGE

"A B.L.T.? SINCE I DON'T HAVE THE BACON IN STOCK, I'D HAVE TO ORDER SOME. AND IT PROBABLY WON'T COME IN UNTIL NEXT TUESDAY AT THE EARLIEST."

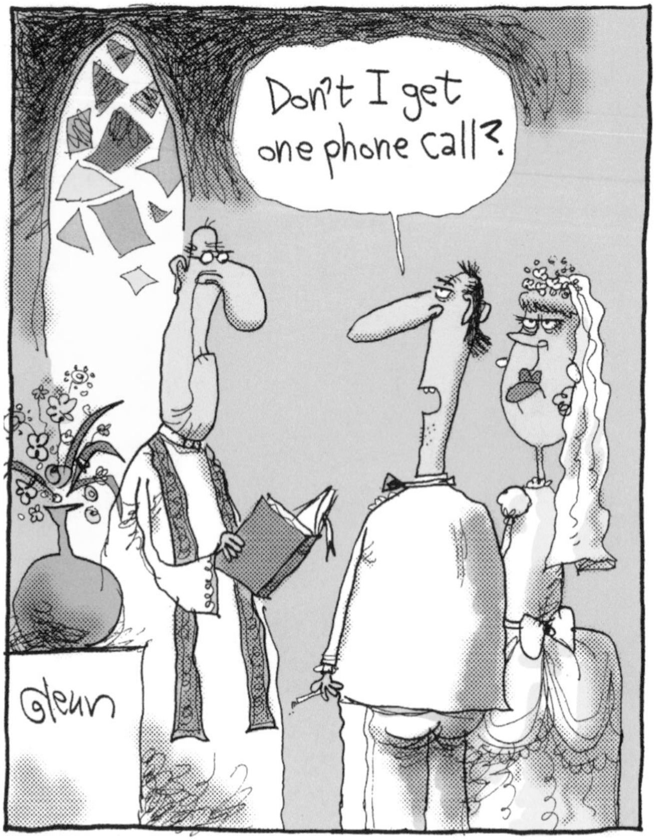
Don't I get one phone call?
Glenn

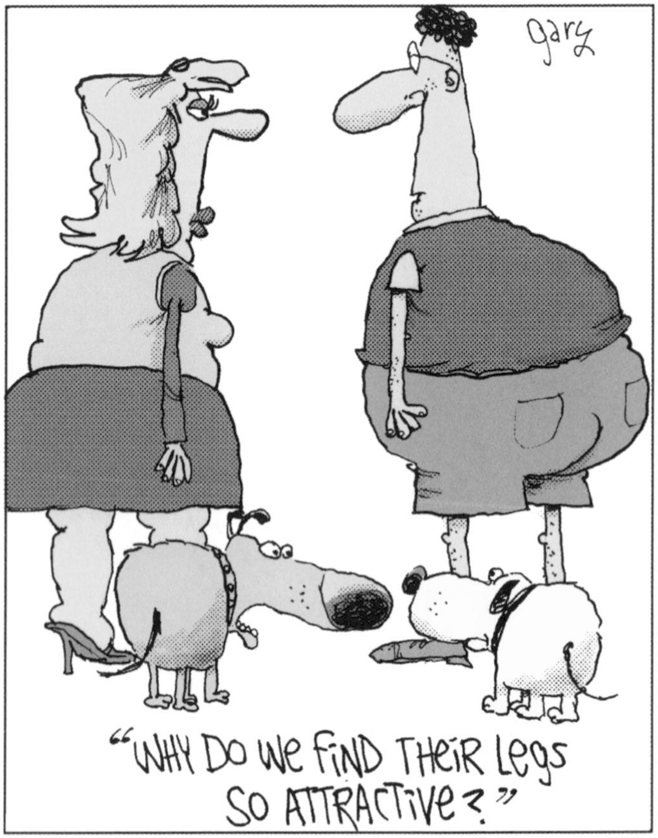
gary
"WHY DO WE FIND THEIR LEGS SO ATTRACTIVE?"

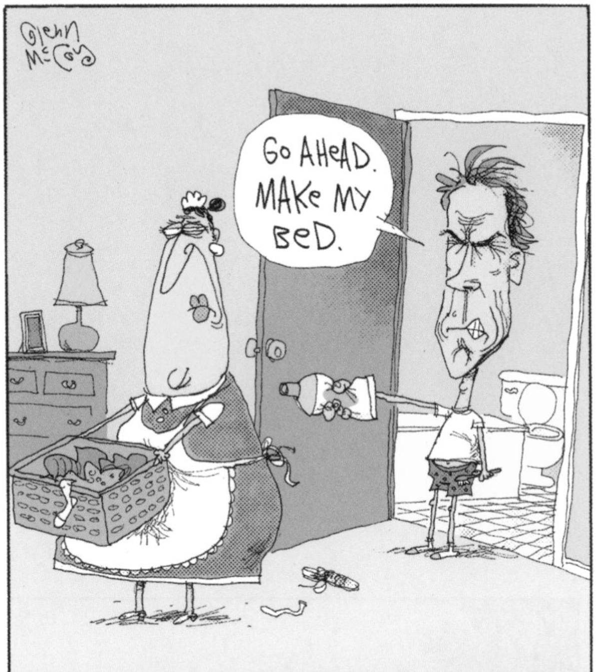
Glenn McCoy
GO AHEAD. MAKE MY BED.

CLINT EASTWOOD GETTING TOUGH WITH THE MAID.

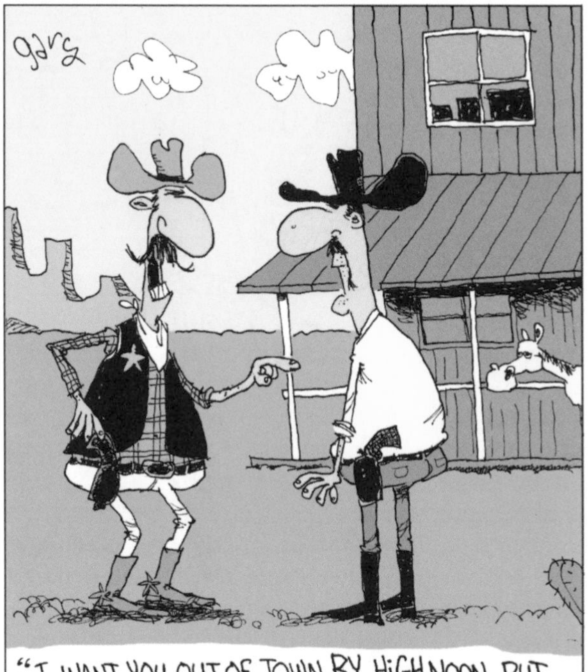
gary

"I WANT YOU OUT OF TOWN BY HIGH NOON. BUT SINCE YOU WANT TO HIT THE HOTEL GIFT SHOP AFTER CHECK-OUT, I'LL COMPROMISE AND MAKE IT 12:45."

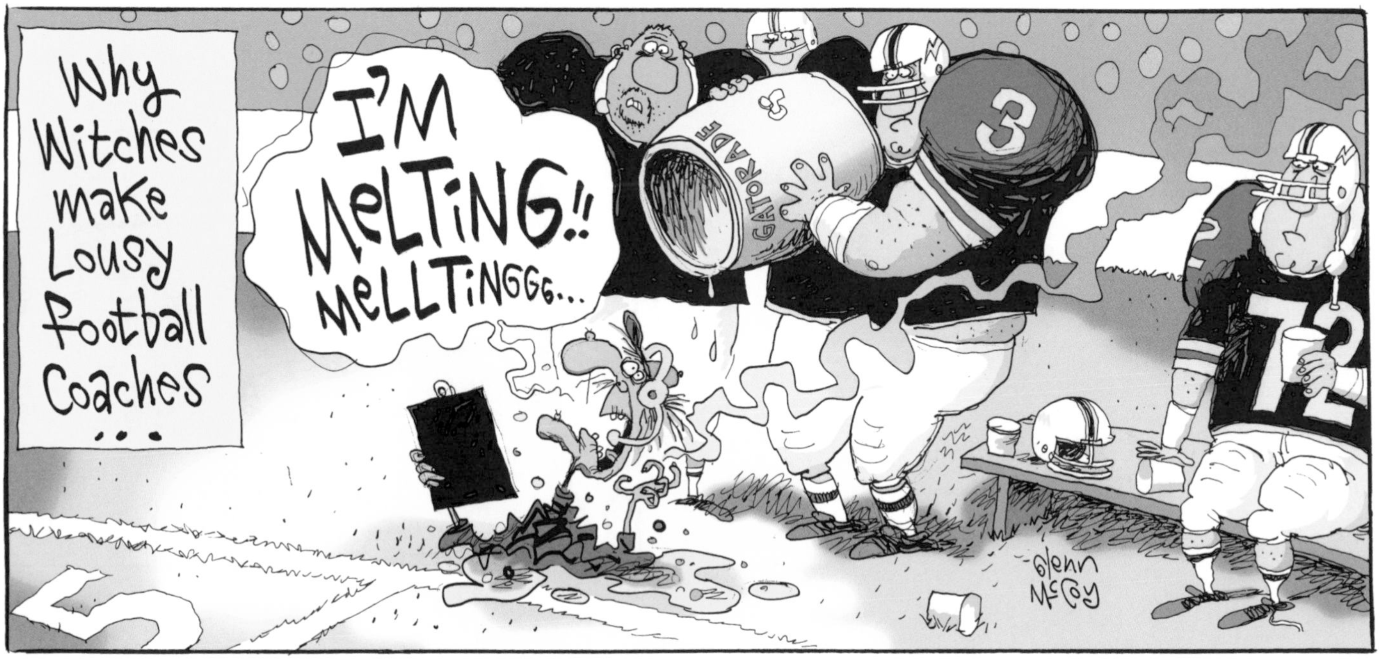
Why Witches make Lousy Football Coaches ...
I'M MELTING!! MELLTINGGG...
GATORADE
3
72
Glenn McCoy

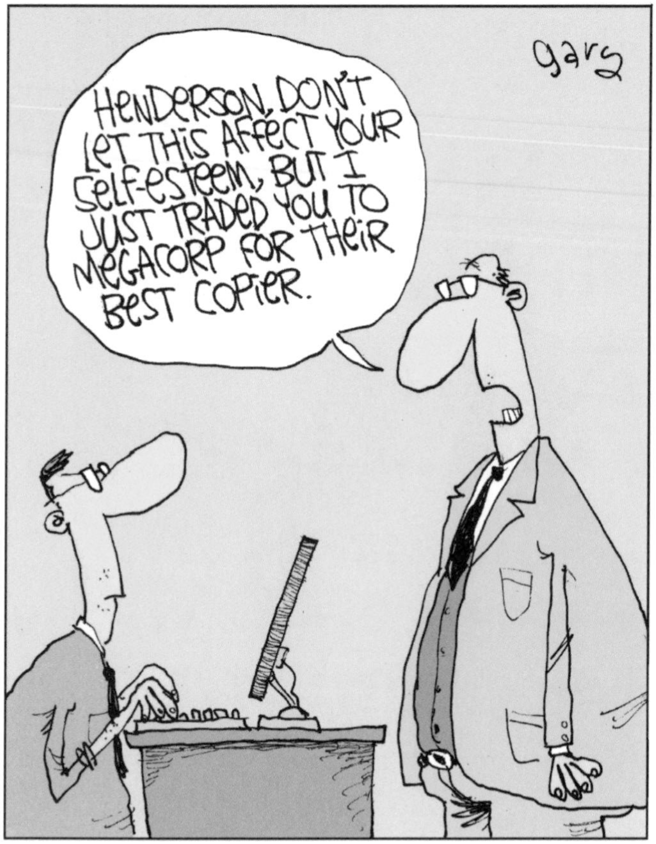
gary
HENDERSON, DON'T LET THIS AFFECT YOUR SELF-ESTEEM, BUT I JUST TRADED YOU TO MEGACORP FOR THEIR BEST COPIER.

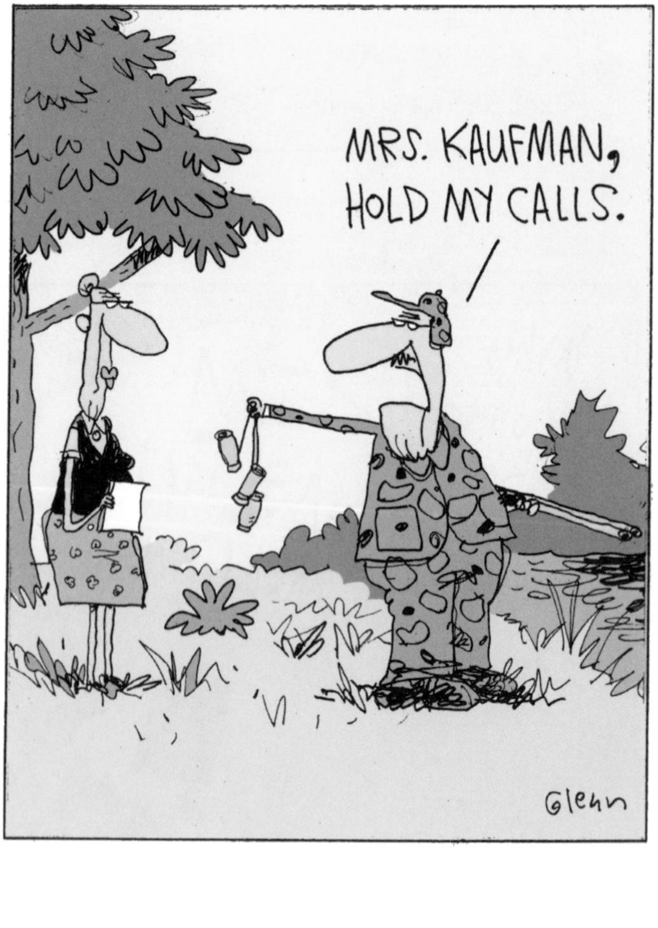
MRS. KAUFMAN, HOLD MY CALLS.
Glenn

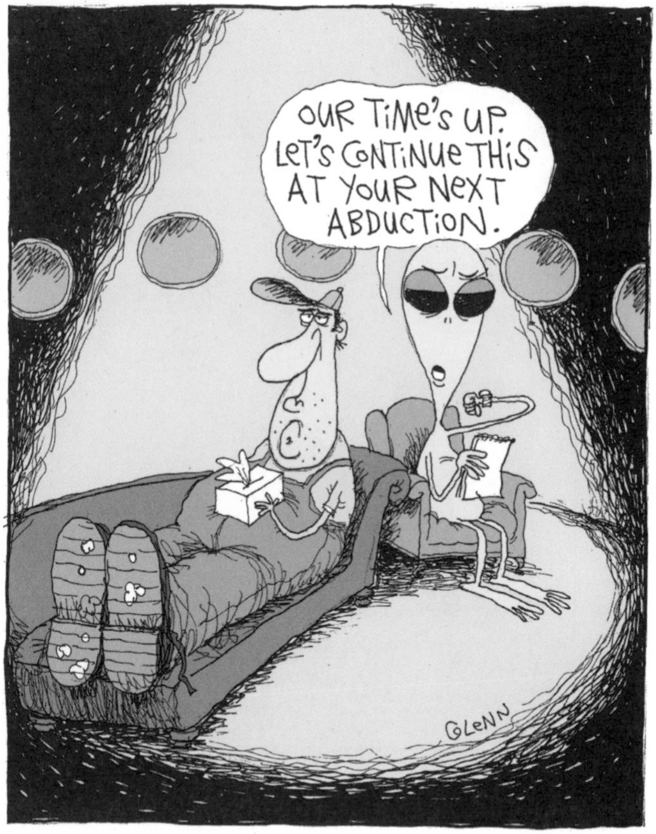
OUR TIME'S UP. LET'S CONTINUE THIS AT YOUR NEXT ABDUCTION.
GLENN

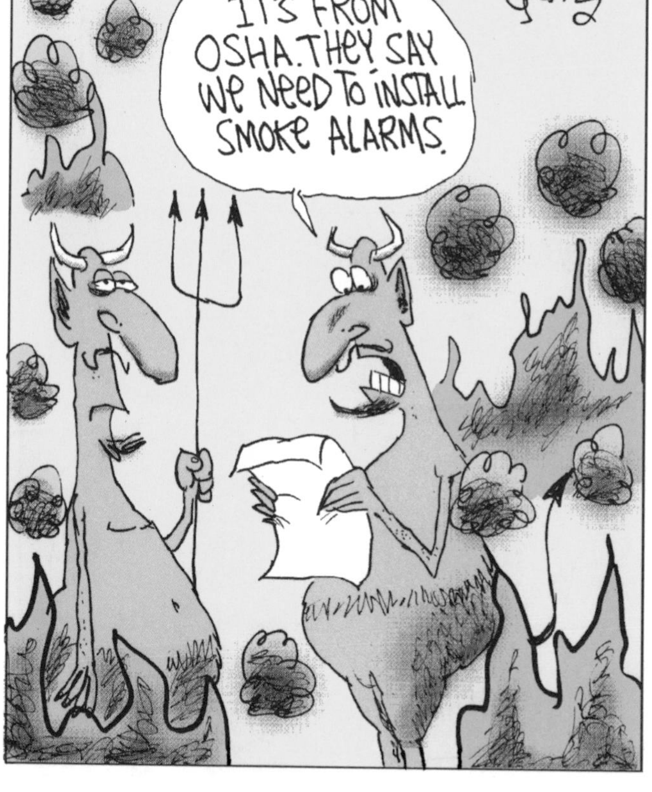
IT'S FROM OSHA. THEY SAY WE NEED TO INSTALL SMOKE ALARMS.
gary

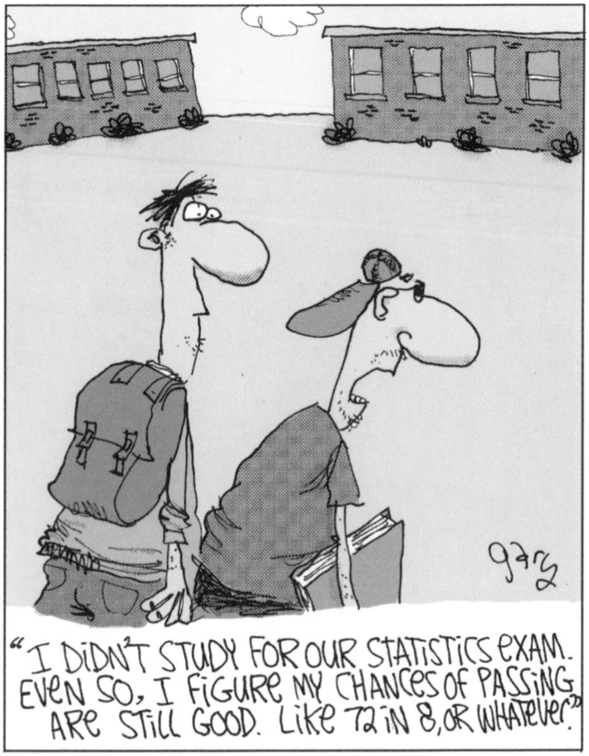
gary
"I DIDN'T STUDY FOR OUR STATISTICS EXAM. EVEN SO, I FIGURE MY CHANCES OF PASSING ARE STILL GOOD. LIKE 72 IN 8, OR WHATEVER."

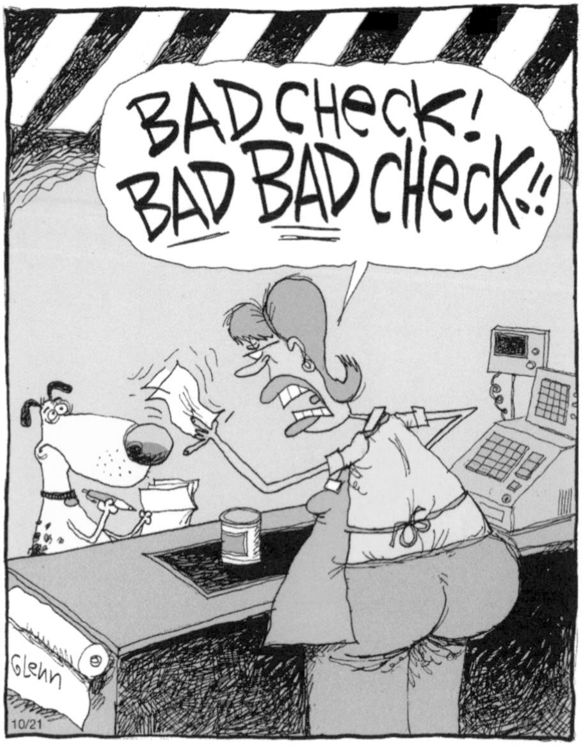
BAD CHECK! BAD BAD CHECK!!
Glenn
10/21

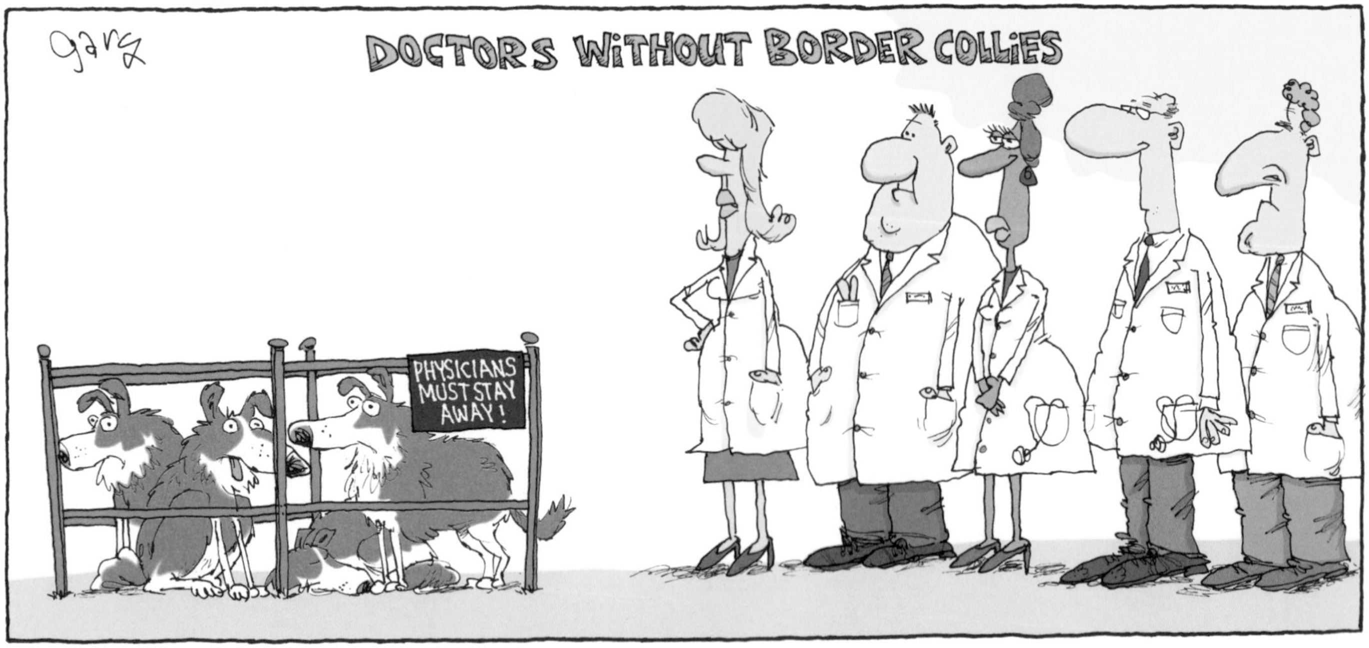
gary
DOCTORS WITHOUT BORDER COLLIES
PHYSICIANS MUST STAY AWAY!

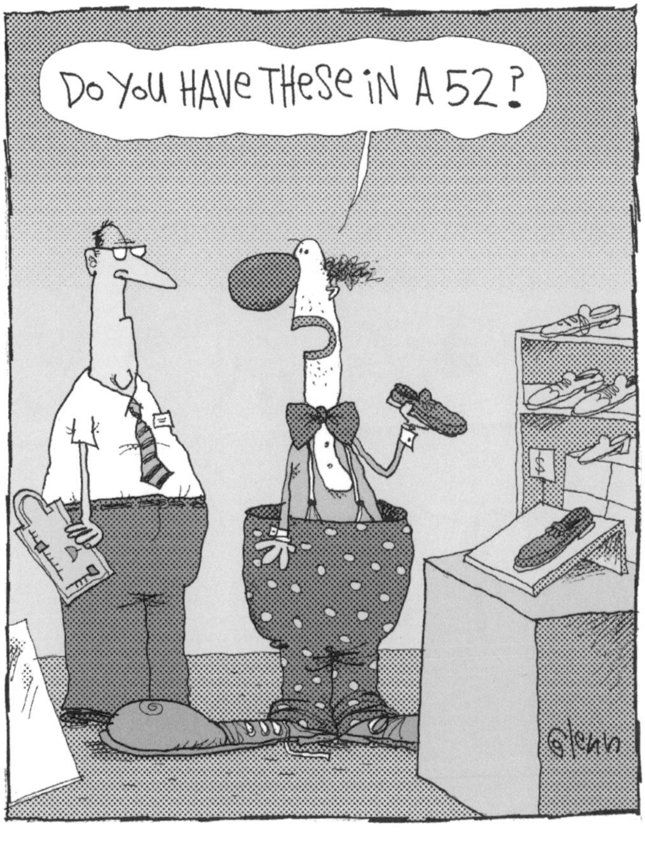
DO YOU HAVE THESE IN A 52?
$
Glenn

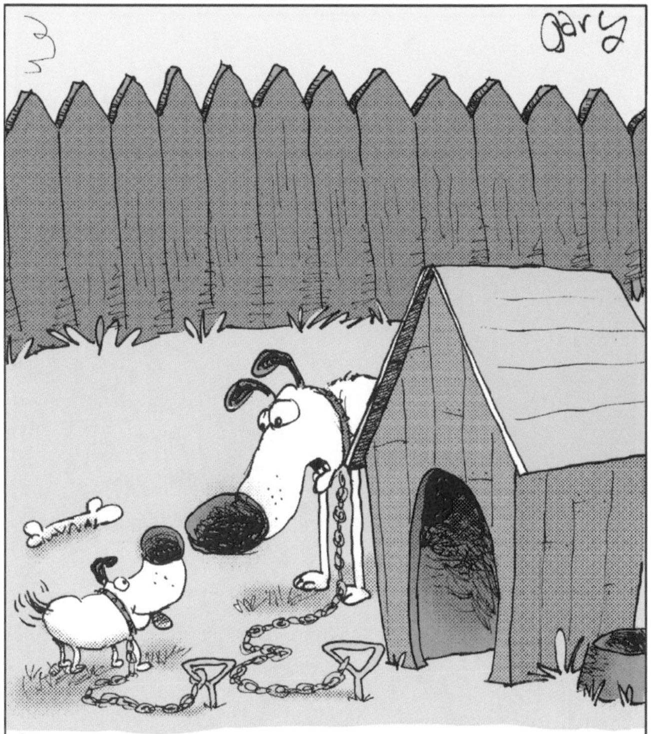
Gary

"SON, HAVE YOU GIVEN ANY THOUGHT TO WHAT YOU'RE GOING TO DO WITH YOUR LIFE?"

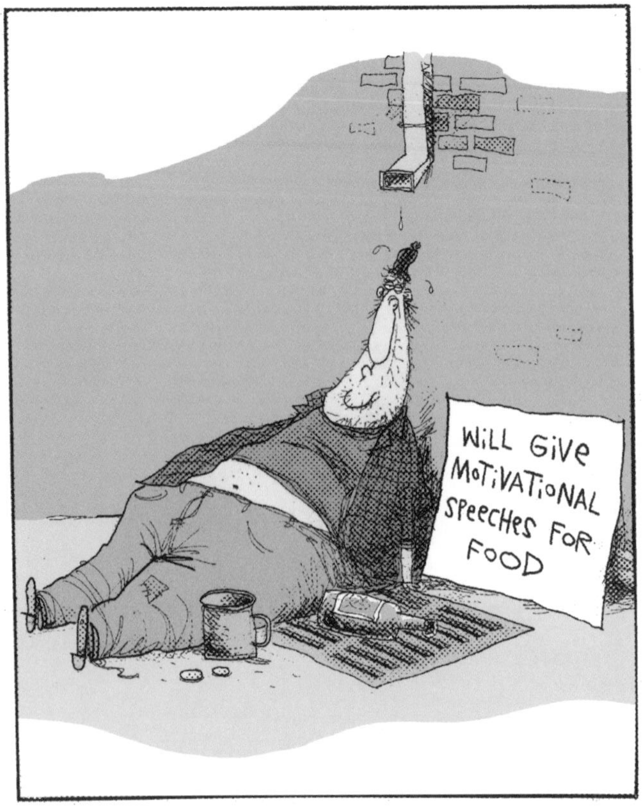
WiLL GiVe MoTiVATioNAL SPeeCHes FOR FOOD

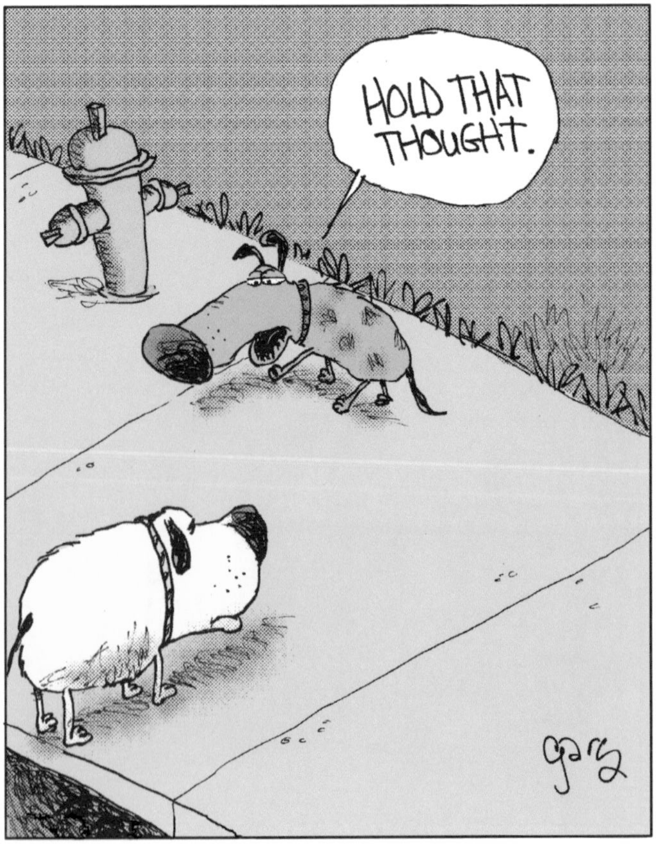
HOLD THAT THOUGHT.

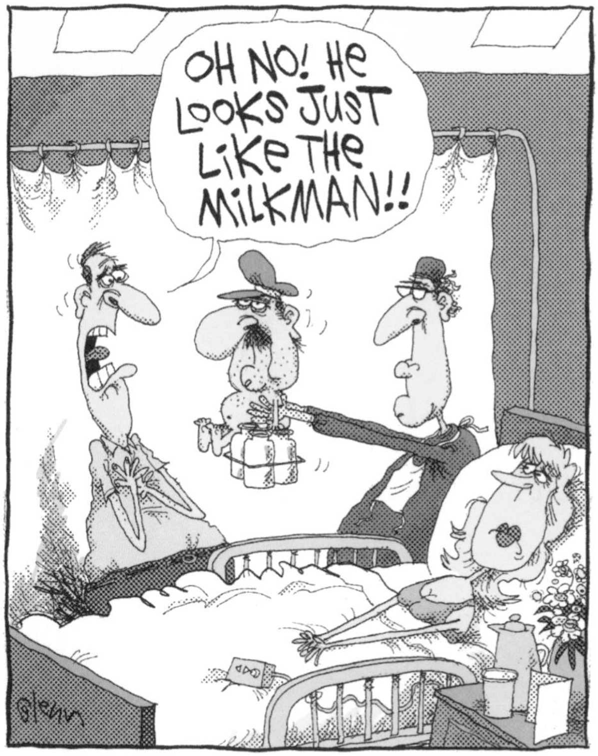
OH NO! HE LOOKS JUST LIKE THE MILKMAN!!
glenn

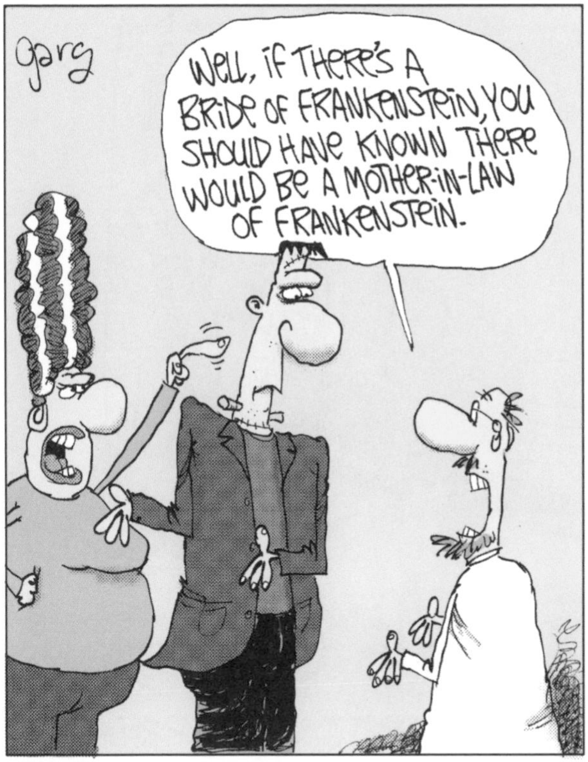
gary
WELL, IF THERE'S A BRIDE OF FRANKENSTEIN, YOU SHOULD HAVE KNOWN THERE WOULD BE A MOTHER-IN-LAW OF FRANKENSTEIN.

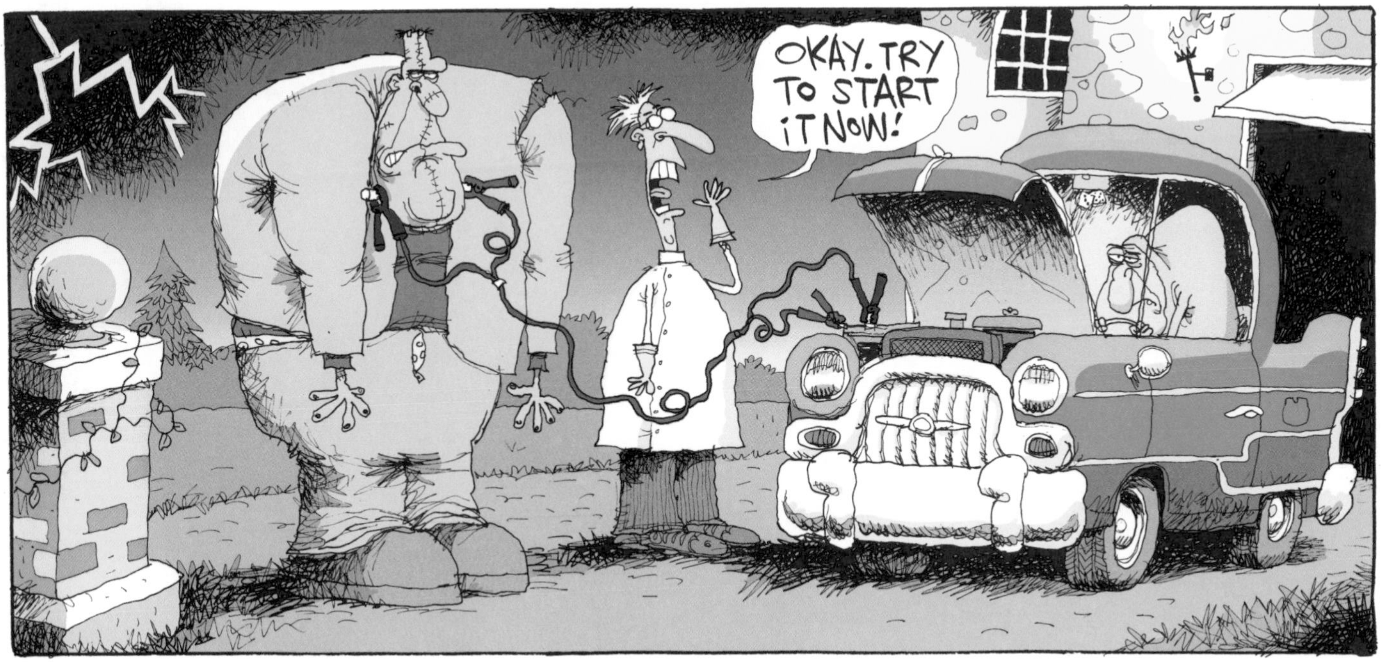
OKAY. TRY TO START IT NOW!

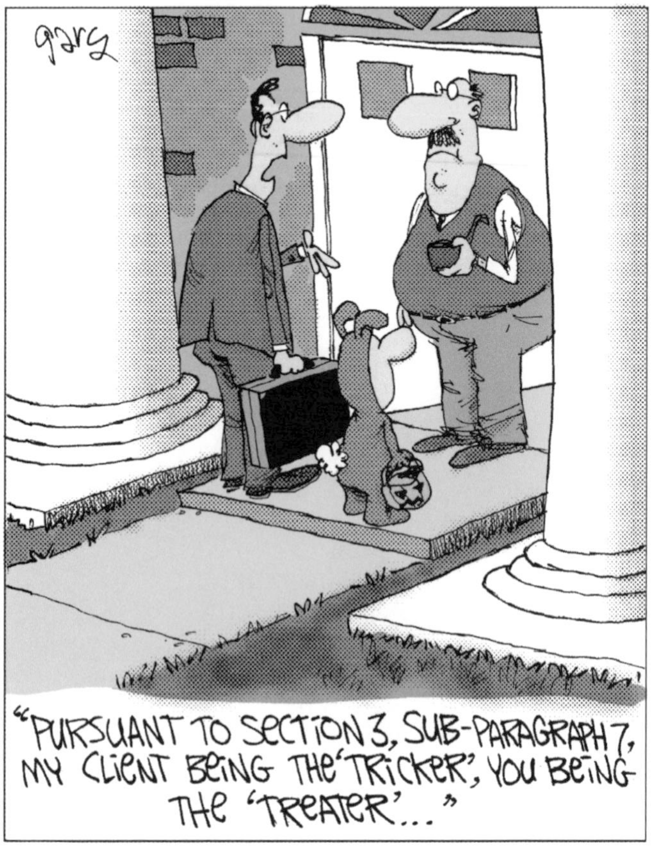
gary
"PURSUANT TO SECTION 3, SUB-PARAGRAPH 7, MY CLIENT BEING THE 'TRICKER', YOU BEING THE 'TREATER'..."

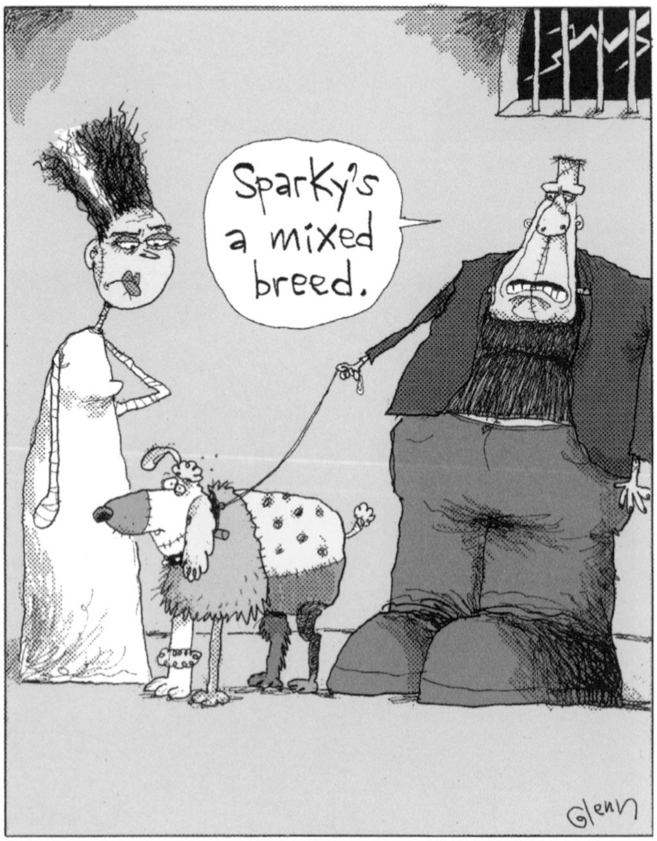
Sparky's a mixed breed.
Glenn

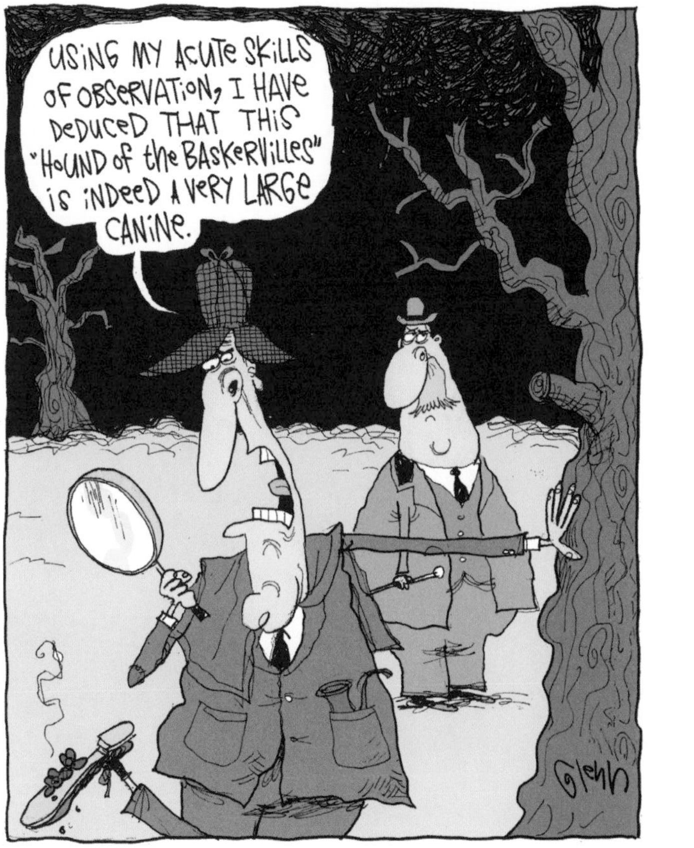
USING MY ACUTE SKILLS OF OBSERVATION, I HAVE DEDUCED THAT THIS "HOUND OF THE BASKERVILLES" IS INDEED A VERY LARGE CANINE.
Glenn

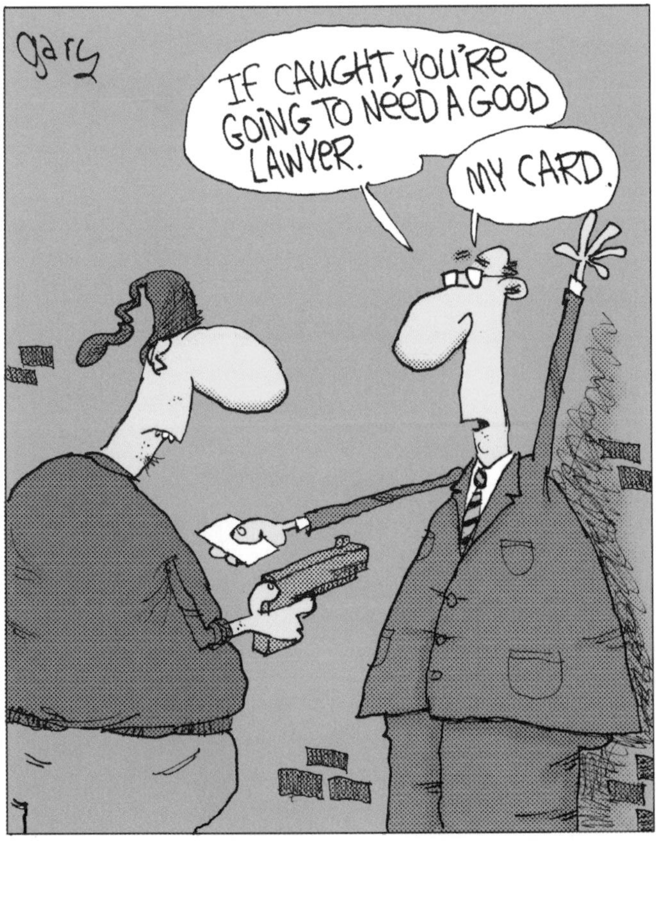
gary
IF CAUGHT, YOU'RE GOING TO NEED A GOOD LAWYER.
MY CARD.

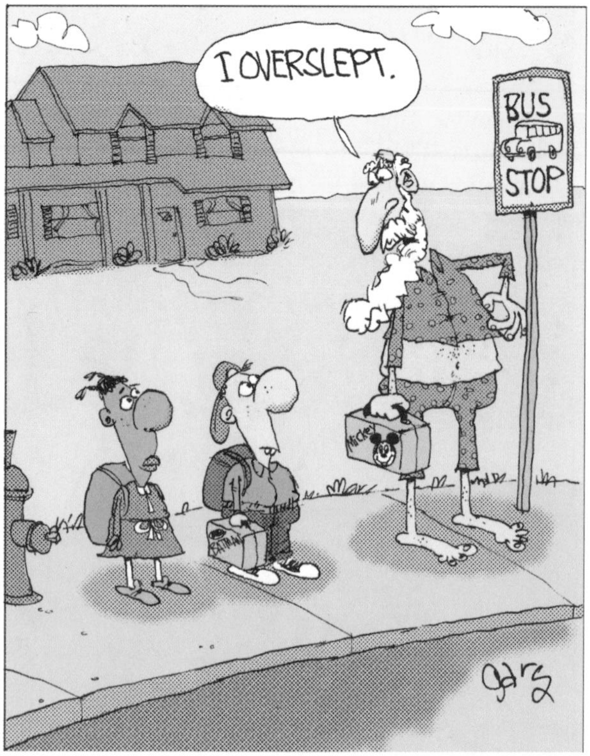
I OVERSLEPT.
BUS STOP
MICKEY
BATMAN
garz

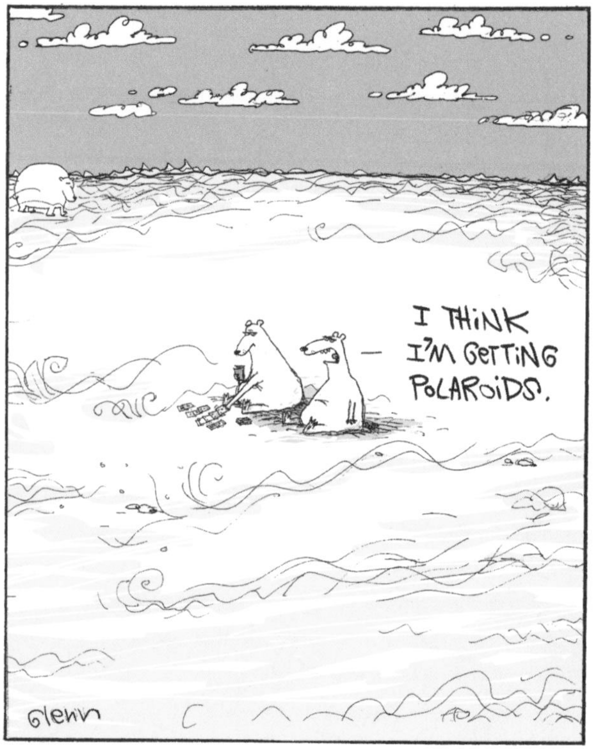
I THINK I'M GETTING POLAROIDS.
Glenn

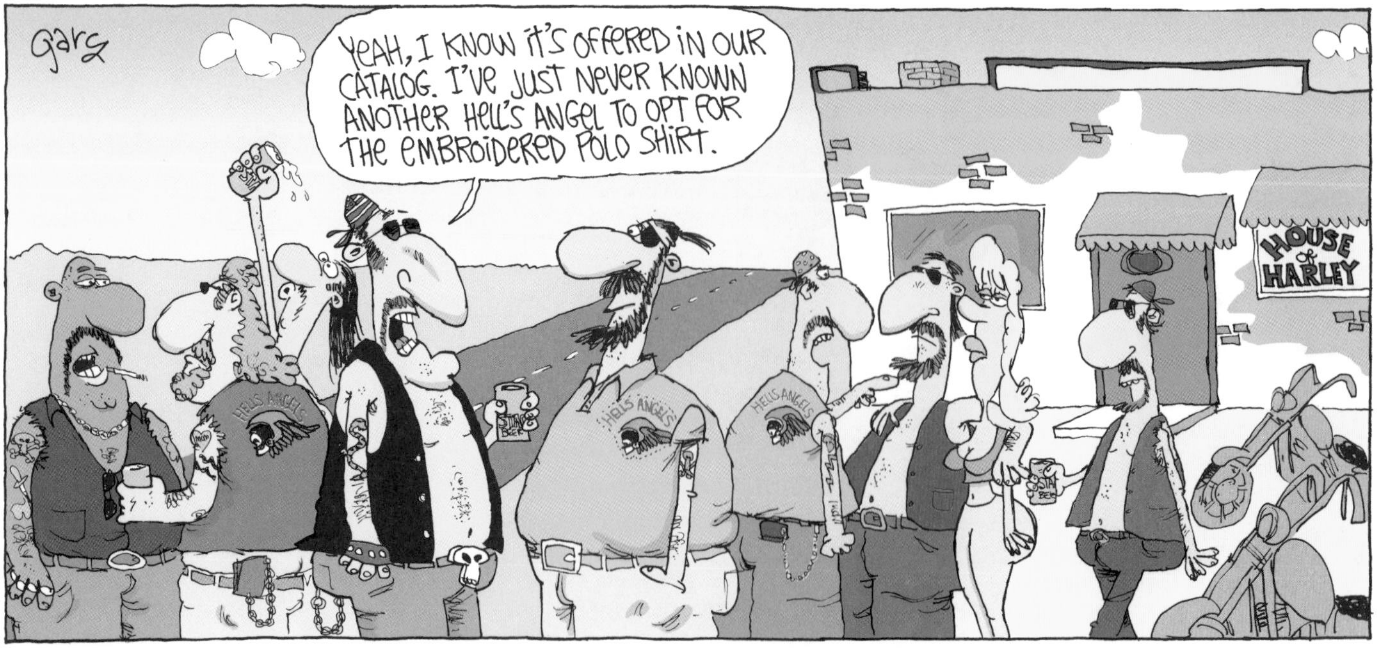
garz
YEAH, I KNOW it's offered in our catalog. I've just never known another Hell's Angel to opt for the embroidered polo shirt.
HELLS ANGELS
HOUSE OF HARLEY

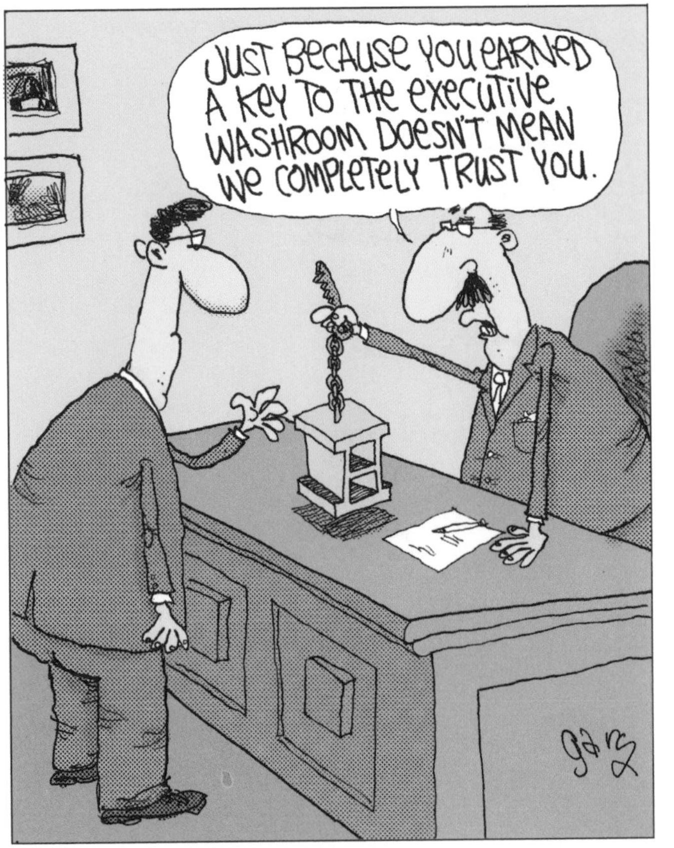
JUST BECAUSE YOU EARNED A KEY TO THE EXECUTIVE WASHROOM DOESN'T MEAN WE COMPLETELY TRUST YOU.

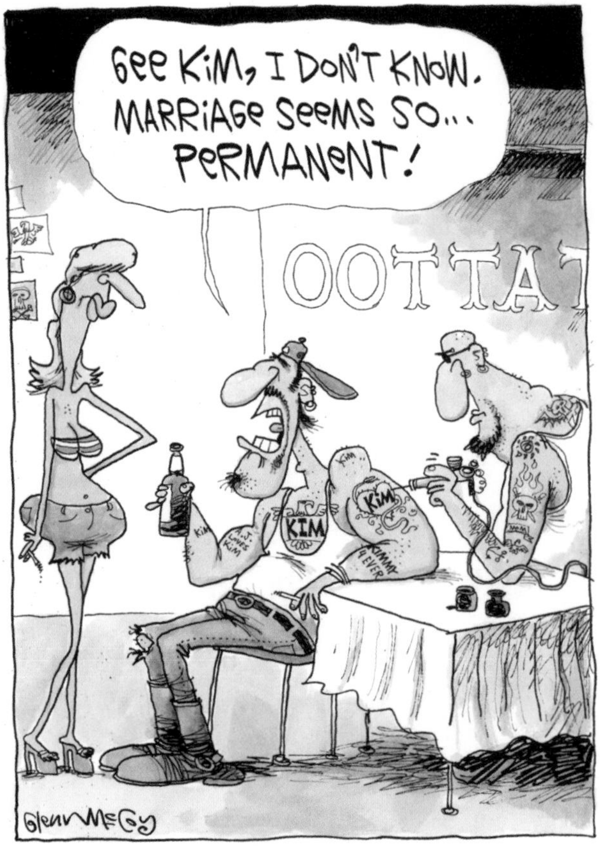
GEE KIM, I DON'T KNOW. MARRIAGE SEEMS SO... PERMANENT!
OOTTAT
KIM

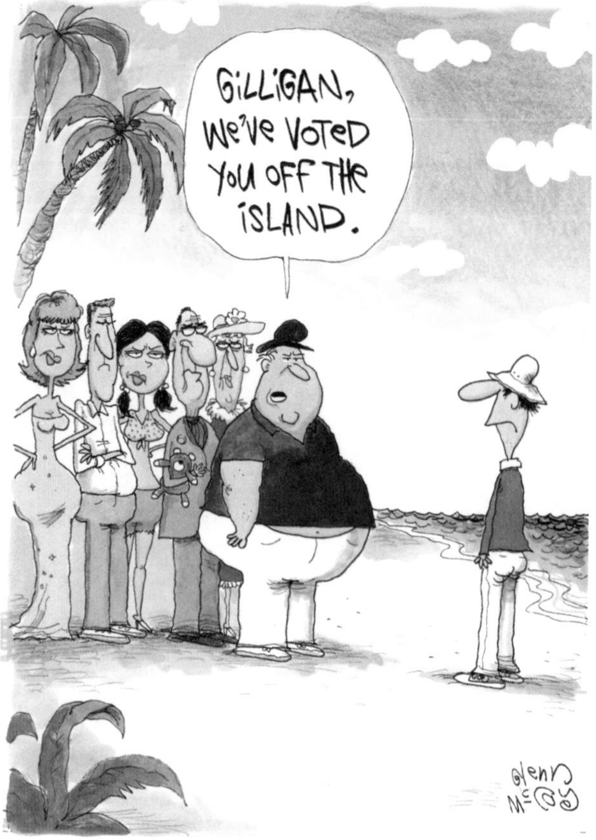
GILLIGAN, WE'VE VOTED YOU OFF THE ISLAND.
Glenn McCoy

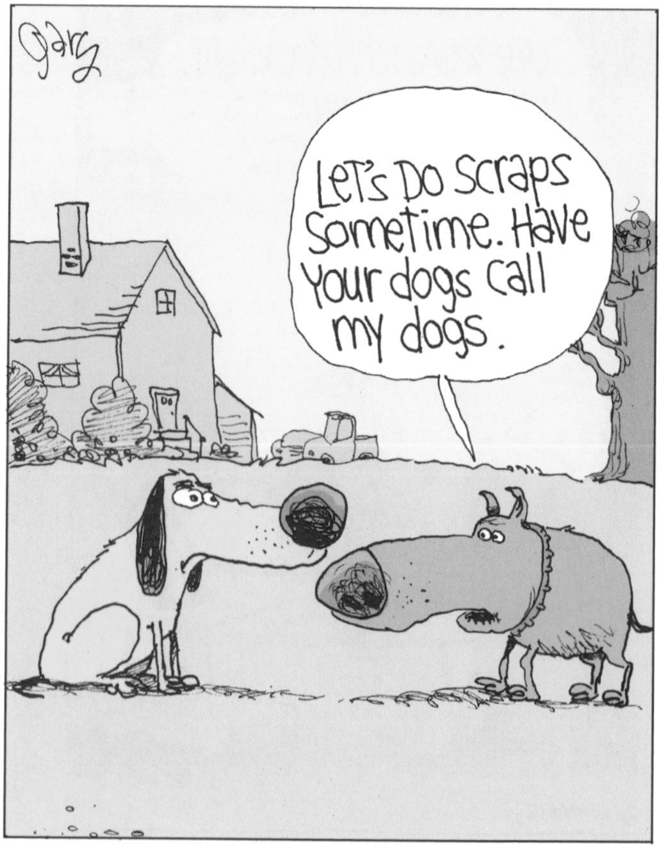
Gary
LET'S DO SCRAPS Sometime. Have Your dogs call my dogs.

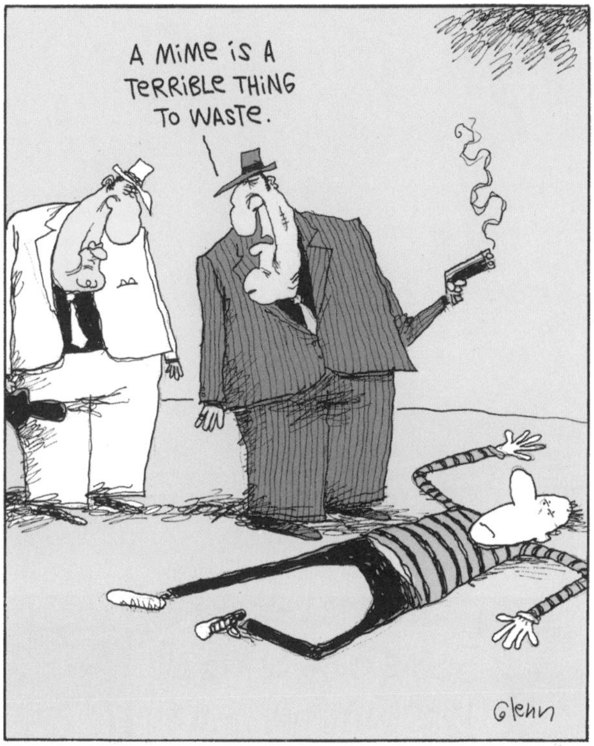
A MIME IS A TERRIBLE THING TO WASTE.
Glenn

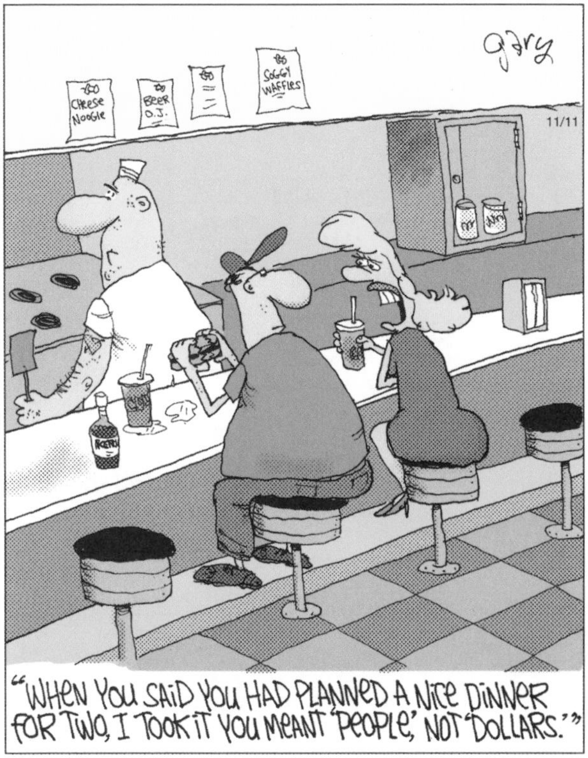
gary
"WHEN YOU SAID YOU HAD PLANNED A NICE DINNER FOR TWO, I TOOK IT YOU MEANT 'PEOPLE,' NOT 'DOLLARS.'"

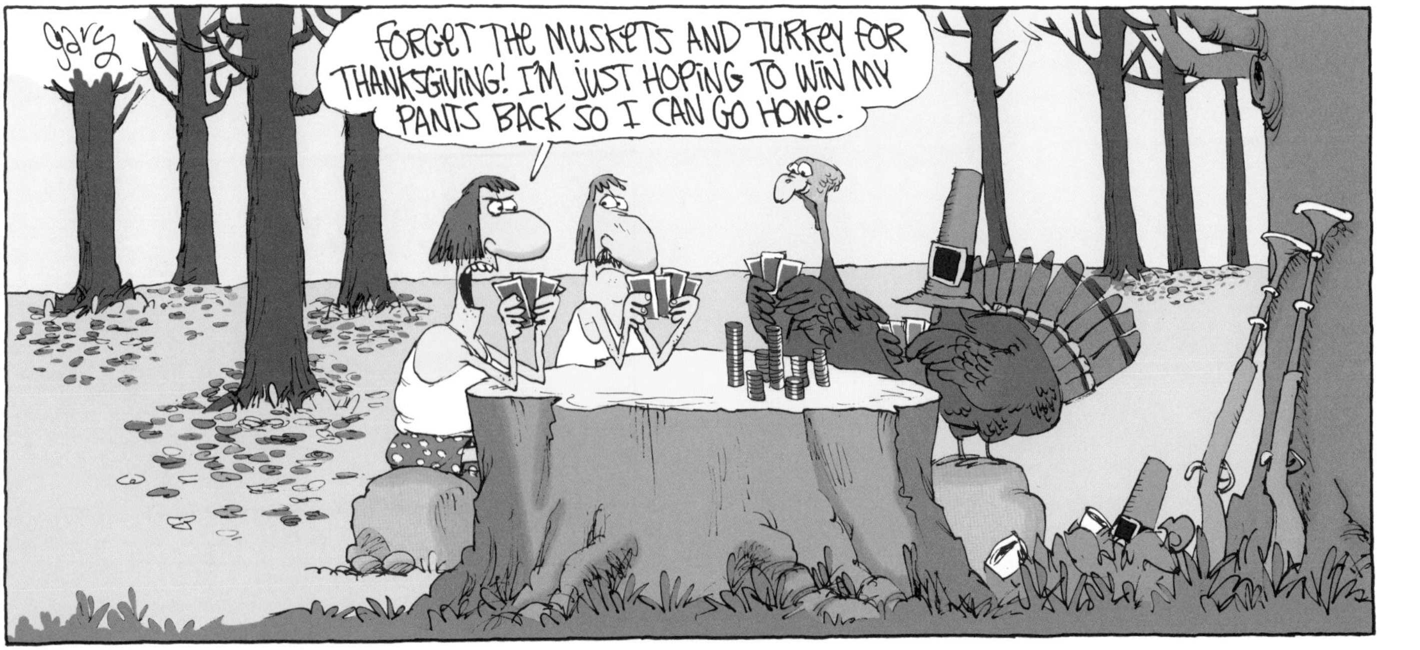
gary
FORGET THE MUSKETS AND TURKEY FOR THANKSGIVING! I'M JUST HOPING TO WIN MY PANTS BACK SO I CAN GO HOME.

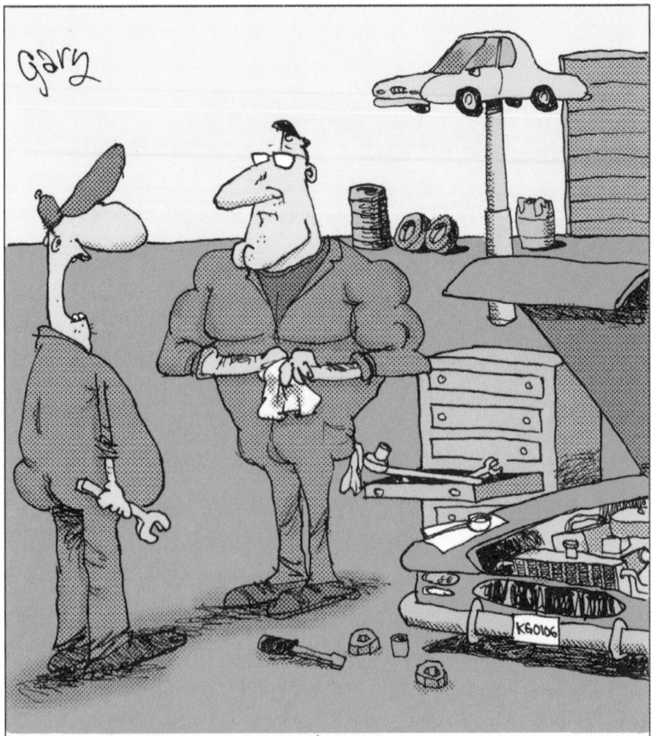
Gary
KG0106

"A CAREER CHANGE?! ARE YOU NUTS, CLARK? YOU'RE A **SUPER** MECHANIC!"

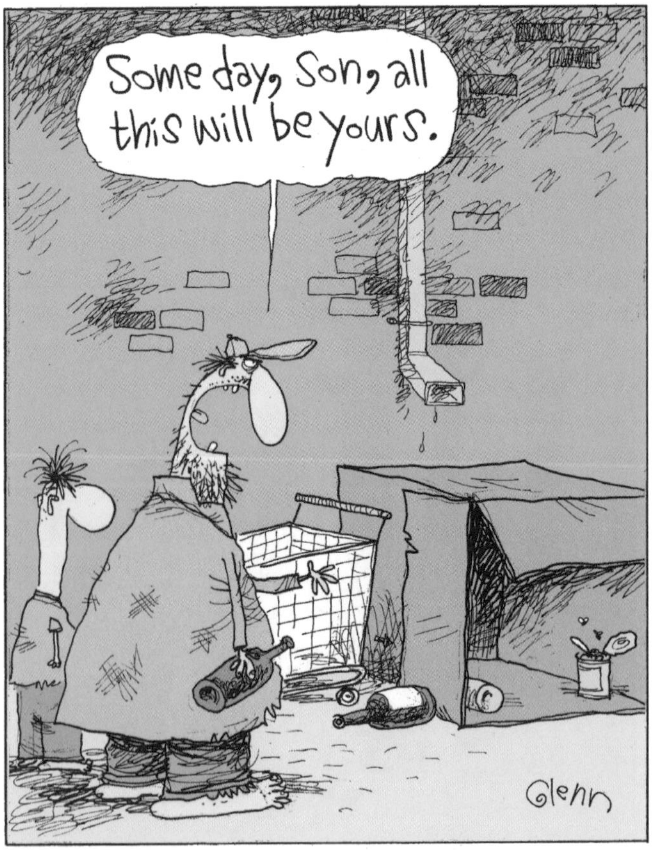
Some day, Son, all this will be yours.
Glenn

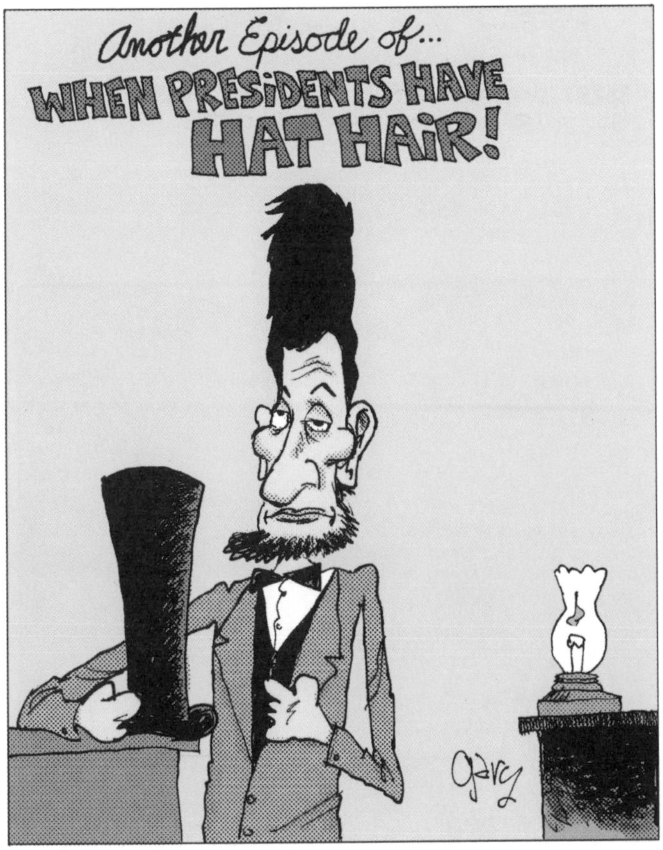
Another Episode of...
WHEN PRESIDENTS HAVE HAT HAIR!
Gary

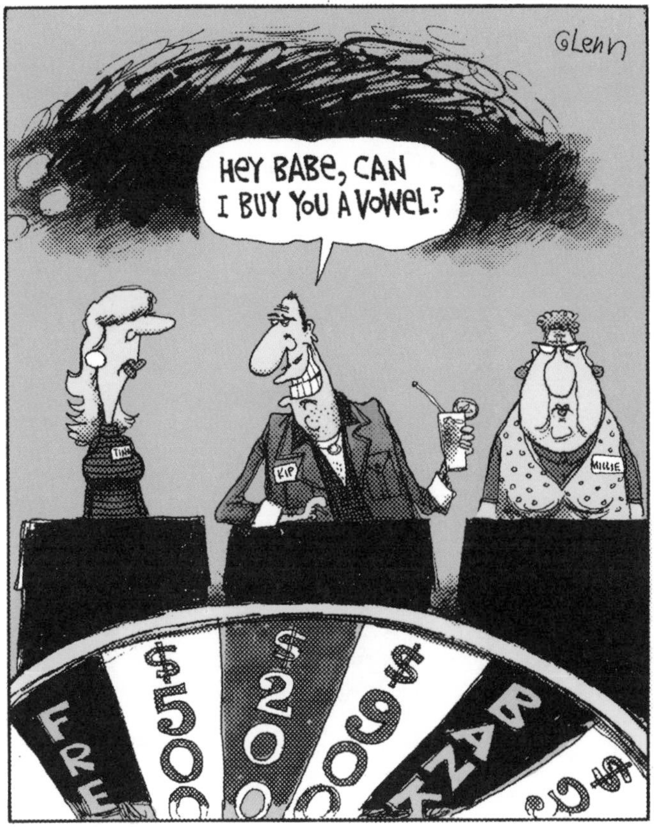
Glenn
HEY BABE, CAN I BUY YOU A VOWEL?

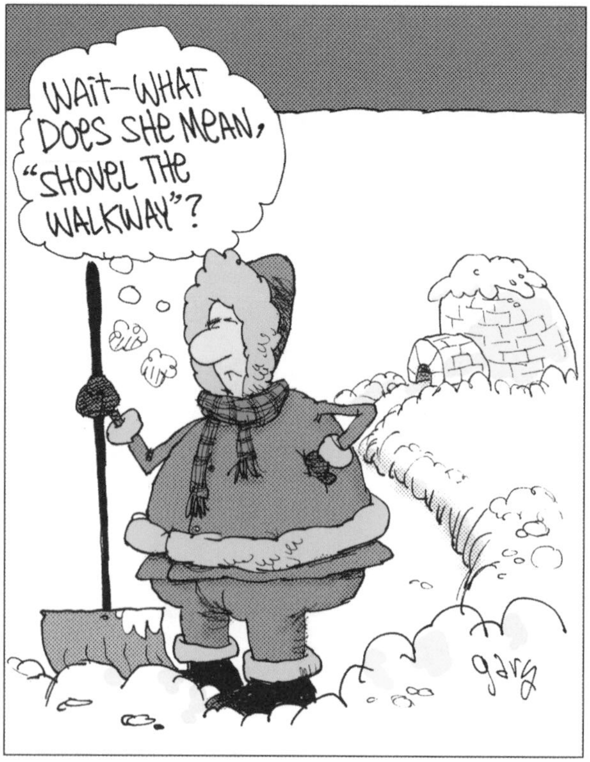
WAIT—WHAT DOES SHE MEAN, "SHOVEL THE WALKWAY"?
gary

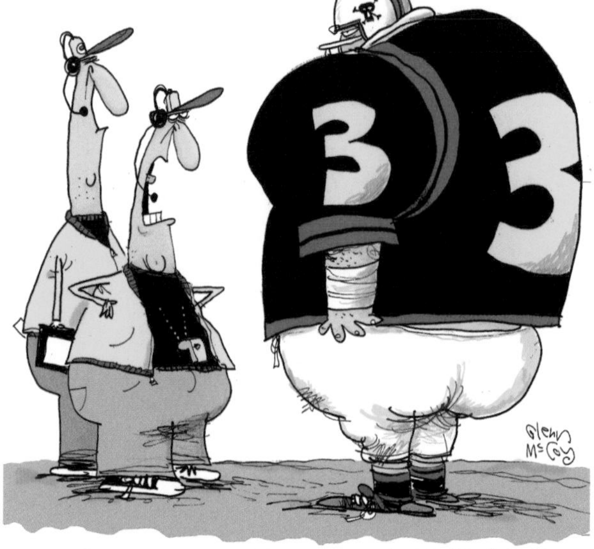
Glenn McCoy

SORRY, McCLARY. WE'RE GONNA HAVE TO LET YOU GO. YOUR END-ZONE DANCE SUCKS!!

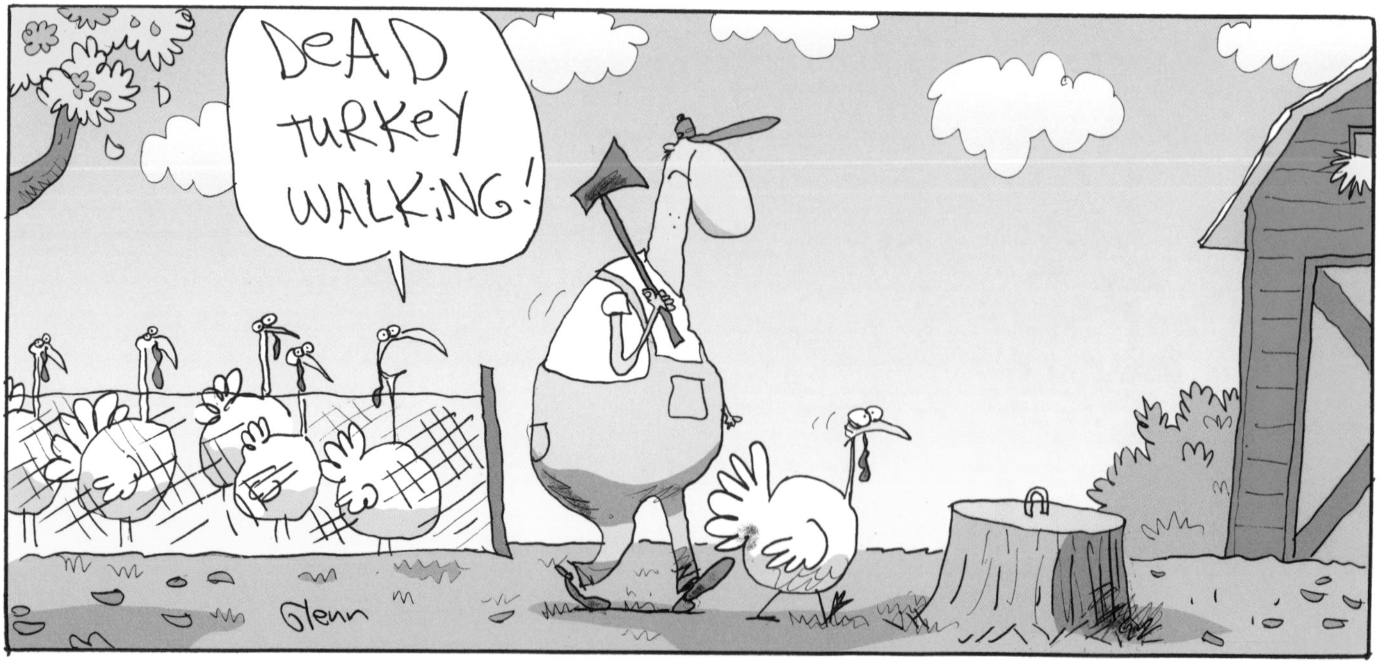
DEAD TURKEY WALKING!
Glenn

"HOW DISRESPECTFUL! WE CALL THEM 'OUR LOVED ONES' REMAINS'; THEY CALL THEM LEFTOVERS!"

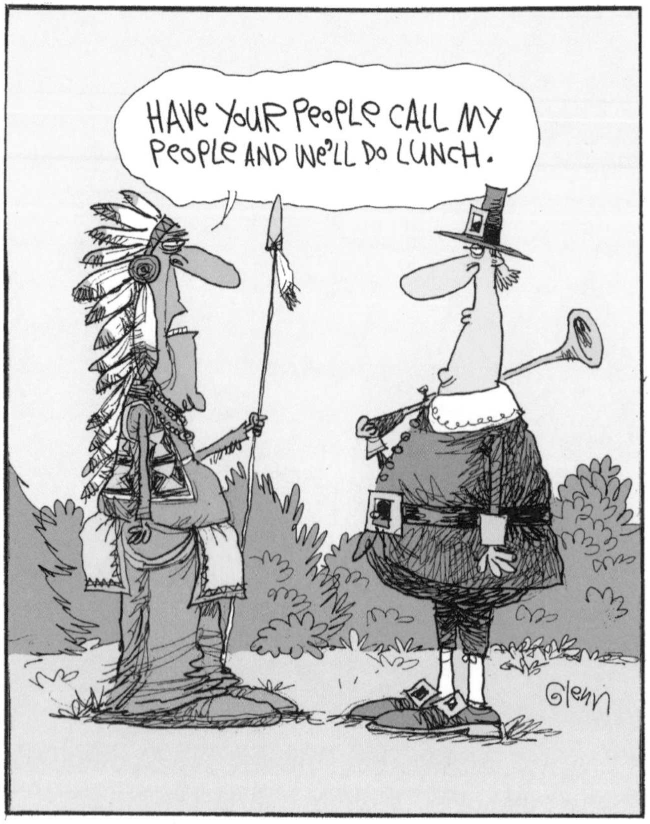
HAVE YOUR PEOPLE CALL MY PEOPLE AND WE'LL DO LUNCH.
Glenn

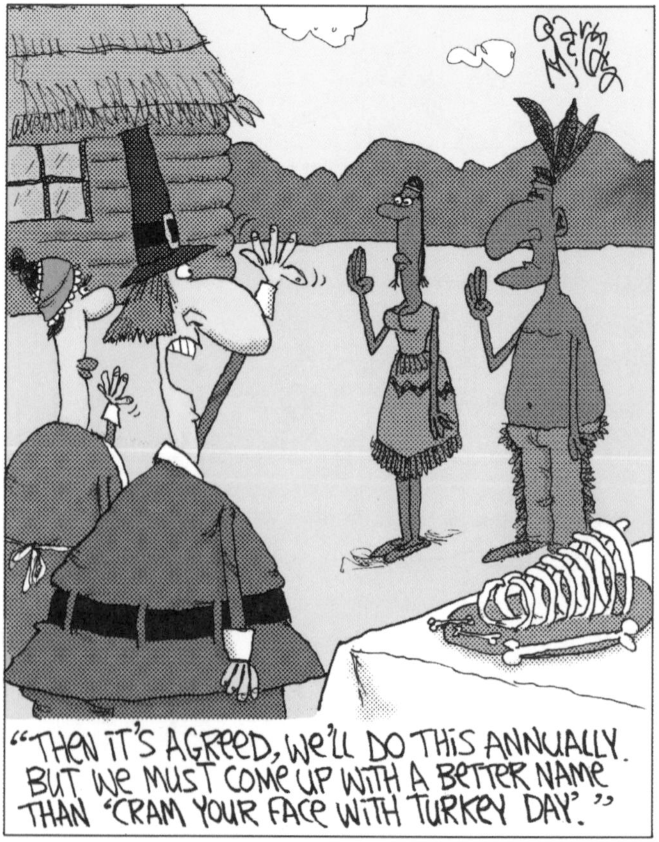

"THEN IT'S AGREED, WE'LL DO THIS ANNUALLY. BUT WE MUST COME UP WITH A BETTER NAME THAN 'CRAM YOUR FACE WITH TURKEY DAY'."

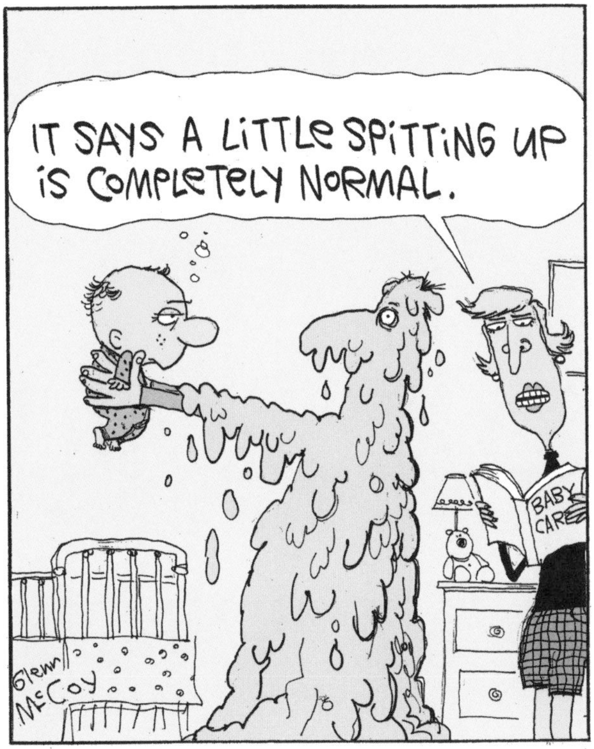
IT SAYS A LITTLE SPITTING UP IS COMPLETELY NORMAL.
BABY CARE
Glenn McCoy

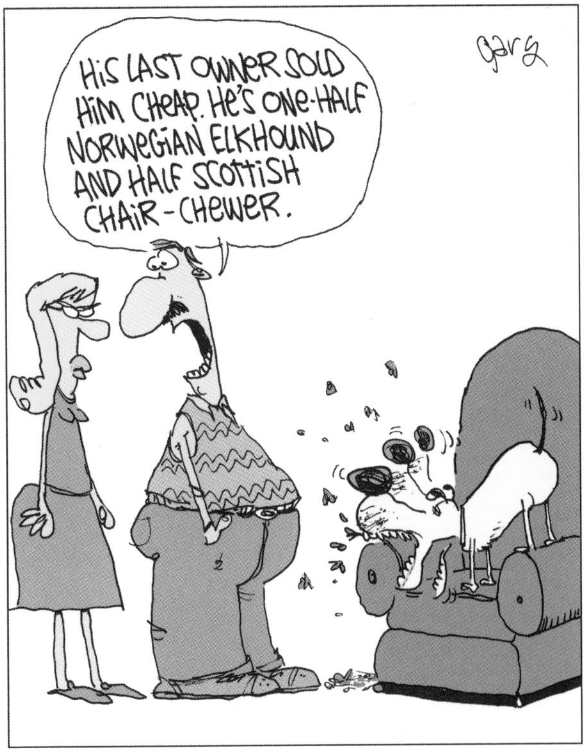
HIS LAST OWNER SOLD HIM CHEAP. HE'S ONE-HALF NORWEGIAN ELKHOUND AND HALF SCOTTISH CHAIR-CHEWER.
gary

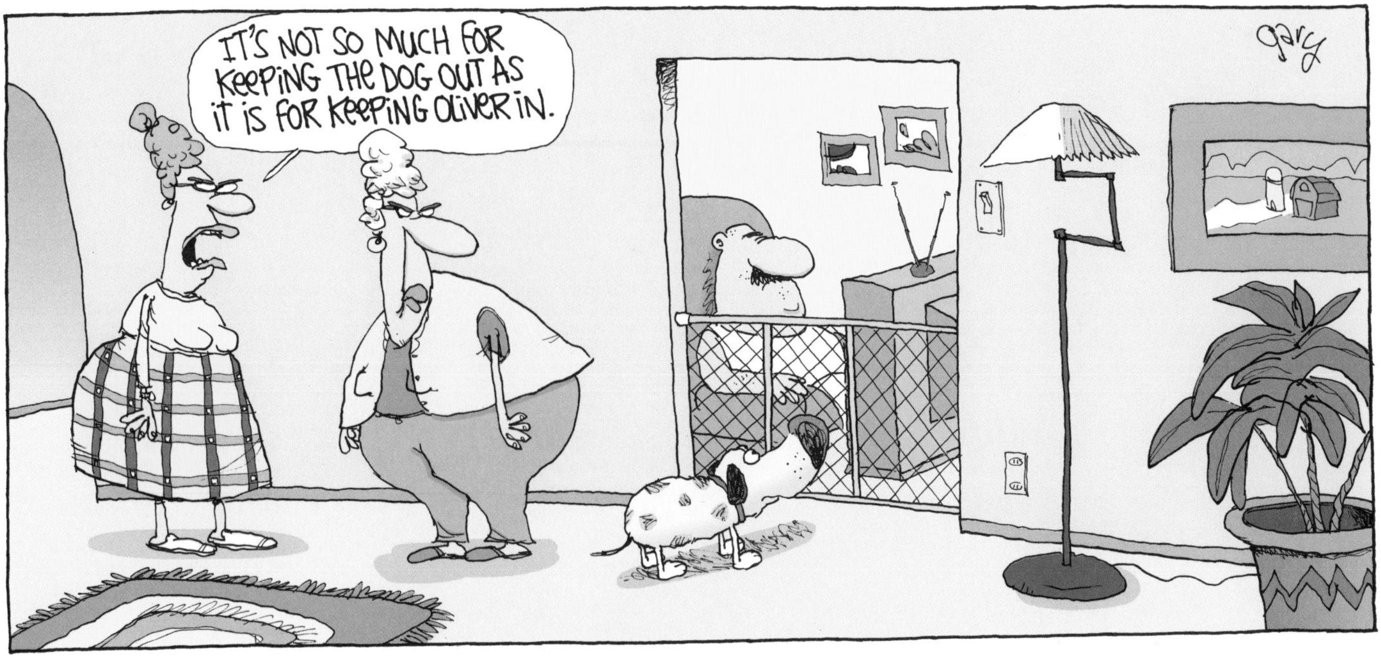
IT'S NOT SO MUCH FOR KEEPING THE DOG OUT AS IT IS FOR KEEPING OLIVER IN.
gary